strategies and tactics for the price action trader

FOREX DAILY

TRADING END OF DAY

The number-one guide for swing trading currencies

Bob Volman

LIGHT TOWER PUBLISHING

Published by Light Tower Publishing

ISBN: 978-90-822786-3-7

Prorealtime charts used with permission of www.ProRealTime.com

forexdailybook@gmail.com

Official Author Website: www.bobvolman.me

Table of Contents

Introduction

In this digital age you don't need to go out of your way to learn all about trading Forex. Articles, websites, guides, and courses are as plentiful as those on the next dietary fad. Yet if you think about it, almost all these publications focus on daytrading. Rarely will you find anything interesting on trading *end of day*, let alone a full method. Well, someone had to break that mold.

One obvious benefit of trading end of day, often referred to as swing trading, is that the Forex markets trade around the clock from Monday to Friday; hence the total absence of gaps during the week on the dailies. And as for gaps over the weekend, you would have to look hard to find even one worthy of mention. No big deal? Then swing trade some stocks, and you'll quickly note the issue.

Perhaps you could argue that there aren't that many currency pairs to actually trade, but that can also be seen as a boon. After all, no sifting through entire indices after the close. Moreover, it is not even necessary to keep track of all currency pairs. A daily scan of the 28 dominant pairs will do and takes only a few minutes to run.

There are also more practical benefits compared to stocks, such as reasonably tight spreads on most of these pairs and less restrictive rules regarding leverage and margin. And not unimportant either, the trading fees are typically a function of volume, allowing retail traders to start on the smallest of accounts and work their way up.

If any of the above strikes a chord with you, I invite you to read on because this guide is all about swing trading Forex. But let it be said that if you'd rather trade stocks, indices, ETFs, bonds, commodities, or any other liquid market, the same strategies can be applied with little adaptation. You might have to craft a few workarounds for trading the opens (ideas for which are offered in Chapter 15), but the method itself is universal as it is all based on solid price action principles.

Please take note that while this book is meant to serve traders of all levels, it is boldly assumed that most readers are already familiar with terms like bull, bear, long, short, support, resistance, and so on. But even if you have no such prior knowledge, you will still be able to follow along; just know that the pace of instruction is not that of an absolute beginner's guide.

Nor is this yet another treatise on Technical Analysis. While we will certainly make use of all the principles that have stood the test of time, it is above all a *trading* guide. So more than anything else, our focus will be on where to place our orders.

As the method in question is based on pure price action, all we really need for analysis are the bars on the chart. Indicators would only clutter our view, and might even lead us astray. Trading solely off a naked chart may take some getting used to, but rest assured, once you learn to appreciate the clarity it offers, you will never want to go back.

In contrast to my earlier publications on intraday tactics, *Forex Price Action Scalping* (2011) and *Understanding Price Action* (2014), there's no reason to elaborate on the trickeries of midsession gameplay; for all that sits pleasantly tucked away within the range of a single bar. That is yet another advantage of trading the dailies!

To provide the most accurate impression of what swing trading can do for your bottom line, it is chosen not to handpick the charts from all over the place but to present them more or less chronologically. Allowing for one exception, we start our research in Part One on the years 2012–2013. This is where we learn all about price action setups and where we effectively create our trading plan.

But to ensure this plan is no one-time wonder, Part Two is all about backtesting our findings on the next four years of price action, on each of the 28 pairs (2014–2017).

These two parts already offer well over a 100 charts with at least an equal number of trades to learn from. Yet as a bonus, in the appendix you will find the charts from 2018–2024 (in annotated format). So all in all there is over a decade's worth of price action setups to get you going on your swing trading journey.

If you have ever imagined trading part-time in a relaxed and fruitful manner, the *Forex Daily* method might be just right for you; or simply use the plans and ideas in this guide to complement whatever method you already have in place.

Alright, enough talking, let's get to work.

Part One

TRADING END OF DAY

chapter 1

Swing Trading Forex

some general thoughts on the task at hand

Our first job is to establish our watchlist. While the number of available currency pairs has risen sharply in recent years, still only a few are truly worth considering. These are the 28 most actively traded pairs comprising the following currencies: the USD, EUR, GBP, JPY, CHF, AUD, NZD, and CAD.

As nowadays most brokers offer competitive spreads on these pairs, I wouldn't worry too much about looking for the absolute tightest offerings. Decent spreads are good enough when trading the dailies. In fact, rather throw in an extra pip than skimp on your entries.

Tip: For analysis, the charts in your trading platform should do, but if for whatever reason you find them unpleasant to work with, do yourself a favor and subscribe to a proper charting service. They offer great value for a modest fee and will make your studying and scanning experience much more enjoyable. Avoid using free charts online as you cannot trust these to be accurate.

If you rent a standalone charting platform, try not to let yourself be distracted by all the flashy features. Just make a template in which the 28 pairs are alphabetically listed, ready to click through. And solely use the daily charts! None of this is to say that indicators or intraday charts couldn't possibly have merit, but let others have their fun. In this guide we go by that timeless motto: simple is best. For let there be no discussion on the dominance of the dailies. Or to phrase it more boldly, if we cannot trust a setup *there*, why look anywhere else?

Without delving into any details just yet, let me give you an example of the task at hand, just to get the gist of it. Say it is early August 2013 and the break in bar 1 on the EURCAD below grabs our attention (the bars afterwards have yet to occur).

Figure 1.1. Several high-odds setups within a few months' time.

First off, note that we only have a few months of data in this chart, which in most instances will suffice for the type of setups we are looking for. And as you can see, all we ever plot in a chart are support and resistance lines.

As will be discussed in more detail later on (Figure 4.1), the break in bar 1 does not call for action yet. What we have is a setup candidate. And so the plan is to wait for prices to pull back to the broken barrier, referred to as a *test*. If granted, we will then keep an eye out for a special bar to "resolve" this test in favor of the breakout. If this resolution is to our liking, as is the case with bar 2, we will refer to it as our *signal bar* for the trade.

Note: A signal bar by itself never warrants an entry. For a trade to be justified, this bar needs to be taken out first as a token that the market agrees with our assessment. A broken signal bar is by no means a guarantee for follow-through, but it is definitely a step in the right direction and as such the safer bet on the whole. Thus, for a long position we place our entry order a few pips above a *bullish* signal bar (white), and for a short a few pips below a *bearish* signal bar (black).

As for managing an open position, unfortunately there's no one plan suitable for all contingencies. For example, using a trailing stop with an open target can work wonders in a trending environment but is not particularly suited for the all too common ranges. Therefore, a more popular approach among swing traders is to place a hard stop and target along with the entry. This certainly has its downsides too, but also some notable benefits, such as always pocketing profits in *strength*. I am a big fan of it myself. And since it is also more practical for educational purposes (little room for debate on what to do), we will use a preset risk and reward in all coming studies. Unless otherwise indicated, the settings are as follows:

We wrap our entry and stop around the signal bar and place our target at twice the distance from entry to stop. So if a signal bar stands 80 pips tall and we factor in, say, 3 pips for the spread on both ends (will do for most pairs), our target will sit at 172 pips from entry (2 x 86). But rather than refer to targets in pips, more practical is to speak of points. Meaning we lose *one point* if stopped out and gain *two points* if our target is hit.

Note: For ease of use, we should always place the stop and target in a so-called *bracket order*, so that if one side is hit, the order at the other end is automatically canceled. You might see this referred to as a TP/SL (take profit/stop loss) or an OCO order (one cancels the other). Another great advantage of a bracket order is that it will only be activated *if* the market triggers our entry.

So in nutshell, once in position, our work is done and the outcome of the trade is out of our hands. Every once in a while it may be justified to close a trade manually, but in principle there is no need for that. Why complicate matters (at the risk of regret), when the worst that can happen is a minor one-point loss.

As for the volume to trade with (specified in units or lots), most order tickets will give us the exact number based on our personal risk-model and what we type in for stop and entry. If by any chance this feature is not offered, look for a standalone *Forex Position Size Calculator.* (We will discuss volume and risk in more detail in Chapter 14 and 15.)

Note: Since currencies trade around the clock from Monday to Friday, there exists some debate on which "close" to use for the daily bars. The argument usually boils down to the following: either let the bars close at the same time the US stock markets close for the day (US close), or two or three hours later, when the Australian/Asian markets open up (EU and UK close respectively).

It's good to know that for *our* purposes it doesn't really matter which close we use because the markets rarely move significantly between the US and UK close. And since the highs and lows of a session are usually set earlier in the day, small differences in closing prices will rarely affect our take on a setup. If ever the differences *are* big enough, for good or for worse, the pros and cons of that will likely balance out over time. So unless your research shows otherwise, why not simply use the setting that scan-wise fits in best with your other activities; as a middle ground option, the bars in this guide all show the EU close (midnight CET or CEST).

While ideally we run our scans just before a new bar opens, so that we can always place our entries at the best possible spot, the markets usually do not break our signal bars right after the close (unless perhaps the bar closes on its high or low). So if you are a little late, or even a few hours late, run your scan anyway; your signal bar may not have been broken yet, or prices may not have moved much since (Asian sessions are notoriously slow).

As already mentioned, if you would rather trade stocks, all the price action strategies in this book are universal and thus applicable to other markets too. (There is a specific section on how to work around opening gaps in Chapter 15.)

Whichever way you go about it, always do your due diligence and make sure to test your findings before you put real funds on the line. That is exactly what we aim to do in this guide. It is not for nothing that Part Two is largely devoted to backtesting.

But let us not get ahead of ourselves. First we will discuss the essentials of the method and learn about the price action principles on which it is based. I hope you will be just as amazed as I was early on (and still am to this day) to see how time and again a small set of recurring themes and motifs will lead to powerful setups, with excellent odds for follow-through.

In Figure 1.1 we briefly touched upon a setup of the so-called pullback reversal variety, which is one of just four types we study in this method, each with a chapter of its own. They are:

1. Range Reversals
2. Range Breakouts
3. Pullback Reversals
4. Trend Reversals

With all this out of the way, let our journey begin. It is time to explore the wonderous world of price action and the hidden treasures within, starting with a personal favorite, the range reversal setup.

chapter **2**

Range Reversal Setup

how to take advantage of failed breakouts

If you have never given ranges much thought, or perhaps appreciated them solely for breakout purposes, you might be surprised to find that there is ample chance for action within the ranges themselves, especially nears the highs and lows. Indeed, it is no secret that the outer barriers are more likely to hold than give way when attacked (the very essence of a range). It is only logical then that we study ways to take advantage, by means of the range reversal setup.

While ranges on the dailies can last well over a year, in our swing trading method the relevant action is usually found within the last five months (about 100 bars). So in most cases we can already spot an interesting range as soon as we open a chart.

Our first task then is to determine its barriers, which in practice are rarely derived from the absolute highs and lows. To find these barriers more easily, the trick is to flatten the chart a bit first as that will "smooth out" the price action (don't overdo it) and give us a better take on which swing points to connect. But rather than discuss such subtleties beforehand, let us simply delve in and look at some examples.

By the way, while for chronological purposes the charts in Part One all stem from the years 2012–2013, as a precursor to our backtest starting in 2014, there is one exception: the GBPCAD on the following page. I couldn't resist including it as it is such a great chart for introducing not only the range reversal setup but some essential price action principles as well.

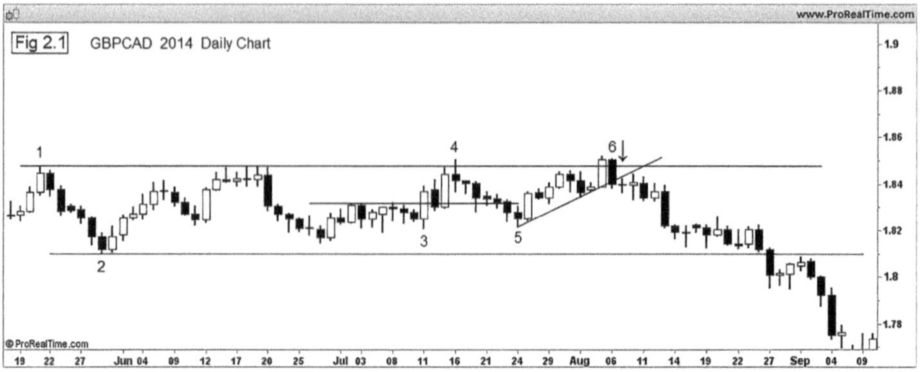

Figure 2.1. Here we have a typical range spanning about three months. Note how its barriers both stem from a swing point early on (1 and 2), which is very common. The top barrier in particular warrants attention as it is perforated twice, yet each time to no avail.

Not surprisingly, false breakouts are potent indicators of a reversal, which is why we generally look for signal bars that stick out of a range yet close back inside, as do bar 4 and 6. However, for any of this to call for action, the conditions as a whole need to favor the trade idea as well, or at least not speak against it.

To illustrate, note the *cluster line* across that block of bars to the left of bar 3. Since that line could serve as a springboard for another attack on the top barrier, the time is not ripe for a short below bar 4. Whether bulls will make use of that block is irrelevant. The last thing we want to do as bears is short straight into an element of support.

See the difference with bar 6, which not only marks a second failure of the bulls to break out (already a major giveaway) but also pressures the angular *support line* (below the 5-6 runup). If that barrier fails, there is no springboard available to help the bulls back on their feet. Now the conditions are ripe for a short.

Note: The fact that bar 6 already sticks through support is a bonus as it grants us an ideal entry in a so-called *confirmation break*. Had this bar merely hit the barrier, we would have still played short, but the risk of counterplay is then a little higher. An entry beyond a perforation bar is preferable because it adds an element of "confirmation" (for lack of a better term) that the break is for real.

There is also a practical reason for why an entry beyond a perforation is preferable over an entry beyond a barrier. The *exact* position of the latter is then less crucial for setup validity.

Not all setups will be so straightforward, but hopefully this example shows that there is no need for price action mastery to spot a high-odds opportunity. On the contrary. Our goal is to scan for the obvious setups and let all the rest be. That's why we stick to the dailies. The simpler the price action, the higher the odds for follow-through.

Note: Follow-through on a trade is not solely a matter of like-minded traders jumping in on the same setup. The best part is that the "enemy camp" often has no choice but to act on our setup too—as in bulls forced to flatten their long positions below bar 6. For any bull that sells out is an extra bear in the orderbook. True, the market will always find new buyers, but right after a failed range break, we can imagine the majority of bulls to now wait for new support. If so, their absence can only benefit our short position as well.

Naturally, as even the obvious setups are no guarantee for a win, it is imperative to always place a stop along with the entry, typically at the other end of the signal bar (or else a bar nearby).

And as for our target, even when everything lines up favorably for a trade, the window of opportunity is best perceived to be temporary. That is why we aim for a target no bigger than twice the distance from entry to stop—for ease of use referred to as a *two-pointer.*

While it might appear more logical to manage our trades manually, to try to squeeze out more profit, I much advise not to go that route until you are at least decently experienced. A set-and-forget plan is far easier to execute and also more practical for backtesting purposes (less room for debate on what to do with a trade). And besides, a two-pointer is by no means a lowball objective; on frequent occasions we will even have to settle for less. But more on that later.

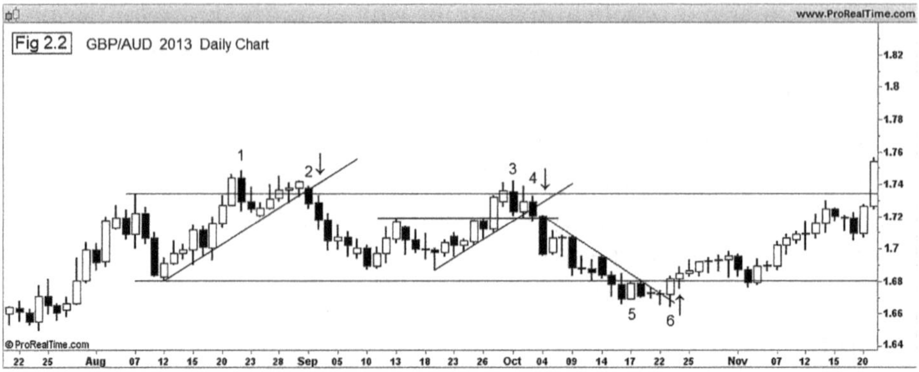

Figure 2.2. This range is a little rougher around the edges, but the barriers are still easy to figure out, again stemming from a swing high and swing low early on. As all attempts to break these barriers are rejected, we know what to look for in this chart.

Things always get interesting after a false break, but they get even better if we can find two such failures relatively close to one another, as in 1-2 and 3-4. As such progressions are known to demoralize the parties hoping for a breakout, they inherently favor those looking for a reversal; for that reason we will refer to such setups as two-step reversals, or *two-steppers* for short.

Tip: A two-stepper only warrants action if the chart as a whole favors the trade idea. At bar 2, for example, the market has only just begun to range. Not a dealbreaker here, but there are instances in which the conditions speak more strongly against an otherwise interesting setup. That is why we will never trade off setups alone.

Our next two-stepper has everything going for it (3-4). At this point the market is clearly ranging and the hardness of the top barrier is more established as well. Besides the false breaks, note also the simultaneous perforation of support (4). But remember, only a dip *below* bar 4 would justify a short. So that is where we place our entry.

To illustrate why a perforation by itself is not a safe sign for action, examine the dip below the horizontal cluster line in the low of bar 4—no selling just yet. If anything, that break is bought. But look what happens next session when bar 4 is taken out. No guarantees of course, yet this perfectly illustrates the power of a confirmation break.

Equally important, however, is to find a good place for our stop. Note that if we opt for protection above signal bar 4, this order would sit right below the top barrier. We might get away with it, but a smarter idea here is to opt for a stop above the previous bar—bulls then have to break the top barrier first to even get to it.

Note: While the benefit of such *insurance* is well understood, it does call for a wider target (to keep our risk-to-reward). That could backfire. Or there may no longer be room for a two-pointer. For example, if due to the safer stop our target on the short would now sit *below* the bottom barrier, we would do well to plan our exit a few pips in front, and thus settle for a lesser reward. So one way or another, there is always a price for safety. All the more reason to choose insurance wisely.

Back in lows of the range, we spot another two-stepper, this time a bullish variant (5-6). Notice in particular how bar 6 sticks its head above the bottom barrier, thus setting up a confirmation break.

Another reason for why this makes for a great reversal setup is that signal bar 6 is a so-called *trap bar*—a bar that first breaks the foregoing bar at one end, only to treacherously spin around and break the other. Trap bars are among the most powerful signal bars we can find because their message is so clear that the opponent often has no choice but to act on them too, or risk serious consequences. (If you were a bear, would you still believe in a range break after bar 6?)

No bar by itself, however, is a ready-made signal bar. Bar 1 and 3, for example, are trap bars too, yet neither calls for a trade because the conditions for a reversal are simply not favorable.

Just two charts in and we have already stumbled upon quite a few interesting principles: swing points, false breaks, signal bars, two-steppers, confirmations, trap bars. Rest assured, these are all features that basically pop up in *any* chart. And that is exactly why it pays to study price action. If the markets were random, why even bother.

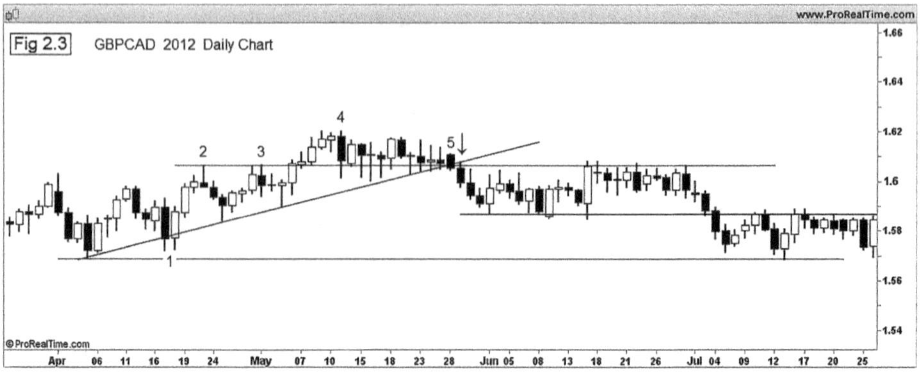

Figure 2.3. It's hard to imagine that not too long ago traders had to go out and buy a newspaper to even see a chart, let alone trade from it. So a big shoutout to the inventors of the online trading platforms. But do yourself a favor and steer clear of the indicator section.

That said, there is one feature among all these bells and whistles that cannot be praised high enough as it is the only "indicator" that pretty much all traders use and respect as is, which of course is the *line tool*. Indeed, no need for fancy settings on this one. All it takes to plot a trustworthy barrier is common sense, as perfectly illustrated by the angular barrier in the chart above (excluding the lows at 1). Would you run that line any differently?

Tip: If you are not too sure about a barrier right away, it is usually best to keep the chart clean; or plot whatever looks decent but keep an open mind for adjustments along the way.

It is actually quite common for a line to "earn itself" only after it is broken. To illustrate, notice how the 4-5 chop keeps bouncing off the 2-3 double top—that is a clear case of former resistance now acting as support, and as such validates that range barrier. (As you can see later on in this chart, this works the other way around too.)

So bulls have their break, but it is only half the work done. If they cannot push prices away from the barrier anytime soon, their break could still turn into a reversal.

Our job then is to rate the post-breakout action (4-5). And frankly, that doesn't look too bullish. Take specific note of bar 5. The session itself may not look that impressive, but make no mistake—this is a key development. For starters, it is the first bar to actually *close* below the 2-3 top (back inside the range). Yet even more provocative is the close below angular support.

Admittedly, nothing is lost yet for the bulls. All they have to do is buy the market back up. From a technical perspective, however, their fate is practically sealed. For even if they manage to break back the top barrier, there is now the 4-5 chop to plow through too. So the irony is that their earlier break effectively works against them. That's what you get when you fail to capitalize on your victories.

Even so, as not much of a counterpush is needed to shake a standard stop above bar 5, a good idea here is to opt for insurance above the previous bar; but not without checking first the consequences at the target end.

Since we are dealing with a fairly wide range, it may seem unnecessary to check if there is still room for a two-pointer, but the range barrier is not the only obstacle to watch out for. As we will soon discuss in more detail, action *inside* a range can also prove obstructive. Not all "bumps on the road" need to be feared (or few setups would ever call for a trade), but if at any time there is a notable swing point or cluster sitting in the way, we would do well to tighten our exit accordingly (factoring in some pips for the spread as well). True, this will affect our risk-to-reward, but better safe than sorry.

Note: Naturally, there is a limit to how far we can tighten our target and still make it worth our while. In principle, we could go so far as to accept a 1:1 risk-to-reward (if given good odds), but such aggression is not for everyone. In the end it is a personal call, but I suggest, if only during these studies, not to deviate too much from standard policy and therefore to set the threshold at 1.5 points. No need to split hairs on it, a rough estimate will do. So if there is *clearly* less room for a trade than 1.5 times the distance from entry to stop, we skip the current setup and look for a more suitable one.

Figure 2.4. After a rally from the lows to the highs, we usually see some profit-taking first (1-2). Whether that allows for a range reversal remains to be seen, but the least we can do is assess the support situation.

Here we actually have two options for an angular line. Which one to use? As a rule of thumb, unless a setup based off a sharper barrier looks too good to pass up, focus on the shallower one because that one cannot block the breakout of the other.

If we follow the above, that false break in bar 2 is not an immediate concern for the bulls as there is still the lower line to help them out. But even if that line is perforated, they may still be able to counter and have another shot at a range break. For example, we can picture at least two reasons for why the dip in bar 3 is rejected: (a) it regards a weak reversal attempt (no signal bar), and (b) we have yet to see a two-stepper to more strongly demoralize the bulls.

It's good to stay attentive, though, because a second failure to crack the top barrier is not likely to get brushed aside so easily, especially in conjunction with a *second* perforation of support, as in bar 4. (Of course, the two-step principle not only works for range barriers.)

Note: Imagine how bar 4 must have shown a proud bullish body at some point, only to close the day near its lows. In candlestick terms that is referred to as a *bearish doji*. The bearish part is not so much the lower close on that small body but the prominent top tail above. Perhaps we would have liked this bar to stick a bit above the top barrier (for an even safer stop), but let's not nitpick on such a fine signal bar, which by the way also allows for our preferred entry in a confirmation break.

If that bearish doji is such a monster, isn't the bottom tail of bar 5 equally alarming for us bears? Not in the least. First of all, we still have the conditions on our side. But more importantly, why worry at all if the worst that can happen is a minor one-point loss.

Note: The fact that bar 4 only *modestly* dips below support is actually preferable over a more prominent perforation because it allows for an entry close to the barrier and stop well above. So if bulls manage to temporarily break back the barrier (quite common), we are not immediately shaken out. An entry further away from the line would make for a trickier stop, and might even force us to skip.

Why then not prefer bar 4 to sit right on support; wouldn't that allow for an even sharper entry? It would indeed—but who's to say that we've plotted our line correctly. If its angle sits just a tad off compared to how most traders perceive the action, we may have set up our entry right *in* a barrier rather than beyond. This risk is logically much lower if a signal bar already sticks through because our entry will likely sit beyond the barrier anyway. Plus there is the aspect of a confirmation break.

Tip: If ever a signal bar hits your barrier spot on, which fortunately is far less common than a perforation, you can always set up your entry a few pips wider (effectively imagining a perforation). Not a perfect solution, but it might just save you a trap on occasion.

As for bar 1 earlier on, that's an easy skip if only for the overhanging cluster line. Bar 6 on the far right is not a trustworthy signal bar either. Even if we picture the bottom barrier to hold, it wouldn't be wise to just ignore the foregoing selloff and take a chance on any first bounce. Another reason for lying low is the tall span of bar 6; note that a two-point target based on this session practically requires a reversal back to the top barrier. Not impossible to accomplish, but to bank on that happening right after a sharp selloff is simply asking for trouble.

Figure 2.5. Even though we can pretty much guess the response to that trap bar at 2, it is not a setup for us as there is too little room for a trade towards the nearest support (1). Still we love to see a selloff to that swing point as then we can look for a reversal in line with the trend.

And that brings us to a variant that may not look so enticing at first yet is actually among the most reliable setups in our toolbox, a so-called *cluster setup* (3-4): a small series of bars tightly grouped together. Their potency stems from the pent-up pressure within, which is bound to pop at some point. (7-9 is another one.)

Note: Given the typical absence of an explicit signal bar, clusters do call for some adjustment regarding the entry. We'll have a closer look at this later on, but here's the basic idea: once we picture a cluster ripe for a pop (usually after only a couple of bars), we set up an entry a few pips beyond the cluster line. So for the 3-4 cluster that would be after bar 4. One thing, we do want the current bar to at least modestly favor a break (so for a long trade this bar should not be bearish).

Sadly, the break above bar 4 falls just shy of a two-pointer, assuming we opted for a stop below the low of the cluster rather than a standard stop. (A fine example of how insurance can backfire.)

A few weeks later the NZDCAD sets up a reversal in the top barrier (6). Not a textbook two-stepper (2-6), but still a high-odds reversal setup. Notice in particular the double perforation of support (5-6). And what to think of bar 6 itself, which is not only a bearish doji but also a trap bar. It also offers an entry in a confirmation break, and the false push above the top barrier allows for an ideal stop to boot.

Yet if for some reason still on the fence, it might help to ask yourself what *you* would do as a bull. Would you still believe in a range break after bar 6 or would you rather sell out and try to buy back in at lower levels? If the latter, here's an idea: instead of merely flattening your position, why not join us on the bear side first, and *then* look to reposition. That in a nutshell is the genius of *swing trading.*

Note: While we're at it, let's take a moment to discuss the actual routine of setting up this short. First we widen the chart a bit for a closer look. Then we right-click on the signal bar and jot down the levels for stop and entry (adding a few pips for the spread on both sides). Once we know the distance from entry to stop in pips (one point), we can project our target in the chart (at two points from entry). If this level still resides above the bottom barrier, we aim for a two-pointer. If below (or right on it), we plan to get out a few pips in front. Do note that the bottom barrier is still best based on the *original* swing low of bar 1, not the lows of the 3-4 cluster. The volume for the trade is always a personal choice. (More on that in Chapter 14.)

Back in support, the generous NZDCAD grants us a second cluster setup (7-9). Note that if we already set up an entry after bar 8 (a few pips beyond the cluster line), this order would have to be canceled in the next daily scan (bear bar). But we stay alert for another try.

A major giveaway of a looming breakout is the way bar 9 first breaks out at the "wrong" side, only to quickly spin around and attack the cluster line instead. While not a trap bar in the literal sense (no break above the foregoing bar), the false dip below support traps bears just the same. But wait, what about the close of this signal bar, isn't that unsuited for a *long* setup?

Note: With its close slightly lower than its open (black body), strictly speaking bar 9 is a bear bar. On a small bodied doji, however, the close is not so relevant if the tail is clearly more prominent. As that is the case here, we may look upon bar 9 as a bull bar.

* * *

Key points to consider when contemplating range reversals

1. Find the relevant range barriers (start with swing points early on and see how these hold up).

2. Look for false breakouts, but keep in mind that it usually takes two failures for the attackers to become demoralized and give up on their breakout aspirations (two-step principle).

3. Figure out the support situation below the latest run to the top barrier, or the resistance situation above the latest run to the bottom barrier; if such lines can be found and still appear relevant for the trade you have in mind, then only look to enter beyond them, never in front.

4. Place your stop at the other end of the signal bar (if safe enough) or else beyond a bar nearby (ideally a swing point).

5. Standard target policy is to aim for a two-pointer (twice the distance from entry to stop). If there is not enough room for it (scan in particular the distance to the opposite range barrier), look to trade for at least 1.5 times your risk.

chapter 3

Range Breakout Setup

how to take advantage of failed reversals

Now that we studied the typical characteristics of reversals, let's have a look at how ranges are typically broken. First a word of caution: given the notorious resilience of ranges, breakouts are not nearly as common as are reversals, so never think too lightly of it. The good part, though, is that the attempts that *do* follow through can often be anticipated by paying close attention to what goes on at the barrier.

Range breakout setups come in all shapes and sizes, yet those that call for a trade need to have at least one thing in common: a barrier fight of some sort, referred to as *buildup*.

The mode of a range (bullish or bearish) may already provide a hint as to whether a breakout is likely, but we should never underestimate the barrier defenders (those banking on a reversal). Hence our policy to always wait for a signal bar to mark the end of the buildup phase, the so-called *resolution*.

Note: Whenever a barrier breaks without us (on account of too little buildup or an unsuitable resolution), our chances to participate are not necessarily lost because we may still be able to hop on after a pullback (a frequent occurrence). As this calls for different tactics, though, we will discuss such setups in our next chapter on pullback reversals.

To get a good grasp on the breakout concept, let's focus on the more textbook setups first, meaning those that (a) harbor some buildup, and (b) resolve by means of a signal bar.

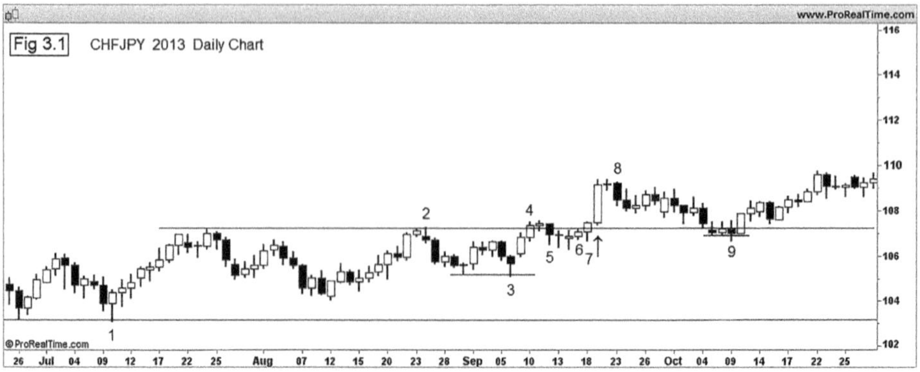

Figure 3.1. Our first example rightfully counts as textbook but not solely on account of the setup. Notice also the series of higher lows on the way to the barrier. As that lets on that bears are slowly pushed aside (modest corrections only), this range is effectively a breakout candidate well before the actual break. Helpful also is the *new-territory* potential: meaning no more obstacles to overcome once the range is left behind. (For a break into *old territory*, see Figure 3.4.) Still, a bet on a breakout would only be warranted after proper buildup.

To see why, let's examine the absence of buildup first, as with the attacks in bar 1, 2, 3, and 4. What do these breakout attempts have in common? That's right, all are hastily set.

Note the difference with the attempt in bar 7. As this one can boast of actual buildup, odds are bears will now not nearly be so confident in their ability to fend off this break. Notice also how bar 7 first dips below bar 6, only to sharply reverse and close outside of the barrier (trap bar). That's not likely to sit well with the bears either. Our take, therefore, is that bar 7 resolves the barrier fight in favor of a break. Whatever comes of it, that is our signal to set up a trade.

The benefit of buildup is easily understood, but how to tell when it is sufficient? In fairness, it depends. Most setups will show at least a handful of bars of pushing and pulling (as in 5-6), but even a few bars could do, as long as there is some fighting going on at the barrier just prior to the signal bar, so that we can speak of an actual resolution. Without such backup, the defenders of the range may not yet see the need to step out of the way (still hoping for a reversal).

Note: When scanning for a breakout, don't be put off if the first attempt is fended off without much ado. This is actually very common and to some degree even benefits the attackers—who then have a chance to prove their resilience (by coming back for another try). Indeed, this is a variant of the two-step principle. If it works great for reversals, then so too for breakouts! But don't forget the key requirement: for a setup to earn our approval, we need to see some buildup first.

Besides paving the way for a break, another great feature of buildup is that it usually allows for a sound stop. To illustrate, first consider the setup at 4. If you trade above that bar, where would you put your stop? Of course, you could place it below bar 4, but if you want to be *technically* protected, you basically have no choice but to opt for insurance all the way below bar 3. Because that is the nearest swing point. By contrast, a trade above bar 7 not only stands a better chance of following through, it also allows for technical protection at a much shorter distance from entry (below the 5-7 buildup).

In fact, if it suits your style you could even place your stop below signal bar 7 itself because this session counts as a swing point too, as do all trap bars and prominent dojis (since their intraday reversals are also visible on the dailies). But do note the following:

Tip: As it is wise to anticipate a pullback, referred to as a test (8-9), it is crucial not to put your stop too close to a broken barrier since the latter is often briefly broken back. But don't think too lightly of opting for insurance either, as any extra safety on your stop will automatically widen your target (assuming the 1:2 risk-to-reward). At some point that could backfire. If at any time the pros and cons appear to balance out, then just set it up one way or the other and have peace with it. (If neither insurance nor a standard stop is to your liking, skip and wait for a better offer.)

Figure 3.2. Here we have a range of the triangle variety. So we already know that a break is inevitable, and it isn't hard to guess which side it will occur. The fate of the bears in bar 1 perfectly illustrates the danger in ignoring the dominant pressure.

That said, bulls still need to play this smartly. They may have the conditions on their side, that doesn't release them from preparing their breakout properly. Examine that silly attempt in bar 2—and look what comes of it. Note also the logical placement of the top barrier, stemming from a swing high early on.

As can almost be expected, it isn't long before bulls give it another try (3). This second attempt to crack the top barrier is definitely a step up from the first, if only for the trap bar element. But not all is rosy with this setup. For starters, we are never too keen on overly tall signal bars as these often call for an uncomfortably wide two-pointer. While that is perhaps less an issue for a break into new territory, it is still something to take into account as we weigh our odds. The real dealbreaker here is the absence of barrier pressure just prior to bar 3. That warns us that things are not yet ripe for a break.

See the difference with the setup at bar 5. Only now the barrier is under serious attack. Note also the two-stepper in this buildup (3-5), and that this time we can put a stop much closer by. Moreover, rather than place it below bar 5, we can opt for a more technical stop below the previous bar (nearest swing point) at the premium of only a slightly wider two-pointer. That should be a no-brainer.

As for our entry, placing this order above bar 5 is inherently sound (confirmation break), but here too we can opt for a more *technical* spot, and place the order above bar 4 instead. While not a strict necessity, it is effectively a plus to have the high of the buildup already out of the way on entry as then it could no longer prove obstructive.

Note: There are no hard-and-fast rules for when or when not to apply insurance, be it on the stop or entry side. It depends on the situation and can even be a matter of style. For a break into new territory, a wider target is generally not an immediate concern, so the risk of insurance backfiring at *that* end is relatively low (within reason). A break into old territory, on the other hand, as we will discuss shortly, always calls for extra caution as sooner or later prices will hit upon an element of support or resistance. In some cases insurance isn't even an option as there would be too little room left for a worthy risk-to-reward. Then we either skip in the hope of a more suitable setup or trade with standard orders (if we still like our odds).

Perhaps you might ask: if the new-territory potential is so promising, why be content with a two-pointer; wouldn't it be a smarter idea to shoot for a bigger target or even trade for a trend? That's a fair question, but it's hard to answer it uniformly. In the end we all have to choose our own path. Just make sure that whichever way you manage your trades, you *always* have an exit plan in place.

Tip: When experimenting to figure out the "ideal" strategies for your personal methodology, try not to get swept into a futile quest for the holy grail. Rather, embrace the idea that there isn't just one "best" way to play the price action game. And welcome the strategies and tactics of your opponents in particular, or no trading opportunity would ever come about. Imagine an orderbook filled with only orders on the bull or bear side. Who then to do business with?

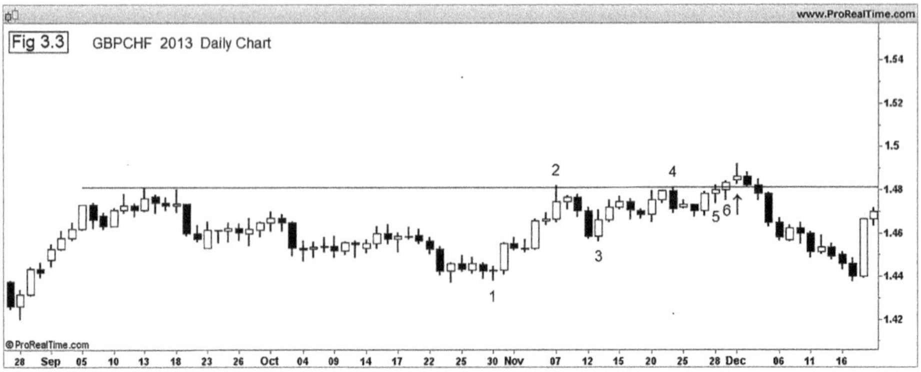

Figure 3.3. Here's a chart to show that things can set up very well but still fail for no apparent reason. Before we get to the setup, first have a look at bar 2. The chances of a breakout there are poor by any standard. But don't do anything silly, like betting on its failure! You never know how far a perforation will push on before it fails—if at all. No matter how well you can "read" the market, never stoop to gambling.

As is customary, it isn't long before bulls come back for another try. Such resilience by itself already raises the odds for a break significantly (two-step principle). But whatever comes of it, for us to join in, we need to see some solid buildup first!

Although we generally refer to buildup as the final fight at the barrier, there are usually several stages of it, as perfectly illustrated in the range above. It always starts with a first attack on the barrier, usually fended off quite easily (1-2). This then sets the stage for a subsequent attack: the *first* stage of buildup (3-4).

Note how this new attack is also thwarted, but not as convincingly as the first, and perhaps for that reason it isn't long before bulls give it another try (4-5): the *second* stage of buildup.

By now things are already looking up for a breakout, but we don't have a setup yet: the absence of pressure on the barrier just prior to bar 5 invalidates the resolution.

So ideally we now see a *final* stage of buildup: a few more bars that really pressure the barrier from below, followed by a resolution in favor of a break. But what to do if the *next* bar already pushes through the barrier, as seen in bar 6?

Note: As much as we would love to solely deal with textbook setups, in the end all that truly matters is whether we like our odds. So whenever we spot a setup that ticks a few boxes, the least we can do is give it a closer look.

In this particular case, I think there is a lot to be said for biting the bullet. The push in bar 6 is perhaps a little hasty, but there is certainly some buildup involved. The fact that bar 6 *closes* above the top barrier is another potent feature (more forcing than a mere perforation), as is the new-territory potential (no obstacles in sight). So for the bulls, the prospects are quite promising.

As for the bears, can you spot their predicament? Not a single one of their shorts is currently trading in the plus, and by the looks of it, the worst has yet to come. Picture the irony: if no new bears come to their rescue, the only way to stop the bleeding is to *cover* their shorts—and thus become *buyers* in the very break they fear!

If you agree that this is worth a shot, then let's go ahead and place our entry above bar 6. The stop on this trade is more a matter of taste. Below bar 6 looks a little tight but might still survive a modest dip below the barrier in the event of a test. We could also opt for a stop below the 4-5 buildup, but that calls for a much wider two-pointer. However, since this regards a break into new territory, this is probably our best bet. A middle ground option is to place the stop below bar 5, but its *technical* merit is debatable (not a prominent swing point).

Tip: The fact that this range break fails is no reason to immediately look for a reversal. It is rarely wise to flip a position after a loss because the conditions are still pointing the other way, or are neutral at best.

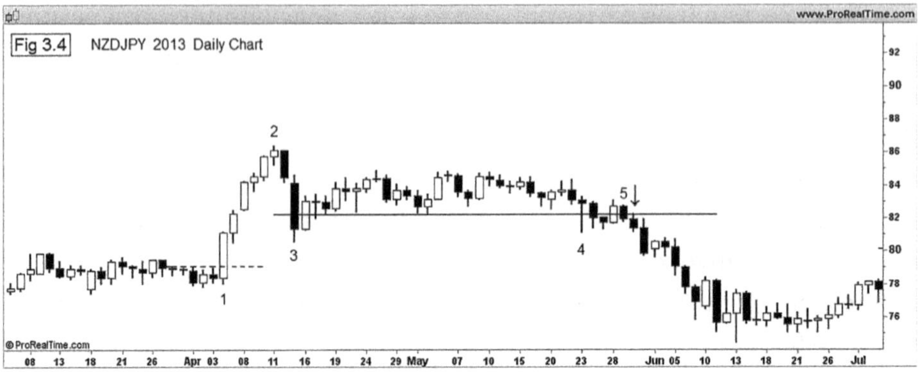

Figure 3.4. Sudden bursts of activity are not as common on the dailies as they are on the intraday charts, but they're no rarity either, often in response to a macro-economic development (1-2). The interesting part is always the aftermath. If the enthusiasm does not return after the inevitable pullback (2-3), it would not be uncommon for prices to trade back to pre-news levels, or worse.

So what to make of that sideways chop following the 2-3 pullback? Well, for one thing it is obvious that the earlier enthusiasm has waned; and note also the gradually declining highs in that cluster.

For as long as support holds up, though, the new trend could still win out. By the way, I chose not to run the support barrier from the low of bar 3 as there are no matching lows further up. The horizontal barrier is a bit of a guess at first but quickly gains relevance thanks to the *false* break in bar 4 and the subsequent barrier fight.

Bulls may have broken back that barrier, but they are not out of the woods yet. Their task now is to *keep* prices above support and force a reversal. Failure to do so should have us on the alert for a range break variant that we shall refer to as a *re-break failure setup.*

Re-break failure setups work best when the odds for a reversal are poor to begin with, as is the case here in view of that fat 3-4 cluster (no easy task for bulls to dig through such chop). Helpful also is when the failure of the re-break doesn't come about immediately but after a few bars of buildup (4-5).

So the conditions appear to favor a short, but what about the resolution. Can we trust a small *inside bar* for signal bar purposes (5)?

Note: An inside bar is any bar that fully sits within the span of its predecessor (the opposite of a trap bar). It is perhaps not the ideal signal bar, but whether or not to accept for the most part depends on the conditions. The more these favor the trade idea, the less relevant the issue of the inside bar. An additional benefit is that inside bars usually allow for a safer stop without immediately compromising the attainability of a two-point target. For example, on a short below bar 5, we can easily opt for a more technical stop above the previous bar.

However, as this setup regards a break into *old territory* (effectively a reversal), it is still important to check if there is room for our minimum reward of at least 1.5 times our risk.

The first hurdle that comes to mind is the low of bar 4, but as it is part of the buildup itself it can be ignored (why else trade). Next up is the low of the 2-3 pullback. I think we can discard that swing point as well on the fair assumption that bulls would rather wait for that cluster on the left to be hit first (to use it as a springboard).

As that cluster still sits within a two-point distance from entry, the recommended call is to exit in front of it. But where *exactly* to do so in the absence of a straightforward horizontal cluster line?

The simplest solution would be to get out in front of its high point; yet even if that would be acceptable reward-wise, we can often plan our exits with a little more finesse (see tip).

Tip: The idea is to look for a technical level within the obstacle itself, basically anything that allows for a barrier. If such a base can be found (dotted line), prices are often seen to travel towards it, courtesy of what is beyond doubt one of the most exploitable phenomenon in price action: the *magnet effect* of barriers. True, in this particular example the benefit is not all that evident, but at least take stock of the principle. As we will soon discuss in more detail, the magnet effect of barriers (and of range barriers in particular) is one of the most potent features in whole array of conditions we could hope to have on our side. In fact, it is often a key reason for considering a trade in the first place.

Figure 3.5. As often seen with stocks in the same sector, certain related currency pairs tend to move in the same direction. They may even form the same type of patterns and break away from them in similar fashion. But not necessarily simultaneously.

Take a moment to compare this AUDJPY chart to its close cousin, the NZDJPY, discussed on the previous pages. I think it's safe to assume that the same catalyst is present in the initial bull swing (1-2) and that the same corrective forces are at work in the 2-3 pullback. Yet the subsequent range forms a little differently, now allowing for an *angular* line. As a consequence, the short on this AUDJPY sets up several days ahead of the short on the NZDJPY.

Again, it starts with a false dip below support (4). As this one is not as prominent as the rejection on the NZDJPY, we could still class this as a regular range break setup rather than a re-break failure, but in the end it is the trade idea that counts. Labeling setups is simply a way to help the typical patterns stick in our minds.

The implications of the 4-5 buildup do resemble those of our previous chart in that the conditions for a reversal are poor at best (with the 3-4 chop hanging above). Hence our focus on a *bearish* resolution.

And there it is in bar 5. Note how this trap bar not only overshadows its direct neighbor but also the two other bars in the buildup. That's a convincing resolution for sure! The fact that its close is back *on* the barrier is perhaps a small boon for the bulls, but their situation is no less dire. After all, the slightest push below this signal bar would technically confirm the failure of support.

While all this looks good for a short, let us not forget that it regards a break into old territory. So first we must check the path to target. This time, though, there is only one real obstacle to consider: that swing point just before the 1-2 runup. So we have to ask ourselves: would that be a logical place for bulls to buy back in?

I think we can make an educated guess that that swing point sits a bit too close to the broken barrier to mark it as a serious springboard. *Modest* buying there should not be an issue as that will likely dry up in or near the broken barrier (as is the fate of many tests). And even if bulls would push on some more, our excellent stop above bar 5 (trap bar) may still hold. Thus, as harmful counterplay is not all that likely here, shooting for a two-pointer looks well worth a try.

Tip: Since this trade sets up several days prior to the short in Figure 3.4, it goes to show that when two related charts display similar action and similar patterns, they can still *set up* at different dates. Hence there is a lot to be said for regarding all charts as unique and for trading them as such. When two similar charts set up simultaneously, however, there is the option of trading both on half volume, so as not to run a risk of a two-point loss on a "single" trade idea; then again, that also takes away your chances of a four-point win; or a mixed outcome, for that matter. My advice on this is not so much to favor one idea more than the other—that's up to you—but to be consistent in the way you manage all such "duo trades." Then you win some and lose some, and in the end it may all balance out.

Note: At this point you may have already noticed that the underlying theme in the range breakout setup is actually very similar to that of the range reversal. It all comes down to the presumed outcome (resolution) of a barrier fight in which either the defenders topple the attackers or a vice versa. Breakouts may not be as common as reversals, but that says little about the skirmish at hand. And lest we forget, all ranges eventually get broken.

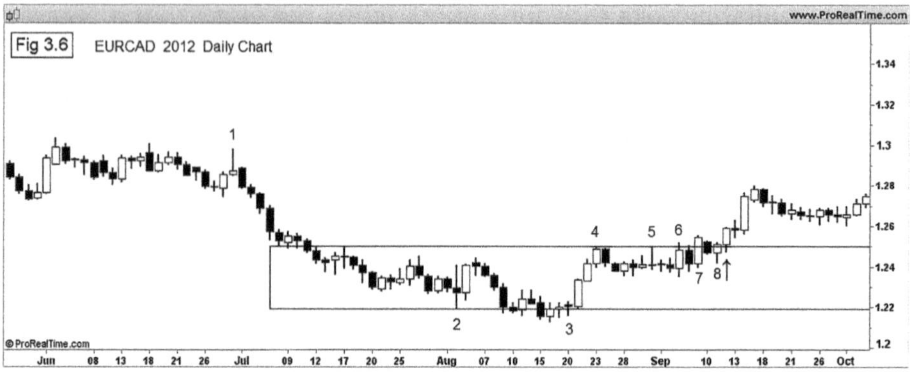

Figure 3.6. As long as there is room for a decent target, a break into old territory can be just as rewarding as any break into new territory. But check first where exactly the break would sit. Here above, for example, the top barrier is situated about halfway a bear trend (1-2). As it is no secret that many traders love to exploit this area for reversal purposes, the conditions for a range breakout are far from optimal. So if we are to look for a setup at all, *topnotch* buildup is of the essence.

Recall the principle of buildup in stages. Progressions 3-4-5 and 5-6 represent the first two stages. Of these early attacks, bar 6 is the first to crack through. Not something to pursue, though, if only for the absence of barrier pressure just prior. And this trap bar stands unpleasantly tall for signal bar purposes as well.

As it turns out, bar 6 is not taken out anyway and instead a bear session forms. Now it is up to the bulls to keep the pressure up. A dip below bar 6 would not be the end of the world, but they would do well to keep prices in striking distance of the barrier.

Bulls indeed don't waste time pushing for another break and even manage to *close* the next bar above the barrier (7). Do we have a setup? Well, this is certainly the best breakout attempt so far, and the preceding buildup also sits closer to the barrier (6-7). But once again the signal bar stands uncomfortably tall. Even if we use a standard stop, a two-point target practically requires a reversal back to the high of the trend. Not impossible to achieve, but far from a promising prospect. And thus we skip the offer.

As the next bar opens lower (can only be a Monday) and never trades above bar 7, the barrier fight is still undecided. But note again the modest rejection. Of course, with now *two* rejected breakouts on the chart, it is even more crucial for bulls to keep the pressure up and not let bears take over. And lo and behold, next session they are at it again (8).

Do we finally have a *valid* resolution? The span of bar 8 is certainly suitable, so no issues there. The bar also allows for a fine stop, at some distance away from the barrier (fairly safe in the event of a test). While the conditions for a break are still not ideal, at this point we can imagine the opposition to no longer feel so confident.

Personally I think there is still a lot to be said for letting this go, but truth be told, a more aggressive trader might think otherwise. For all of you in that camp, think for a moment about how you would set this up. Would you opt for a slightly riskier entry above bar 8 or arrange to enter above bar 7 instead (the only hurdle left) at the premium of a wider two-pointer?

Tip: As there exist no rules on the matter, you can only answer this for yourself. Keeping your target well within a "doable" limit is generally a good idea, and even more so for a trade into old territory. Yet in the end it all depends on the conditions at hand. One thing, though, never accept a risky entry or stop for the sole purpose of an easy target. Then either opt for insurance and hope it doesn't backfire or stand aside and wait for a better offer.

Figure 3.7. Let's wrap up with an interesting variant of a triangle breakout. Contrary to the one discussed in Figure 3.2, this one breaks on the bear side. By the way, while we will be looking at the setup from a breakout perspective, note that we are effectively dealing with a reversal inside a range. More on that in a moment.

It all starts with that false break in bar 1. Not a happy sight for the bulls, we can imagine, and not their first failure either. But with support not far below, nothing is to make of it yet. One thing we do know at this stage in the triangle, a break will soon come.

The fact that the market fails to bounce meaningfully after bar 2 is a first tipoff that we might be seeing a bearish resolution. We shouldn't expect bulls to give up so easily, though, if only for the quality of support (spanning multiple months). As we like to see some decent buildup first, a short below bar 3 is clearly not an option.

At bar 4 the buildup has fattened up a bit, but the jury is still out on the winner of this barrier fight. Consider also the following pointer, an extra reason not to do anything rash:

Note: As you may have noticed, the final barrier fight often revolves *around* a barrier rather than sit right on it (or below). This is crucial to observe because whenever there are several perforations that appear to line up, chances are there is a so-called *buildup line* in play (as shown). If so, this little barrier will very likely function as a line of last resort for those still banking on a reversal. And so it naturally follows that we no longer concentrate on the failure of the main barrier but on that of the buildup line instead.

One extra note, if at any time the perforations appear quite erratic, or otherwise fail to connect, it might be wise to focus on the main barrier still (or wait for new perforations that match).

At some point all barrier fights demand a resolution, be it for a break or a reversal. While we usually have a preference for one side more than the other, we must never underestimate the resilience of the opponent. Even when we spot a seemingly valid resolution (bar 5), it is always wise to check if we are not missing anything.

So let's do just that, starting with the trade idea. As bulls repeatedly failed to break the top barrier (despite the higher lows on the way up), it's safe to state that the odds now favor a bearish resolution more than a bullish comeback. So far so good. As for the buildup, no issues there either as the action on the barrier now looks "fat" enough for a breakout (2-5). The perforation of the buildup line in bar 5 is a welcome feature too as it allows for our preferred entry in a confirmation break. A more subtle find, also in bar 5, is the total disrespect for yesterday's trap bar (warning bulls not to have their hopes up). And as for our target, despite the fact that it regards a break into old territory, there is ample room for a two-pointer still, even if we opt for a stop above the high of the buildup (recommended). So yes, we're definitely good to go.

Note: Moreover, if there is ever a valid reason to deviate from standard policy and shoot for *more* than a two-pointer, this could be one such occasion. Remember what we talked about earlier regarding the magnet effect of barriers. This time we can see the phenomenon in all its glory. Note that once support is finally given up, the market drops like a stone towards the nearest support. In this case the magnet effect of the bottom barrier immediately kicks in, but the speed of the drop is not so relevant as long as that magnet gets hit. Needless to mention, you don't *have* to aim for the range barrier. Being content with a two-pointer here is still perfectly fine and principally advised.

* * *

Key points to consider when contemplating range breakouts

1. Locate the relevant barrier.
2. Look for stages of buildup.
3. If a first break fails due to poor buildup, anticipate the attackers to come back for another try.
4. Look for serious pressure (one or more barrier touches) just prior to the signal bar.
5. In the event of a break into old territory, check closely the available room for a trade.
6. In choppy barrier fights, consider the possibility of a buildup line that may have taken over from the main barrier.
7. When setting up your trade, be mindful not to put your stop too close to the broken barrier, to minimize the risk of a shake in an otherwise harmless test.

chapter **4**

Pullback Reversal Setup

how to take advantage of corrections

As we all know the dangers of chasing a trend, a popular strategy even among non-technical traders is to wait for a pullback first and *then* try to hop on. There is obviously a little more to it, but the idea itself makes sense. Not so well-known perhaps is that this same strategy is equally applicable in a ranging environment. And that's great news for us swing traders because ranges in Forex are far more common than trends, and the next pullback is never far away.

Whichever type we are dealing with, the basic tactics work the same for all contingencies: meaning we never guess the turn of a pullback but always wait for some reliable signs that a reversal is "brewing."

Note: A key idea for this setup is that we want to see *two* notable reversal attempts before hopping on ourselves, not unlike our plan for the range reversal. In certain conditions a one-stepper might do, but it can safely be stated that the vast majority of pullback reversals to have our attention will be of the two-step variety.

Of course, and this goes for all setups, a trade can only be considered in conjunction with a convincing signal bar, so that the tension in the turn is properly resolved.

Given the wide range of possible variants, let us not delve too deep into any particular subtleties just yet but really focus on the underlying themes and motifs. Once we know what to look for, individual specifics are not that relevant anyway as we mainly focus on the resolutions. Let's have a look at some examples.

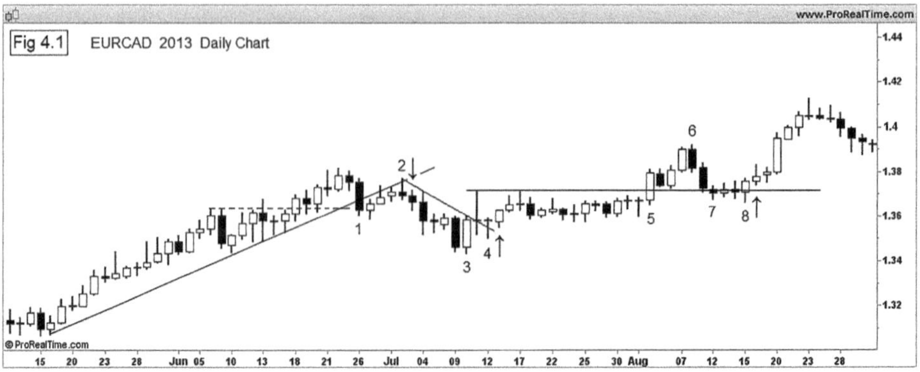

Figure 4.1. Our first setup is actually a bit of a misnomer as it regards a reversal of a rally, not a pullback. But as it offers a perfect illustration of a two-step reversal, let's simply imagine this bull run to be a pullback in a much bigger bear trend.

The setup effectively starts with the perforation of support in bar 1. As prices rarely follow through on a first probe, this development is not likely to turn the tables around. Even more so as there is support from a cluster nearby (dotted line).

To keep the pressure in their favor, however, bulls would do well to reclaim their broken support. If all they can muster is a test, and that test resolves bearishly, that would count as a *two-step* reversal. And that is exactly what happens in bar 2. So in a nutshell, bar 1 sets the tone, bar 2 blows the whistle.

Note: As for that cluster to the left, practice has it that such obstacles rarely prove a nuisance *twice* (unless very fat). So with a hit on that block already out of the way (which triggered the test), it is no longer a dealbreaker for a short. This is not to say that it couldn't prove obstructive again, but we trust our stop above bar 2 to hold.

The location of our next setup is beyond debate as it occurs in the popular *halfway area* of a rally (meaning after a pullback of about 40 to 60 percent). This one starts with bar 3. As we calmly wait for more info, we can already scan for a *pullback line*, but always with an open mind for adjustment. If no solid line can be found, or a line no longer seems relevant (as with our trade above bar 8 later on), then we do without and take it from there.

Assuming we have plotted a line as shown (2-3), there are effectively two ways for a two-stepper to form. Either a new bull bar will soon attack this barrier from below (pushing against it or sticking through) or, as is the case here, there is a significant break first, followed by a test. If this test resolves to our liking, as happens in bar 4, we have our signal bar. All we have to do then is set up the trade.

Note: The fact that our signal bar dips below the pullback line first is not only commonplace in a test, it is actually preferable over a mere hit-and-bounce, in that the failure of a re-break attempt can only help to demoralize the opponent. Note also how the bottom tail of bar 4 forms a nice swing point for our stop. So no need to opt for insurance all the way below bar 3.

If the setup at 8 looks familiar, well noted. We already took a peek at it in Chapter 1 (to introduce the concept of the signal bar). The idea for this trade starts with the break in bar 5, which by the way also hits our target on that earlier trade above bar 4. An immediate re-entry above bar 5 would be too optimistic, though; but we may see chance to hop on if the break gets tested.

A brief test right after bar 5 doesn't offer much, but when the market pulls back a second time (6-7) and then goes sideways for a bit (buildup), we are granted our favorite resolution, the ever-potent trap bar (8).

So there you have it, no less than three pullback reversal setups in a single chart, all a bit different, yet the two-step principle is remarkably consistent (1-2, 3-4, and 5-8). And as you can see, there is no need for a classic trend-and-pullback scenario to find interesting reversals. A test of a breakout can be just as promising.

Figure 4.2. Pullback reversals in a trend are a little harder to anticipate than the test-type variants, but the area in which to look for a setup can safely be guessed: about halfway the latest rally. It gets even better if we can find some sideways action in this halfway area. That cluster at 1, for instance, could not only serve as a magnet for the pullback but also as a springboard for a later reversal.

In this example, however, both bar 2 and 3 are far from ideal signal bars. The former is only a one-stepper and sits way too close to the top of the trend to even think of a trade. Bar 3 couldn't be a signal bar either, if only for the pullback line situation. While we could run that line more sharply, and have the bar stick through, that looks a bit contrived. The pullback is also still quite shallow.

Then how about bar 4? As that is now the third attempt of bulls to reverse the pullback (2-3-4), in conjunction with an actual perforation, things are indeed looking *up*. So in that light the shallow pullback is no longer a major concern; but that doesn't automatically warrant an entry; first we have to find a good place for our stop.

Note: As you may recall from our discussions on range breakouts, it is crucial not to put our stops too close to a broken barrier—to avoid a shake in an otherwise harmless test. *Angular* breakouts require even more caution because the meeting point with the barrier is not fixed. For example, a stop below bar 4 (already a bit tight) might survive a hit on the barrier in next few days, but less so if the test takes a little longer to come in. Because the meeting point will then sit *lower*.

Why then not place our stop below bar 3? Alas, that is not really an option as the premium for this insurance is a much wider two-pointer. With the trend as backup, we could perhaps take our chances, but in most such cases we simply skip and hope for a test.

Tip: Always be mindful of the *way* a test comes in as that will have a big say in the type of setup to scan for. Aggressive pullbacks generally take more time to reverse than the calmer varieties. How to tell the difference? Compare the bars in the breakout to those in the test. If the latter clearly look stronger, don't look for a swift reversal back in the barrier. Wait for an extra step or some other form of buildup to indicate that the earlier break will likely hold. And should you ever spot a session like bar 5 in a test—aptly coined a *powerbar*—it might be wise to drop the reversal idea altogether. Granted, the example here obviously shows otherwise, but it's the principle that counts.

Throughout July, the USDCHF forms a so-called *head-and-shoulders* formation (6-7-8), a triple top variant widely regarded as the mother of all reversal patterns. And it should be said, these patterns tend to live up to their reputation quite well. Unfortunately, the tall span of bar 8 (effectively a *favorable* powerbar) is unsuited for signal bar purposes; so here too we hope for a test.

There are many ways for a break to get tested, one of which is by means of an almost instant re-break, as in the 9-10 sequence. Do recall that in such choppy skirmishes a buildup line may have taken over from the main barrier, as looks to be the case here. Hence we must now look for a bar to either attack or stick through this buildup line.

Of the two bear bars in the test, bar 10 is clearly the more suitable signal bar (trap bar). We could also call this a re-break failure setup but in the end all that matters is that we place the short.

Note that it still takes a few days for this trade to take off, which is actually fairly common. So don't fret, trust your stop.

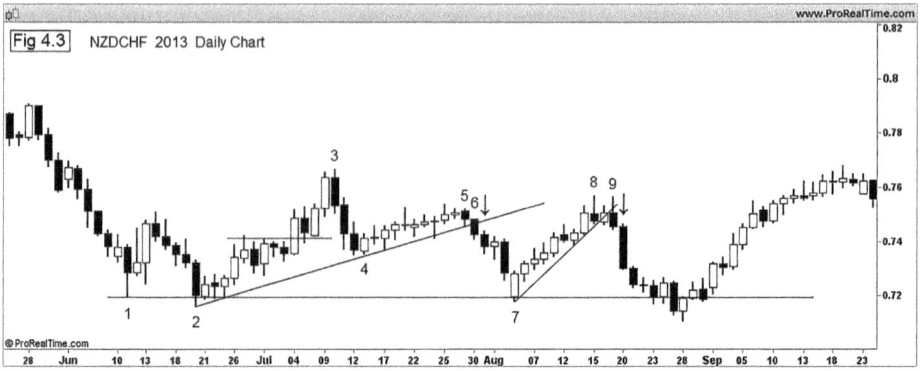

Figure 4.3. Pullbacks come in all shapes and sizes but not all are suited for reversal operations. Focus in particular on the orderly, diagonal corrections, often referred to as *flags*. Be mindful of pullbacks of the choppy type or those that harbor clusters within (2-3) as these rarely allow for smooth reversals.

The good part is that an unsuitable pullback can still morph into a suitable one. Note how the 2-5 action is now more orderly and diagonal, resembling a *bear flag*. As it is no secret that flags tend to break in line with the trend, surely we are not the only bears looking for a failure of the pullback line (or *flagline*). An extra incentive is of course the looming magnet effect of the bottom barrier.

A short below bar 5 looks premature, though. The 4-5 buildup does add to the pressure, but we cannot speak of a proper resolution.

Bar 6 is more up or alley, but the perforation of the flagline is a little deeper than we like to see. Can we still short below this bar? It depends on what is needed for protection.

Since a standard stop is not really an option (too easily hit in a test), ideally we would opt for a stop above the highest bar in the 4-5 buildup. But as that would only leave room for little more than a one-pointer, we either have to make do with the lesser stop above bar 5 (no swing point), or skip and hope for a test. Given the situation, however, there is a third option worthy of mention:

Tip: Since the room for a trade is capped by a barrier, the only downside of using the best stop available is a smaller *profit*—because the target is the same. For that reason, there is a lot to be said for playing such trades in the safest fashion, even if the risk-to-reward is under our chosen threshold (but no smaller than 1:1). If you'd rather stay principled, then by all means go for the weaker stop or stand aside. But don't just discard occasional deviations by default. As a trader, always think logically, with your own best interests at heart.

Note that if we do trade below bar 6, we should still base our exit on the low of the earlier trend (1), not the *false* low shortly after (2); and for good reason (examine the bounce in bar 7).

Not much later the NZDCHF calls for attention again, thanks to the 7-8 bounce in the lows of the range. As this runup effectively still counts as a test of the earlier broken flagline, we may have another shot at the bottom barrier magnet (which remains active for as long as the conditions are bearish).

Given the relative aggression in the 7-8 runup, an immediate short below bar 8 would be too aggressive here. But see what a little patience can do. Two bars later, we not only have a two-stepper in the top of the test (8-9) but also another popular reversal pattern known as the *M-top.* Here we see a classic three-bar version (bear bar/bull bar/bear bar), but that is certainly not the only M-pattern to appreciate as we will discuss in later examples. (The same goes for the *W-bottom.*)

Granted, the M-top is essentially a bonus because the resolution in bar 9 by itself is already well worth a short (trap bar). No need to place our stop above bar 8, a standard stop is fine. And judging by the space between bar 9 and the bottom barrier, it looks like we can play this for a standard target too.

Note: If on closer inspection a two-point target would sit a tad *below* the bottom barrier, again we should plan our exit a few pips in front. Even though it is common for range barriers to get perforated prior to a reversal, to actually bet on that is a terrible idea (remember bar 7). Never risk a good trade for a few extra pips.

Figure 4.4. If you have never traded the dailies before, I hope you are pleasantly surprised to find that most currency pairs show fairly orderly price action. If on occasion the action gets a little fickle (1-2 and 2-3), just wait for things to calm down and become more "tradable" again. In general, the more orderly the pullback, the more likely the reversal setup will be spotted by others as well.

Note: When looking for a pullback line, plot whatever you deem relevant at the time but keep an open mind. It is actually not uncommon to have to wait for a break and a test before you can confidently plot a barrier (3-4).

Interestingly, a re-break in a test is no reason to question your trade idea. On the contrary, it is preferable over a mere hit-and-bounce in the barrier because it allows for a stronger setup (re-break failure), and typically for a safer stop as well. And that is exactly why we love that resolution in bar 4 (trap bar).

About a month later, the AUDJPY switches gears and even goes on to form a giant W-pattern (4-6), which puts us on the alert for a reversal in the halfway area of the 5-6 rally; we can already spot a very promising *bull flag* (6-7).

At first the flagline is pretty straightforward (hence the exclusion of the push in bar 8), but then the action gets a little scruffy, hinting at the presence of a buildup line. Just to be safe, we should now keep an eye out for a signal bar that either hits this new line from below or sticks a bit through. The latter is preferable as that would allow for a stronger entry in a confirmation break; but either way is fine.

Which brings us to bar 9. Is that a worthy signal bar? Personally I prefer more potent resolutions (like the one in bar 4 earlier on), but there is perhaps something to be said for it. Do note that if you set up a trade above bar 9, your entry would still be pending following session and the setup itself would no longer be valid. Then just cancel.

Tip: As a sidenote, examine the false break in bar 10. While in principle never an issue for us, this perfectly illustrates why I strongly advise not to check your charts intraday—as you might get tempted into playing such midsession breakouts yourself. The same goes for checking your open positions. As it is all too easy to freak out and do something silly, why expose yourself to such risk. As swing traders we all best stick to what we do best, which is to trade *end of day*.

After the false break in bar 10, there are essentially two possibilities. Either the reversal attempt will fail completely or bulls will regroup and try again. We might prefer a breakout but either outcome is fine because we have no *need* for a trade.

As it turns out, the next bar already shows another push above the buildup line, and this one holds firm (11). That's a signal bar. However, since bar 11 is an inside bar, a good idea here is to place our entry above bar 10 instead, to have that hurdle already out of the way. The premium of this insurance is only a marginally wider two-pointer anyway. (Entering long above a *bear* bar does not violate our policy because bar 11 still counts as the signal bar.)

Should we then base our stop on bar 10 as well? That is actually a fair question if you think about it. Here's how to answer it for yourself: imagine a break above bar 10 and then a drop below bar 11. Would you still believe in a good outcome? If so, place your stop more safely away. If not, then you might as well go for a standard stop as that one comes with the tightest target.

Figure 4.5. Before we head over to the next chapter on trend reversals (the last in our series of four), let's wrap up with a few more pointers on pullback reversals inside a range. Setup-wise these work the same as in a trend, but keep good track of the magnets in play. For example, if you trade long above bar 2 (not a setup), base your exit on that swing point on the far left (the later top barrier), not the *false* break in bar 1.

Similar tactics apply to our short below bar 4. As the exact level of the bottom barrier has yet to be decided on, there we base our exit on the low of bar 3 as it is the first swing point (potential support) in sight. Once again it is a matter of better safe than sorry.

Tip: When having to tighten your target due to a barrier or a notable swing point, rather than plan to exit *in* such magnets, plan to get out *a few pips in front* (to account for the spread). Play it even more safely, if you like, but whatever you do, don't shoot for a perforation. You might get away with it, but there is simply no point in risking a good profit for a few extra pips.

Bar 4 is a fine example of a one-step resolution (of a test), although you could also look upon it as a two-stepper with the break of the cluster line earlier on (the first step is somewhat hidden in the break). Of course, labeling setups is purely for instructive purposes. All that truly matters is that we spot that powerful trap bar and act accordingly. Yet if for some reason we missed our scan, it is not too late to short below bar 5, which now forms a two-stepper with bar 4.

The trade idea for the short on the far right is pretty much a copy of the one earlier on. With prices again below a cluster line in the midrange area, we logically look for a bearish resolution of the subsequent test, in anticipation of another selloff to the bottom barrier.

At a casual glance bar 7 already forms a two-stepper with bar 6, or if you will an M-top variant (bear bar/bull bar/bear bar). This one, however, is not particularly suited for a setup because the bar in the middle is actually the strongest of the three. How's that relevant? It regards the unconvincing resolution. Or to phrase it more practically: for as long as we can picture bulls to still believe in a re-break, we shouldn't be looking for a short.

The next two bars would hardly be worth mentioning if not for the fact that they warn of a buildup line beneath what looks to be a test of a test. Nothing to write home about, but it does give us a line in the sand beyond which to look for an entry. Which brings us to bar 8.

While bar 8 by itself is of modest standing, this resolution is already more convincing as bulls now failed to break back a *second* time. That's a two-stepper (7-8). The "bullish" close of this doji is not an issue either as the bearish top tail is more telling. Perhaps we would have preferred this bar to stick through support rather than sit right on it, but that too is no reason to postpone a short. (If you prefer, place your order a little wider to ensure an entry below the buildup line.)

For protection, we could either play this with a standard stop above bar 8, the latest swing point, or with an even safer stop above bar 7, the high of the test. If *that* gets hit, we truly have no business staying short. The safer stop does require a wider target, but still very doable. Set it up as you deem best.

* * *

Key points to consider when contemplating pullback reversals

1. Identify the pullback or test for a reversal play.
2. Scan for a logical pullback line; and take into account the possibility of a buildup line.
3. In most cases, wait for two distinctive reversal attempts before hopping on a reversal.
4. Make sure your stop isn't too easily hit.
5. Be extra wary of aggressive tests as these rarely allow for a swift reversal and might even spell trouble for the break itself.
6. When looking to trade inside a range, see if you can exploit the magnet effect of the nearest range barrier.

chapter **5**

Trend Reversal Setup

how to anticipate the turn of a trend

Since our aim is to have setups in place for all kinds of markets, our studies would not be complete without a good look at trend reversals. At first glance this may seem a bit odd because we all know the danger in fighting a trend. But what if we let the market do the fighting first? As we will see, that opens up a whole new range of possibilities.

It should be said upfront that we are not going to find trend reversals all over the place since the conditions for this setup are not easily met. Chances are we may only locate a few high-odds scenarios per year; but that's more than enough for any type of setup to deserve a place in our toolbox.

To a large extent, the tactics resemble our pullback reversal strategies discussed in the previous chapter. But there is a major difference: a typical trend is much harder to turn than a typical pullback. Bar an occasional exception, we can be fairly sure a two-stepper won't do. Enter the three-stepper!

Indeed, what many trend reversals have in common is that they come about in *threes*—as in triple tops and triple bottoms, or any variant thereof. The individual steps could sit days, weeks, or even months apart (depending on the trend), yet the three-step element should clearly stand out for a setup to be valid. Of course, there will be exceptions, but the trend reversals demanding our fullest attention will be of the three-step variety. So let's familiarize ourselves with that first.

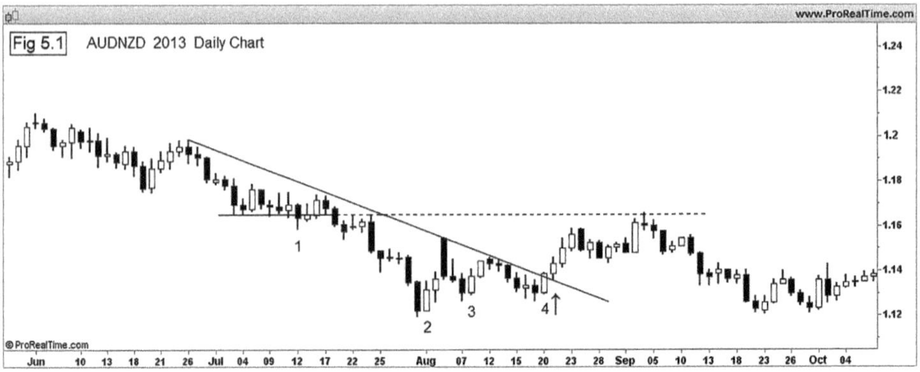

Figure 5.1. Whenever we have a trend on the chart, our first trade idea should be a pullback reversal (in line with the trending conditions). At some point, however, we may start to consider a reversal of the trend itself. This usually happens after *three* notable reversal attempts in the highs or lows (2-3-4).

Not all three-steppers are equally interesting, though, because we also like to see a certain "harmony" between the trend and the reversal attempts. For example, if the three steps sit only a few days apart, that probably won't do for a serious trend. The setup here above is decently spread out in view of the relatively modest bear trend. Do note that the harmony element typically regards the *latest* trend. So it is not necessarily a problem if the total trend is much bigger.

Note: Contrary to what the name suggests, trend reversals rarely call the end of a trend; more likely they are pullbacks. Hence it is important not to overstay our welcome in any such trade. Ideally we aim no further than the halfway area of the latest rally as that is where so many pullbacks are known to reverse. But what we need to avoid at all costs are obstructive elements in that tricky area, such as that cluster from which the dotted line is drawn.

Mind you, such barriers (let's call them *halfway barriers*) need not solely be feared; they can even be seen as an ally, thanks to their magnet effect. But as we can see in this chart, once that effect runs out, things can quickly take a turn for the worse.

Tip: As for the exact position of that barrier, in principle you could also base a line on the low of bar 1. Recommended, however, is to first look for a more technical exit. If you find a line worthy enough to earn a place in the chart (two matching bounces might already do), consider targeting *that*, as it will likely prove a magnet.

Assuming we plot the halfway barrier as shown, there looks to be ample room for a trade, but that ultimately depends on what is offered for an entry and stop. In that regard it is nice to see that the *trendline* (similar to a pullback line) leaves little room for debate; so at least on the entry side there is no need for insurance.

As for our stop, we would love to place it below bar 4 as that would easily allow for a two-pointer, but that may not be the wisest call here. Even though we enjoy the backup of a three-stepper, the perforation of the trendline is only a first and as such quite prone to get tested. Not a dealbreaker, but the possibility of a test always calls for an extra sound stop, more so when it regards an *angular* breakout—as we cannot know beforehand where a test will hit. (And even if we knew the exact meeting point, a test doesn't necessarily reverse on impact.)

Tip: Truth be told, there is only so much we can do to avoid a shake in a test. My advice therefore is to keep it very simple by using the already familiar tactic: if at any time a standard stop won't do, look for a stop beyond the foregoing bar first; and if that won't do either, a swing point nearby. But keep in mind that too much safety on the stop could backfire at the target end!

For the trade in question, a stop below the session prior to bar 4 should be a no-brainer as that bar also forms the nearest swing point. Then it is a matter of checking if there is still room for a two-pointer. If not, arrange to exit a few pips below the halfway barrier.

Figure 5.2. The first half of this chart clearly shows the bulls in control. With higher bottoms throughout and orderly pullbacks on the way up, there is no reason to even consider a short.

As it is unlikely for a trend to turn without good fight first, the market usually grants us several tipoffs that warn of a nearing reversal. One is that the action from bar to bar has become more choppy. Another tell is an increasing number of tall bars, at least taller than what is average for the pair. Yet by far the strongest giveaway is a series of potent reversal attempts, typically *three*, in the highs or lows (1-2-3).

Although the three reversal attempts sit quite close to one another, there is still decent harmony between this three-stepper and the trend (as it regards a breakout rally, not the long-term trend).

Tip: As for a trendline, not all trends allow for a long-lasting barrier, but that doesn't necessarily mean that there is no support or resistance in play. So grab your line tool and see what you can find. A small cluster line can have just as much say in things as any big trendline, if only to warn us *not* to enter prematurely—as here below bar 3.

And so our first plan is to wait for some buildup. Should the barrier break without it, as is the case here, then we switch to Plan B and hope for a test (after which we effectively look for a pullback reversal; not that it matters how we label our setups).

Recall that an ideal test not only hits a line from below but breaks back a bit first—as that offers the possibility to exploit a re-break failure. How can it be then that a short below bar 5 is marked as valid when the cluster line isn't even hit, let alone broken back?

To answer that, first note bar 4. At *that* point we still anticipate an actual attack on the cluster line. Two bars later, though, the expected test appears aborted, what else to make of that bearish doji (5). In fact, we can even look upon the 4-5 sequence as a mini two-stepper, which makes this resolution even more worthy. And as for the close of bar 5, that is not an issue either in view of the bearish top tail (which allows for a fine stop to boot).

If all this is still not enough to take a chance on a short, consider also the magnet effect of the halfway barrier below. Moreover, note how that barrier is effectively still "waiting" for a test of the breakout rally. Taking all the bearish features into account, not the least of which the three-stepper that started the reversal process, a short below bar 5 looks well worth a try.

Tip: Thus, a *minor* shortcoming in a setup can at times be forgiven as long as the odds for a win are still to your liking (a personal call). But whatever you do, never downplay a *major* issue, as with bar 3 earlier on. Remember, support had yet to be broken.

If we quickly double the span of bar 5 in our mind's eye, it looks like there is room for a two-pointer before support would come into play. But it is wise to check that closely because we don't want our target to accidently sit *below* that halfway barrier (best based on the first swing high of that January cluster).

Note: When determining the room for a target, always factor in a few pips for the spread on both ends of the signal bar, and if you wish, throw in an extra pip for good measure. So say bar 5 stands 100 pips tall and you add 4 pips on either end, a two-point exit will sit at 216 pips from entry (2 x 108). Project that in the chart and you have your answer on whether or not you need to tighten.

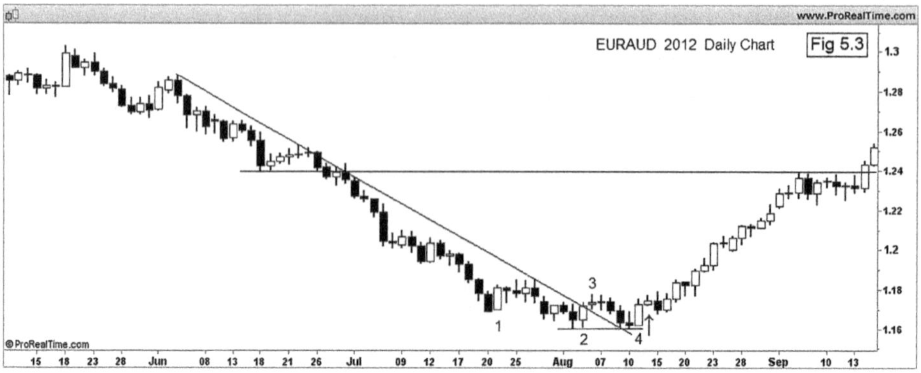

Figure 5.3. The stronger the trend, the harder it is to force a reversal. So even when a trendline is broken, expect a test or at least a barrier fight of some sort. And if you do trade, make sure you always have a sound stop in place.

Tip: Given the nagging resilience of trends, here's an idea: each time you consider a reversal, rather than look for features that confirm your intention, do the opposite first. It's good practice. Or think of it this way: one shake avoided is effectively a point *won.*

Just to illustrate, take the situation at bar 2. There are at least three reasons for why things are not ripe for a reversal. First, we only have a two-stepper as buildup (1-2). Second, a cluster to the left sits in the way (could easily provoke a test). Third, the odds for follow-through are not great to begin with since the perforation of the trendline is only a first. And there you have it. No need to look any deeper as it is already clear that a reversal above bar 2 is not a safe bet.

The fact that we skip a setup doesn't mean that the trade idea itself is invalid. So let us keep a close watch on the action to see if we can find a better deal. And indeed, six bars later we not only have a more potent three-stepper on the chart but also a test of the trendline out of the way (1-2-4). That is no small improvement! That little cluster is no longer a real threat either as it already "served its purpose" (blocking the break above bar 2, which led to the test).

Aren't there any drawbacks to this setup? To be fair, one thing does call for attention: the false break above bar 2 left behind a potentially obstructive swing point (3).

Note: Recall that the odds for follow-through are always the highest when both sides of the market are likely to act in unison—as in bears *buying* out when bulls are *buying* in. Since it is reasonable to assume that the majority of buy orders will sit above bar 3, the most technical spot for an entry would be above that bar. But that isn't necessarily our best option.

While it is true that *most* buying will likely come forth above bar 3, only *modest* buying is needed to break that swing point and hit all those pending orders. So there is something to be said for a standard entry above bar 4 as well.

It is not always easy to determine the ideal course of action; it might even be a matter of style (say conservative versus aggressive). But just in case you are overlooking something, consider *all* options. This should not take long as there are only four brackets to choose from. They are:

1st: A standard entry and stop.

2nd: A standard entry with insurance on the stop.

3rd: A standard stop with insurance on entry.

4th: Insurance on both the entry and stop.

Personally, I lean towards the second option, with a stop below the low of the trend. The fourth option is also doable as there is still ample room for a two-pointer before the halfway barrier would come into play. True, there are some hurdles to overcome on the way to that magnet, but keep in mind that only a *new* low on the trend could shake us out. While we have a stop in place just for that occasion, it is fair to reason that after such a windfall selloff and the now looming reversal, bears will be more concerned with not letting their profits slip away. And lest you forget, any bear that buys out is an extra bull in the orderbook.

Figure 5.4. What to do with a trend reversal that is also a range reversal? Should we wait for a three-stepper, as advised for trends, or could we already take a chance on a two-stepper, as is common for ranges? In fairness, it depends on the situation at hand. Yet if ever on the fence, it is generally better to wait for extra buildup (at the risk of missing out) than act on too little of it.

Earlier on we discussed a two-step reversal known as the M-top (Figure 4.3). The most classic variant is a three-bar pattern (bear bar/ bull bar/bear bar). But an M-top can also be of the *cluster* variety, as seen in the 1-2 sequence. Note that we still have a bear bar on either side of it but extra bars within. This cluster variant is certainly not inferior and in some cases even preferable (think buildup).

Yet even more potent than this wider version (all else equal) is the so-called *Mm-top* (1-2-3), in which a second and usually smaller M-top follows the first (2-3). (Its bullish counterpart is the *Ww-bottom.*)

Note: Before we go on, say we liked the first M-top enough to place a short below bar 2. As the next bar opens higher (Monday) and never trades below bar 2, it appears we would not have been filled. Probably so, but consider the following:

Since the Monday open is not standardized in Forex, you may already see some activity on your platform on Sunday. (Should you even see a Sunday bar *printed*, uncheck the "show weekend data" box in your chart settings.) Steer clear of such pre-open action or you will certainly be hit with ridiculously wide spreads. Hence it wouldn't be wise to already set up a trade over the weekend. In principle, it is best to treat a Friday bar like a Sunday bar, and thus to set up your trade as soon as the Monday bar opens. But before you do so, wait a few minutes for the spreads to come down a bit.

Tip: If you find that your broker keeps the spreads uncomfortably wide (well past 15 minutes), that is still no reason to switch platforms if you are otherwise content. Friday setups are relatively rare anyway and the nuisance typically regards a few pairs only. And remember, tight spreads are not that crucial when trading the dailies. (For a few more pointers on how to handle the open, also in regard to stocks, see the Questions and Answers section in Chapter 15.)

Back to our setup. The marvel of the Mm-top, a three-step variant, resides in the fact that it is a very visual pattern. Even traders not familiar with the three-step concept are likely to grasp the implications of any such sequence (and hopefully act on it too).

You never know what lurks in the dark, but from where we stand, bulls are pretty much done for after bar 3. The one thing to decide on is whether to set up the short below the signal bar itself or below the previous bar. Taking into account the rejected range break, the Mm-top, the strong signal bar, and the very likely magnet (dotted line), personally I see little reason for insurance, but either way is fine. If you prefer a safer entry, check if there is still room for a two-pointer. If not, tighten your exit accordingly.

Tip: In case you never traded Forex, you might be wondering how exactly we calculate the volume for our trades in view of all the foreign currencies involved. Fortunately, on most platforms this will automatically be done for us in the order ticket, based on (a) the levels we type in for entry and stop, and (b) on what we are personally willing to risk per trade (more on that in Chapter 14). If this feature is not offered, or you prefer to prepare your orders away from the platform first, you can use a *Forex Position Size Calculator*, freely available online (that is also a great tool for practicing with dummy orders).

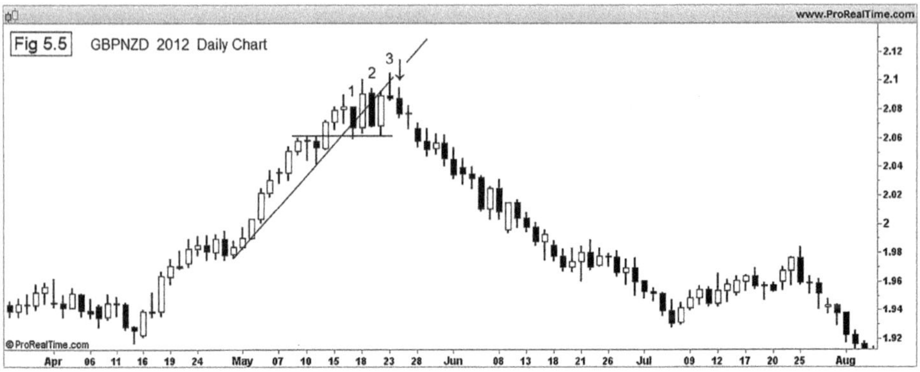

Figure 5.5. As trend reversals take time to form, a signal bar rarely marks the absolute high or low. In a bull trend, for example, the last thing we want to do as bears is short the very top of the market. Then we might as well carry a sign on our backs saying *shoot!*.

Be as that may, here above we have a situation in which the signal bar sits right in the top of the trend and is still marked as valid (3). It's important to grasp that this cannot solely be a function of the signal bar itself, no matter how strong its message or how overextended the trend in question. So let us take a closer look to see what exactly went on in that reversal.

Starting with the conditions, a first cue that the trend might be up for a turn soon is that the action has become more choppy. Another tell is that the last so many bars are notably taller than the average bar earlier on. And of course the double perforation of the trendline is a bearish case in point (1-2).

At bar 2 things are obviously not ripe for a short yet. Besides the fact that we only have a two-stepper as backup, this signal bar also stands unpleasantly tall, yet is still an inside bar to its bigger neighbor. Plus there is support from that cluster to the left. Even though that block is already tested (1), shorting right into it couldn't possibly count as a *high*-odds bet.

Bulls indeed stand their ground and even set a new high shortly after (3). That speaks well of the trend—or does it? On closer inspection, this run to new highs is also a test of broken support, and rejected at that. So, which feat earns more credit?

Taking everything into account (unsustainable rally, three-stepper, broken trendline, several re-break failures, bearish resolution of a test), I think it can safely be argued that the conditions now favor a reversal. If you agree, then the signal bar in the top can even be seen as a *boon* in this setup because it allows for the best stop in the entire chart (only a new high could shake it).

Once again, do see that any signal bar is merely the icing on the cake of a setup already in the works. If you take position on account of a promising bar alone, you are bound to find yourself regretting your entries more often than not.

* * *

Key points to consider when contemplating trend reversals

1. Figure out the trendline (or any relevant barrier).

2. Look for a three-step reversal in the lows or highs.

3. Look for relative harmony between the reversal pattern and the latest trend.

4. Figure out the most likely magnet (usually in the halfway area).

5. Make sure your stop is not too easily hit in a test.

chapter **6**

Understanding Conditions

things to keep in mind when scanning for setups

Now that we have built our method, our next task is to put it to the test, which will be the subject of Part Two. Before we go there, it will be good practice to first recap what we covered so far. But rather than just discuss more setups, this time we will pay extra attention to situations that may look tradable at first but are best left alone on closer inspection. The more we understand the subtleties from the get-go, the less we have to learn the hard way later on.

By the way, the charts in this chapter too still stem from the years 2012–2013, as a precursor to our backtest over the next four years of price action (2014–2017). As a bonus, the years 2018–2024 are included in the appendix (in annotated format). So rest assured, by the time you finish this guide, you will have more than enough proof of the amazing potential of the *Forex Daily* method. Whether it suits your swing trading purposes is of course a personal matter.

Whatever method we ultimately make our own, the best we can do is prepare ourselves for all contingencies. Especially in situations where the call to action is not immediately clear, it is imperative that we know what to do, be it to trade or stand aside. True, even after mastering our craft, small oversights may still slip in (we're only human), but let it be our goal never to indulge in big mistakes, as that would mean we haven't done our homework. In the following examples, therefore, let's focus in particular on that somewhat elusive concept of *conditions*.

Figure 6.1. Let's start with an obvious skip. Can you spot the issue with bar 1? Besides the fact that we are not too keen on signal bars that are notably taller than the average bar earlier on, a short below bar 1 would be a bad idea on account of that cluster not far below (potential springboard). The same goes for a short below bar 2.

As for a trade above bar 5, it's nice to see that there are no obstacles to overcome in the 3-4 downswing, but this setup too leaves a lot to be desired, mainly because the only place for a stop is right below the range barrier. As we have yet to see a (proper) test, the risk of a shake is simply too high. The market clearly thinks otherwise, but that has no bearing on our assessment.

Then how about a short below bar 6? While the trade idea is sound, given the looming failure of angular support (aided by a broken cluster), again it is hard to find a safe place for a stop.

Note: If a standard stop above bar 6 would be too easily hit, why not opt for insurance? To answer that, picture any safer stop below the top barrier, or even right above it, and ask yourself to what extent you would be better off in the event of a test. Not by a whole lot, I'm afraid, because if bulls have it in them to break back that cluster line, the magnet effect of the top barrier could quickly kick back in, in which case you probably get shaken out anyway. So rather than trade and *fear* a test, the advice here would be to skip and *hope* for one.

Again the market refutes our reservations and even goes on to push through the bottom barrier (7). Should we finally give credit where credit is due and become bears ourselves? Not so fast!

Tip: One reason not to think too highly of a range break is of course the absence of buildup. But there is another aspect to take into account, a variant of the three-step principle that we already came to appreciate for trend reversals. The premise is that any *third* visit to a range barrier is more likely to lead to a reversal than a breakout because the barrier already proved sound (note the earlier bounces in October and December). But keep in mind this distinction: while the three-step principle is often suitable for *setup* purposes in a trend, in a range it is best regarded as *backup*—meaning we anticipate a reversal, but if the buildup proves otherwise, we can still switch sides.

So let us see what goes. Starting with bar 7, it is nice to see a false dip below the barrier (a possible swing point for a stop), but that's about it. When not much later bar 8 comes along, we have a more potent two-stepper on the chart (7-8), plus a chance to enter in a confirmation break (note the perforation of the angular line). Yet even such otherwise interesting features do not make a setup per se. At least one element of concern is the aggression in the 6-7 selloff. With that still fresh on the chart, a test of some sort can almost be expected. Hence I would suggest to bet on that first and take it from there.

Bar 9 in that regard clearly ticks more boxes. Now we not only enjoy the three-step backup as mentioned earlier but also within the setup itself (7-8-9). And no reason to fear a test either because we already have one out of the way. A small drawback is that high of the test now sits in the way, but that can be solved by opting for an entry above that swing point (at the premium of a wider target, but still doable).

As for that little cluster halfway the 6-7 swing, it might hinder our trade a bit, but most likely not for long (no real match for a potent three-stepper). Yet even if it forces prices back to the bottom barrier, bears still won't have an easy time shaking us out as then they would have to venture out *well below* support (our stop sits below bar 9). This perfectly illustrates the benefit of a stop beyond a false break versus one directly beyond a barrier (as with bar 4 earlier on).

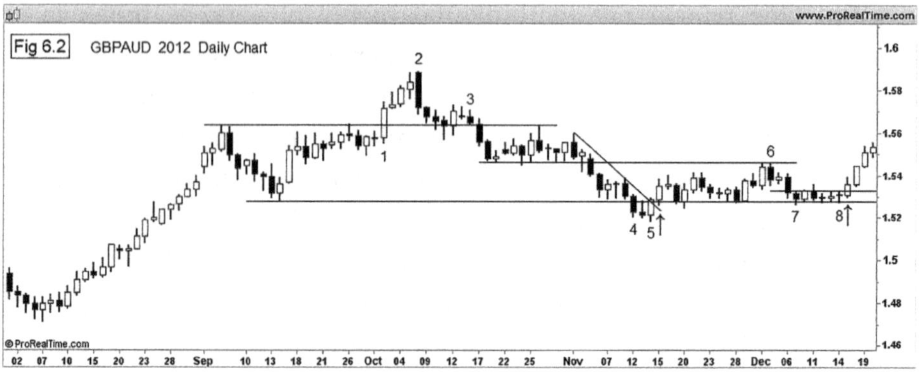

Figure 6.2. The attraction of a break into new territory is easily understood (1): no obstacles anywhere in sight. But don't discard the buildup part; and take into account as well that not *all* resolutions are suitable for a setup. For instance, if the signal bar is a powerbar (notably taller than the average bar earlier on), or sticks out well beyond a barrier (1), we have no choice but to wait for a test.

But not all tests are immediately suitable for setup purposes either. Always be extra cautious if the bars in the test are more aggressive than those in the breakout. Then at least wait for an extra step or some other form of buildup to back up the reversal. And if you ever spot a powerbar in a test, be even more cautious or drop the trade idea altogether (2).

If aware of the above, you might feel tempted to play short instead, say below bar 3, but keep in mind that the trend itself is still up. Meaning bulls in position may not wish to sell out; and their buddies on the sidelines may still plan to buy in, possibly as soon as the action stalls. In sum, the conditions are far from favorable.

While a short below bar 3 can perhaps be forgiven, the same cannot be said of a short below bar 4, against the halfway barrier of a powerful trend. What were these bears thinking!

If that break is almost destined to fail, a logical plan is to try to take advantage. But as we are surely not the only ones with this idea, this is one such situation in which a *one-stepper* might actually serve us better than the generally more reliable two-stepper.

Tip: If you ever go the one-step route, make sure to have at least two features strongly in your favor: (a) a highly convincing signal bar and (b) a great spot for protection. While a sound stop is crucial for all types of setups, it is even more important in this context since one-step reversals are quite prone to get tested.

In fairness, even though bar 5 meets both requirements, this setup is strictly seen a skip as the max reward is under 1.5 times our risk (due to the halfway barrier of the 2-4 pullback). But at least take stock of the concept.

Over the next few weeks the halfway barrier of the bull trend is repeatedly tested but holds up fine. When then a cluster appears (7-8), we trust it to break on the bull side. By the way, rather than run the cluster line across the highest bar, more principled is to exclude that one perforation. (Do note that this tightening is most effective when there is only one bar sticking out.)

Note: A pleasant bonus of tight cluster setups is that they usually allow for an easy two-pointer, even if we place our stop at the most technical spot (as here below bar 7). A disadvantage, if you will, is the typical absence of an explicit signal bar. But recall that for these occasions we devised an alternative tactic that is almost just as effective: as soon as we deem a cluster ready for a break, we place an order a few pips beyond the cluster line and hope for a fill next session. We do want the current bar to at least *modestly* favor a breakout, as with bar 8. (So we wouldn't look for a bull break after a bear bar.)

As for the overhanging cluster line, in principle it is no longer a concern as it already proved obstructive earlier on (6). Then again, it does stem from a fairly fat block and there is almost room for a two-pointer anyway. Alright then, let's be wise and tighten our target accordingly. There is no point in risking a good trade for a few extra pips.

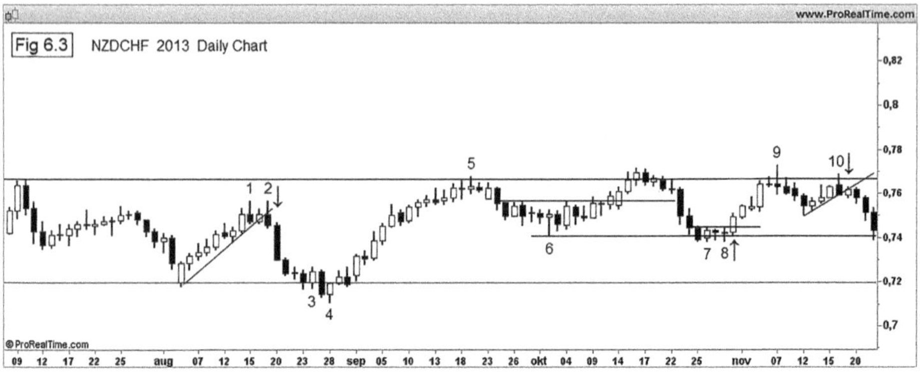

Figure 6.3. M-tops and W-bottoms come in all shapes and sizes. Quite popular are the three-bar versions (1-2 and 7-8). We are always happy to spot these too, but not all are created equal. In the 3-4 progression, for example, the *middle* bar is clearly the strongest of the three, which effectively ruins the setup for us. The conditions still favor a reversal, but the resolution in bar 4 is a bit too weak to accept.

When it comes to ranges, we typically focus on the outer barriers, be it for a break or reversal. Every now and then, however, the *midrange area* too can make for great opportunity. Consider the 4-5 bull run. It is not hard to imagine a pullback to stall about halfway that rally. And not only are prices likely to stall there, they might quickly find their way up again, aided by the magnet effect of the top barrier!

Now that we have a trade idea, the waiting is for a decent setup. At first it looks like we're out of luck as bar 6 doesn't really do it for us, but when prices pull back a second time we may have another shot.

An immediate entry above bar 7 is not advised because at that point the pullback has only just petered out. Two bars later, however, we have a cluster as backup and even a W-bottom within (7-8); support is more established as well (note the false dips). That's our setup.

Note: If you would rather shoot for the top barrier here, recall that your exit is still best based on the original swing high on the far left, so ignore the false breaks in September and October. (The same goes for the short below bar 10 later on; there we base our exit on the low of bar 6, not the lows of the 7-8 cluster.)

Tip: Imagine for a moment that our entry above bar 8 is not yet filled next session. Should we cancel or leave the order pending? It depends. Consider the following: if the new bar is either neutral or bullish, nothing in the setup has changed for the worse. If anything, the extra build-up is a boon. So no reason to cancel, unless perhaps this new bar prints a lower low *first* and *then* turns bullish (think doji); then it makes sense to reinstall with a stop below this new low. Is the next bar in the cluster a *bear* bar, however, then we no longer anticipate a break next session. That is when we cancel. We can always put the trade back on if a new bull bar shows up.

Back in the top barrier, a trap bar strongly warns of a range reversal (9). This is still a skip for us, though; partly because there is not enough room for our minimum reward, but consider also the relative aggression in the 8-9 rally. So as much as we anticipate a reversal, we have to be patient here and hope for a test. Should it fail to come about, we accept and move on.

Fortunately, a test is granted and so too our desired resolution (10). Note also the two-step element (9-10) and that this time there *is* enough room for a worthy risk-to-reward.

Tip: As a final note, examine the wavy action in the 8-10 sequence; can you spot that M-pattern in the making (the right leg has yet to form)? Make it a habit to keep an eye out for such partial M-progressions (and their W-counterparts) because in the right conditions they tend to complete more often than not (as here below bar 10).

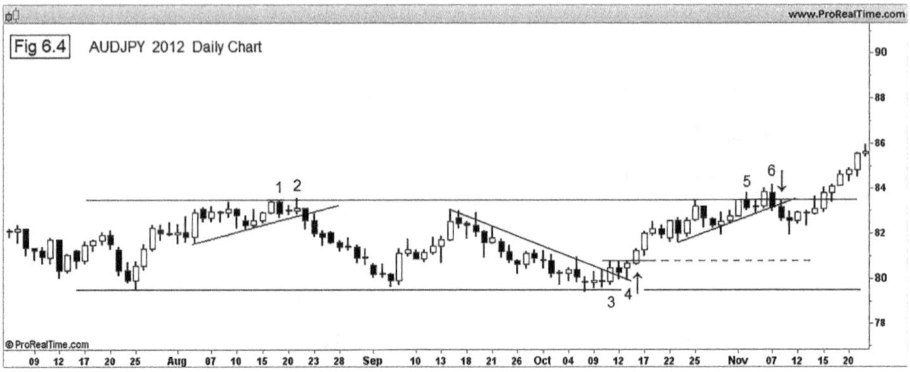

Figure 6.4. As we scan through our charts, it's good to keep in mind that outcomes have no say in the validity of our setups, or we might as well conclude that we skipped a rightful two-stepper (1-2) and traded a false one instead (5-6). Yet the latter setup is not only more potent (*two* false breaks), it is the only one valid—for the simple reason that bar 6 offers an entry below support, whereas bar 2 does not.

When planning a reversal trade (which always has to travel through *old* territory), first thing to check is if there is enough room for a target. Not every obstacle needs to be feared, but always be mindful of anything that allows for a barrier, and if necessary tighten your exit accordingly. For that short below bar 6, for example, a good plan would be to aim no further than the dotted barrier.

As for a trade above bar 4, at first glance this looks like a skip because the best place for a stop is right below the range barrier, so quite vulnerable in the event of a test. An important consideration, however, is that we already have a test *out of the way* (3-4). While still no guarantee for follow-through, the risk of a bad start is now far lower. In that light there is also little point in placing our stop below the range barrier, below bar 4 should suffice (technically speaking).

A bonus is that the test allows for a neat little cluster line, the failure of which will likely have more traders respond in our favor. A final boon is that this setup comes about after a third visit to the lows of a range (three-step backup). The more favorable features we can spot, the better our chances of success on a trade.

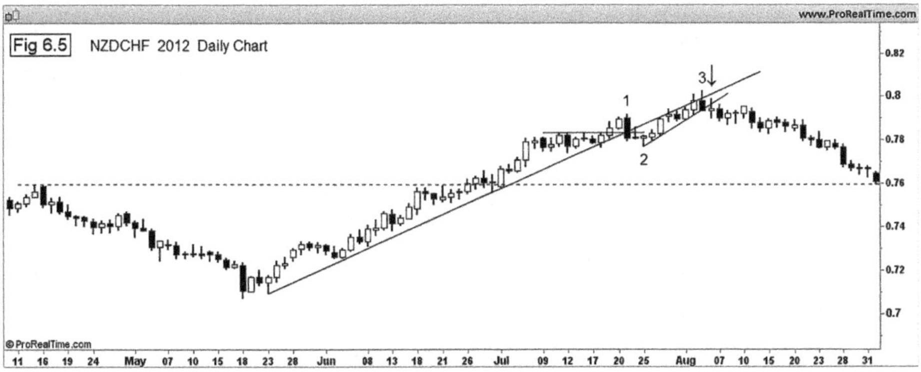

Figure 6.5. Every now and then a trend just marches on as if there is no tomorrow. When the reversal finally sets in, we often see an equally one-sided pullback—as trend traders quickly bail out to save their windfall profits and clever contrarians step in to take advantage.

We would love to exploit such reversals ourselves, but then we need to find a convincing setup first, ideally of the three-step type. The perforation of the trendline in bar 1, for example, couldn't possibly do as it is only the first serious reversal attempt on the chart.

If the trend is any good, then two-steppers too are best looked upon with suspicion (1-3). The same goes for signal bars in the top or bottom. If all this is common knowledge, why then short below bar 3; would that not be asking for trouble?

I specifically included this exception to show that we always need to keep an open mind. Can you see what's going on in the top of the trend? Despite the bear trap below bar 1 and the run to new highs shortly after, no bar in the 2-3 leg manages to close back above the broken trendline. So technically we are merely dealing with a *test*. And by the looks of it, that test is about to roll over (3).

If not yet convinced, consider also the looming failure of the buildup line, plus the magnet effect of that halfway barrier below, which by the way is also a broken range barrier still "waiting" for a test.

Would bulls have it in them to discard the writings on the wall and push for new highs as if nothing happened? Possibly, but that's for our stop to worry about.

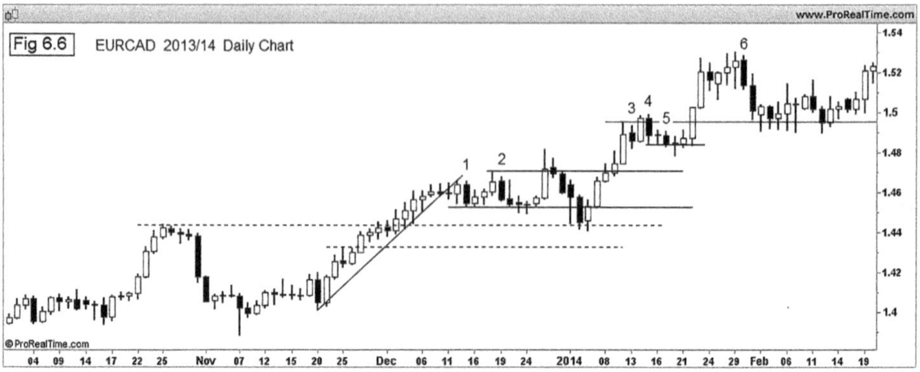

Figure 6.6. Much unlike the optimistic bull run in our previous chart, here's a trend that follows a stairstep pattern as a consequence of repeated pullbacks on the way up. This type is generally more dangerous to counter due to the many areas of potential support, such as former tops and halfway corrections of the latest swings.

To illustrate, consider the 1-2 two-stepper (M-top variant). Despite the fact that the angular barrier is broken, the conditions are unfavorable for a short—because there is support not far below (upper dotted line). And not much further awaits another level of support, the halfway area of the latest runup (lower dotted line).

A short below bar 5 would be equally misplaced, notwithstanding the otherwise interesting three-stepper (3-4-5). A setup like this might work for a pullback reversal in a bear trend, but here the trend is *up*, and the tops of the foregoing rally sit in the way as well.

Similar concerns regard a short below bar 6.

The message is clear: think twice before you take position *against* a trending market.

Tip: When finally a situation arises in which everything lines up for a trend reversal, always assume that the pullback will be short-lived. So plan your exit wisely, ideally no further than the halfway area of the latest rally. And don't even think of defying any *serious* obstacles in that tricky area.

Figure 6.7. Come Monday morning the market may not open where it closed on Friday, but noticeable gaps are quite rare in Forex. Even less common is for a big gap to occur and then to transpose into a trap bar of epic proportions, as seen in bar 3. Perhaps a better term for such a pompous powerbar is a *freak bar.* (Bar 5 is another one; no gap there because that came along on a Thursday.)

As much as that selloff will have hurt all bulls in position, it could prove a boon to their buddies on the sidelines. After all, the trend itself is still up. Consider also that the freak bar has already eaten back half of the latest rally (1-2). What's more, the three *bottom tails* in the lows of the pullback let on that the USDJPY is being bought again rather than sold in panic (3-4). Which then begs the question: should we take a chance on a reversal ourselves—say above bar 4?

Note: Let us simply call this a skip on account of the aggression in the pullback. But here's something to remember for future purposes: when a freak bar shows up *against* a trend and *fails* to follow through, there is a good chance the anomaly is discarded as a one-off event—which then favors a turnaround to where prices were trading before.

For the sake of argument, then, say we give it a shot above bar 4: should we go for a stop below the signal bar or the freak bar instead? The most technical spot for protection is of course below the freak bar. But bar 4 is a potent swing point in its own right and allows for a better risk-to-reward to boot. My preference goes out towards the tighter stop, with a target just below the high of bar 2.

In conclusion: The main takeaway from this chapter, or basically from everything we covered in Part One, is to always look at any chart from both a bearish and bullish point a view. It is all very nice to anticipate a break or a reversal, but none of that will prove beneficial if the trade in question is placed too aggressively and fails as a result.

Playing too conservatively, however, may not prove very productive either. This happens when traders are so focused on avoiding risk that they can no longer pull the trigger. In fact, it's not unthinkable to rotate between either folly, simply as a function of whether one is up or down on the month. To be honest, I believe that no trader is ever fully safe from these and many other self-destructive tendencies. The trick is to minimize their impact.

A lot has been written on the topic of trader emotions, and most of that is well researched and makes perfect sense. But in my opinion a key issue in these studies is often overlooked: the emotions that wreak havoc on a trader's mind are largely a *symptom* of the problem, not the cause. More likely the real culprit is a lack of preparation. For it is no easy chore to stick to a plan that is only partially worked out, especially when the going gets tough.

Where do *we* stand? I'd say we're on the right track. At this point we have the foundation for an encouraging end-of-day method. But it is only half the job done. Now the time has come to put our findings through a rigorous backtest to see how well this method holds up over time. We need to know for sure whether we truly have an edge in the field. Trade without such faith at your own peril.

Part Two

28 CURRENCY PAIRS, 2014–2017

chapter **7**

Backtesting 28 Currency Pairs

Some thoughts before we get going

Save for one exception early on, the charts discussed in Part One were all taken from the years 2012 and 2013. This already suggests that there are plenty of good setups to be found in a small list of 28 currency pairs. Yet it would be foolish to assume that such setups will pop up on a daily basis. As end-of-day traders, we do best to think in terms of opportunities per *year*—not per week, and not even per month. So try not to get discouraged if on occasion you have to wait for what seems like an eternity for a setup to come along.

Skeptics might argue that since most setups worked out favorably, these two years were simply exceptionally fruitful, perhaps in the same way a raging bull market tends to be generous even to a newbie investor. Fair enough. While it is not our mission to convince these skeptics, we do need to verify for ourselves whether we can truly build on our findings for future use. For this purpose, we will now run a detailed backtest on the next four years of price action (2014–2017), on the same 28 pairs (all the combinations of the USD, EUR, GBP, JPY, CAD, CHF, AUD, and NZD).

Note: Before we dig in, it is important to understand that all we can hope to derive from a test (any test) is whether the method under review harbors an edge if traded according to plan. The actual results can only provide an indication as to how effective the edge in question is. But they should never be extrapolated.

A notable advantage of our personal backtest, though, is that it rules out what is arguably the biggest issue with backtests in general, and those on stocks in particular: would the charts in the tested period have been spotted in realtime? This is not an issue for us because we always have the same 28 charts on our daily radar. That is not to say we will never miss a setup, but we can honestly state that we will never miss a chart.

Another big plus is that we are not at the mercy of an occasional mega trade to offset a whole series of small losses. Missing a setup is never a big deal because the impact on the yearly bottom line would be relatively small. Trading for a preset reward may not be everyone's cup of tea, yet it works wonders for the reliability of a backtest.

Here's another thing we can do to minimize the chances of painting a too rosy picture. When in doubt as to how we would have handled a certain setup, we simply assume to have selected the least favorable option in terms of outcome (be it a skip, a loss, an adjusted target, or what have you). This will compensate, at least to some extent, for outcomes elsewhere in the test that may have been skewed inadvertently the other way around.

To maintain a pleasant read, I have chosen not to bother you with meaningless charts but to only show the ones that actually set up for a trade (both the winners and losers). Rest assured, with a minimum of at least three months per chart, that is plenty of data still.

As we make our way through the test, I will point out the rationale behind the setups and share notes and tips on the general picture—as done in Part One. Of course, with the basics down pat, there is no need to repeatedly drill on the obvious; the vast majority of explanations will therefore fit on the same page as the chart.

Undoubtedly, you won't agree with everything that is put forth. Perhaps you find some of the setups too aggressive for your taste, or even plain off. At other times you may wonder why a certain situation isn't acted on. It is inevitable. Price action trading is not an exact science and as such there is always room for debate. For the most part, though, the setups should make sense, or you might as well conclude that there is no viable edge in this type of trading to begin with.

Now with all that out of the way, let's get down to the fun part. We will run the test on the 28 currency pairs in alphabetical order through the years 2014–2017, starting with the AUD pairs, ending with the USD pairs. So first up is the AUDCAD, and last on our list is the USDJPY.

chapter **8**

The AUD pairs

AUDCAD, AUDCHF, AUDJPY, AUDNZD, and AUDUSD

AUDCAD 2014–2017

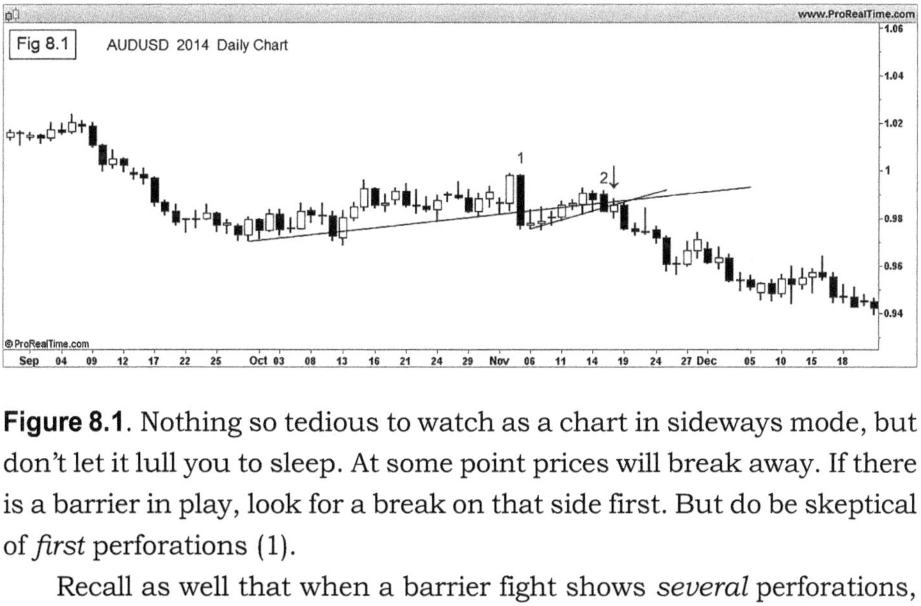

Figure 8.1. Nothing so tedious to watch as a chart in sideways mode, but don't let it lull you to sleep. At some point prices will break away. If there is a barrier in play, look for a break on that side first. But do be skeptical of *first* perforations (1).

Recall as well that when a barrier fight shows *several* perforations, a buildup line may have taken over from the main barrier, as looks to be the case here. Its exact angle isn't even that crucial since the signal bar already pokes through (2). Notice also the two-step element in this resolution (1-2). Surely we have seen all this before.

For protection, most logical is to play this with a stop above the high of the re-break as it marks the nearest swing point.

Figure 8.2. With the chart in bearish mode, that bold attack on the highs is not likely to trigger much follow-through (1-2). Which of course is not to say that we should therefore jump on any first sign of a reversal. Our plan is to wait for a two-stepper of some sort, or for anything that could make these brave bulls lose confidence.

One such development is the 2-3 cluster, which can also be seen as a stretched-out M-top (note the bear bars on either side of it). An immediate short below bar 3 would be premature, though, as there is no pressure on the barrier in the days prior to this signal bar. By the way, due to the choppy underside of that cluster, I opted for a barrier beneath its low point first. In this case, however, there is no need for some tweaking later on as both the break and test confirm its relevance.

In our previous chart we saw a test break back the barrier only partially and then resolve back out. All else equal, that is the ideal scenario for a setup. Here above, the re-break is stronger, with several bars fully back above support. We still anticipate a bearish resolution, but we can imagine bulls not to give up on *this* re-break so easily. For that reason, the resolution in bar 4 is up for debate. Yet when bar 5 shows up next, it is fair to reason that bears have taken over.

How exactly to set this up is a matter of taste. If we opt for the safest stop (above the high of the re-break), we would have to shoot for the low of bar 1, the nearest magnet, for a little less than a two-pointer. A standard stop above bar 5 would allow for full two-pointer, and also a much tighter target, but the risk of a shake is obviously much higher. Set it up as *you* deem best.

Figure 8.3. Always think twice before you take position in the midrange area as that is where the action can get awfully choppy. A possible exception is when a range contains a trend. Then you may have two things going for you right off the bat: the underlying pressure of that trend and the magnet effect of the nearest range barrier.

So let's see what we have to justify a trade above bar 2. For starters, there is indeed a strong trend in play. The top barrier stopped the rally short, but there is a good chance bulls will come back for another try, more so as the earlier broken cluster line could serve as a springboard. The false dip in bar 1 is proof of that support, and already offers a nice swing point for a stop.

And as for the resolution, no issues there either as bar 2 not merely perforates the pullback line but *closes* above it, which sets up an ideal entry in a confirmation break (as opposed to a perforation). The magnet effect of the top barrier could kick in any moment as well.

Given the way things stand we could perhaps opt for standard protection below bar 2, but more logical is to place our stop below bar 1. The only downside of this insurance (or *premium*, if you will) is a slightly smaller reward as there is no longer room for a full two-pointer.

Note: Keep in mind that a barrier within a two-point distance from entry is not necessarily a negative feature in the assessment of a setup. You may have to settle for a lesser reward but in return your chances of success are a little higher. After all, the closer the magnet, the stronger its pull.

Figure 8.4. The first half of this chart shows a bear trend that is actually a pullback in the Jun/Nov bull trend (not shown). Hence the plan here is to wait for bears to run out of steam (possibly in bar 1) and then look for a reversal.

The fact that both bar 2 and 3 fail to trigger new selling already favors a reversal more than a breakout, but the real giveaway in this test is the resolution in bar 4, which forms a two-stepper with bar 1.

A standard stop could do, but more logical here is to opt for protection below bar 3 (nearest swing point) as there is ample room for a two-pointer still. Given the bull trend as mentioned, perhaps you might feel tempted to let this trade run to the dotted magnet. If the plan succeeds, you would indeed reap an extra point. But is that worth the extra risk? Consider the following:

Say you had a chance of bagging 20 two-pointers in a certain year, but five of these you left to run for a three-pointer, only one of which resulted in a loss. Looks like a pretty good score. Yet if you do the math, all this amounts to is *one* extra point (41 vs 40). And mind you, that is the rosy scenario! True, a trailing stop might have prevented that loss, but such tactics might have also cut some of your winners short.

I guess the real point is (pardon the pun), no methodology is perfect. Flexible targets have more potential, but don't dismiss the ease of simply sticking to two-pointers. And don't forget, such price swings are far more common than their three or four-point counterparts.

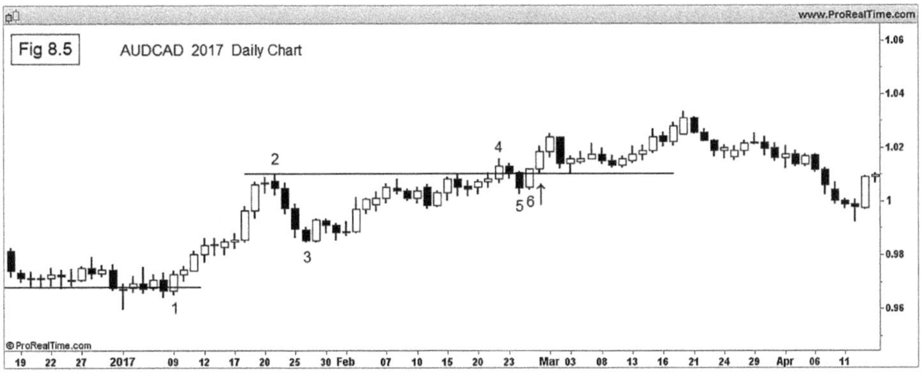

Figure 8.5. Every time you open a chart, first take a step back and see if you can detect the dominant *theme*. Very few charts, if any, show random price action! Monitoring themes will not only keep you more alert for an eventual setup, you are also less likely to look for one in the wrong places.

A fine example of thematic action is shown in the AUDCAD above. First we have a runup and a typical halfway correction (1-2 and 2-3). Then follows a more cautious rally back to the highs (3-4). Notice also how the action slowly tightens up below the top barrier (extended from the first rally), which grants us the preferable buildup in stages. So the obvious theme here is that bulls are heading for a breakout.

But that's not all. Equally fascinating is that our setups often follow a thematic pattern too, as in the 4-5-6 sequence. First there is a brief perforation (4), then comes a test (5), soon to be followed by a resolution in favor of an actual break (6). If we miss such setups, we simply haven't done our homework.

Note: Since it is largely a matter of style whether to play this with a stop below bar 6 or bar 5 (the latter is advised as it marks a swing point), it's nice to find that both would have led to a win. But how to book this trade had the safer stop backfired? As you may recall, my suggestion for all doubtful outcomes in a backtest is to always book the least favorable setting by result. Because a few unfortunate outcomes should not destroy the edge in a sound trading plan. And if it proves otherwise, that is good to know too! For what better hint that we are not yet ready for the markets. Then it's back to the drawing board.

AUDCHF 2014–2017

Figure 8.6. Choppy as this chart appears at first sight, the overall mode is bullish (higher lows throughout), which favors a break into new highs a little more than a range reversal.

That said, after two failed tries not too far apart, the odds for a break no longer look that good (1-2). Yet just when it appears that the bottom barrier is up for a visit next, bulls come back for another try. And so we have to ask ourselves: is that a mere test of a reversal attempt or should it be regarded as buildup for a breakout?

While it's hard to tell for sure, the *sideways* nature of this comeback and the mounting pressure on the top barrier (3-4) favors a bullish resolution. And for what it's worth, the dotted line also supports a breakout (broken and tested).

An entry above bar 4 looks a bit too aggressive, but let's say we took our chances there. As bar 5 never trades above bar 4, we basically have two options: either leave all orders be or cancel and reinstall with now a stop below bar 5 (new swing point) for the benefit of a slightly easier two-pointer. These choices largely come down to style.

Tip: This setup also nicely illustrates that an unfilled entry is never a reason for disappointment. Quite the opposite: see it as a gift instead because it grants you a chance to reassess your trade idea with an extra bar. That's like a free card at the poker table!

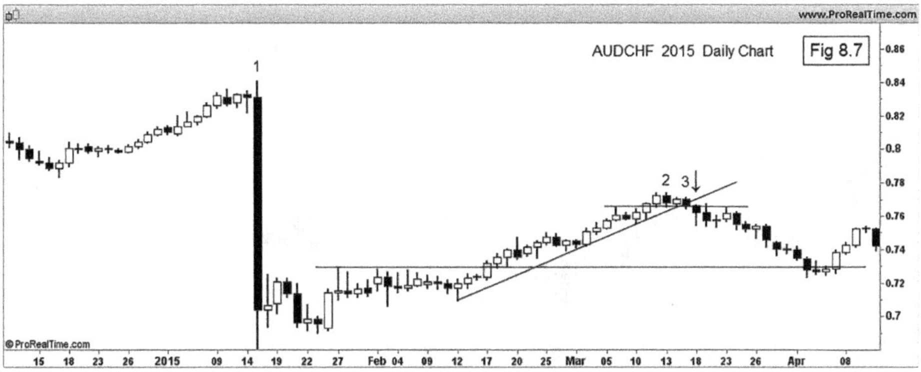

Figure 8.7. Much unlike the stock markets, Black Swann events in Forex are extremely rare on the dailies. Yet one notorious session earns that label fair and square: January 15, 2015 (1). Just look at the size of that freak bar, and that's not even all of it. Let this be a warning to always trade with a hard stop. You might incur some slippage on the fill, but at least you live to fight another day.

All this came about in response to sudden policy changes from the Swiss National Bank, which rapidly appreciated the CHF against all other currencies. (Hence the AUDCHF selling off.)

Once the dust settles down, however, it is simply business as usual. And so our first trade idea is a trend reversal. Should that fail to set up, as appears to be the case, we switch to watching the pullback and look for a reversal of that. So how about that two-stepper (2-3)?

Although we are not too keen on first perforations, this does have all the makings of a valid short setup. But let's think for a moment how to best set this up.

Since first perforations are quite prone to get tested, a standard stop would be too risky. The only proper alternative is to place the stop above the pullback high, but that would widen our target by no small margin. Fortunately, this safer stop is still perfectly doable as there is more than enough room for a two-pointer before the next support would come into play. So if that cluster below has a say in things at all, it can only be to our advantage (magnet).

Figure 8.8. There would be little point in studying price action if the sequences and patterns we see on our charts weren't so amazingly repetitive. Take the 1-2 M-top and the 3-4 W-bottom in the AUDCHF above. Who could possibly label these two-steppers as random.

Not all such patterns are setup worthy, though. While we can have no issues with the M-top here, the W-bottom leaves a lot to be desired. Its first drawback is the rather tall signal bar (4), but consider also the unfavorable entry point, *far* above support. And since it regards a fairly sharp re-break as well, a test of some sort can almost be expected (never mind the outcome).

All good, but what's wrong with the setup at bar 5?

To its defense, this tiny inside bar does improve the setup to some extent, if only for withholding a test; and the fact that its high lines up with the high of bar 4 is a nice feature too (allowing for a mini barrier). But look where our stop would sit!

Note: The risk of a tight stop is of course partly compensated for by a smaller than average two-pointer, or by shooting for a higher reward. All good if your plan allows for it, but don't opportunistically incorporate alternative ideas in the midst of a *backtest*! Or do so only when it proves disadvantageous. The point is, when you test a method, you don't want to go gentle on it. If anything, skew the results adversely, to ensure that your plan can withstand the occasional setbacks. Trade without such confidence and you will almost invariably lose faith in your chosen path when the going gets tough. And then the search for the holy grail can start all over again.

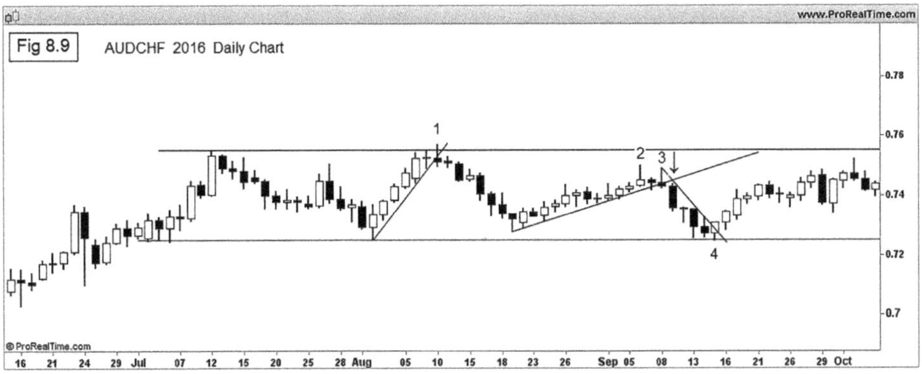

Figure 8.9. At first glance a short below bar 1 seems like a no-brainer, but what about the enthusiasm in the preceding bull run? And would you say the chart is predominantly bearish? Far from it. So this is not the time or place for a bet on a one-stepper. (See Figure 8.11 for a valid example.)

While the 2-3 two-stepper is no guarantee for success either, this little M-top has everything going for it. Besides threatening to crack a bear flag, it also forms a lower top next to the earlier tops of July and August (a popular triple-top variant). The bottom barrier magnet further adds to the potency of the setup.

Not much later, bar 4 hints at a reversal in the halfway barrier. We can have no issues with the conditions, but the prepwork is rather weak, especially in regard to the foregoing selloff. Note also the tricky spot for a stop, right below the barrier (easy game in a test).

Fact is, both a short below bar 1 and a long above bar 4 would have worked out nicely in this chart—and surely this is not the first time our natural caution leaves us emptyhanded. Which then begs the question: would it really be to our disadvantage to accept these “so-so” setups?

Tip: Since at its core *all* trading is a matter of odds, even the smallest edge on a setup is essentially acceptable. But get your priorities straight. If you have yet to show a consistently profitable bottom line, do yourself a favor and focus on the *topnotch* setups first. Do not go the aggressive route just to speed things up—or worse, in a last-ditch effort to revive an all but dead account; that’s like stepping on the gas when you *know* your breaks don’t work.

AUDJPY 2014–2017

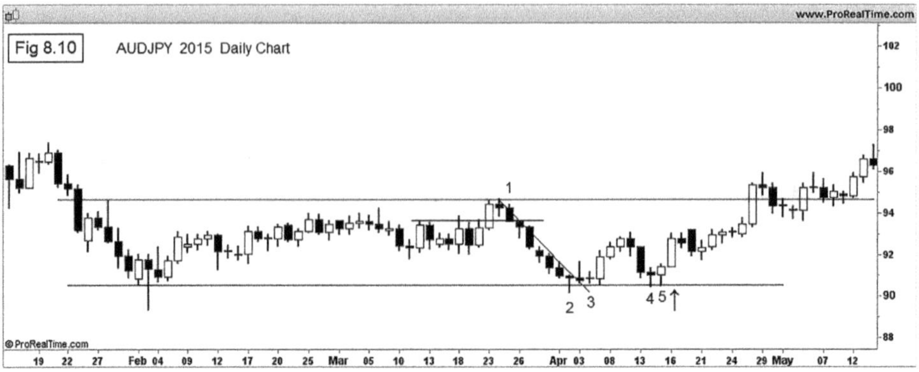

Figure 8.10. In a way, it is strangely ironic that range reversals are far more common than breakouts because whichever way you look at it, reversals always have to plow through former price action, of the days, weeks, or even months prior to the setup. Yet such is the magical force of support and resistance, most notable at the edges of a range.

That said, let us not gullibly jump on any first reversal attempt (1). Even though an entry below bar 1 would sit below a cluster line, there is still the cluster itself to pass through, not to mention all that chop from the month prior. And as the cluster line is currently *tested*, the resolution could still prove bullish, even after a dip.

Examine the difference with the space above bar 5, with only one minor swing point in the way. (As for the 2-3 two-stepper earlier on, at that point the bottom barrier is more a guess than a certainty, and the signal bar too is not very convincing.)

After the bounces in bar 4 and 5, the support situation looks solid enough for a bet on a range reversal. Consider also the partial W-bottom (1-5): it is not hard to imagine this pattern to be completed above bar 5, more so if the top barrier proves a handy magnet. Interesting to note as well is that this reversal attempt regards a *third* bounce in the lows of a range (three-step backup).

So all in all a pretty decent setup. We could probably trade it with a standard stop below bar 5, but more logical is to opt for protection below bar 4.

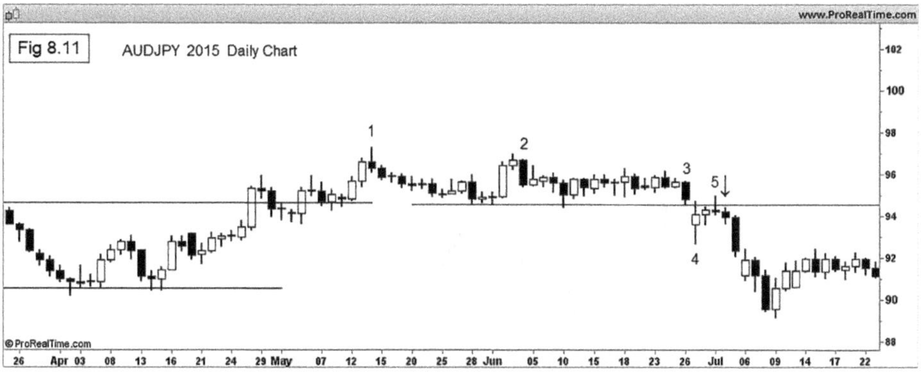

Figure 8.11. In May 2015, bulls have clearly broken away from the range in the previous chart. By itself a worthy accomplishment. But do note that instead of using the broken top barrier as a launching pad for their next runup, bulls are forced to seek refuge in it, for weeks on end, with no sign of reprieve (1-3). Adding to their plight is that the lengthy fight on the barrier shows an Mm-top, the fatter cousin of the already illustrious M-top (1-2 plus 2-3).

Notwithstanding the bearish implications, which we love to exploit, it wouldn't be wise to fire short below bar 3 right away given the absence of barrier touches in the days prior.

In this case, however, bar 4 opens well below support (note the gap, suggesting a development over the weekend, either bearish for the AUD or bullish for the JPY). As now our only chance to hop on is a test, let's hope bulls are not too demoralized yet.

The good part is that an eventual test is almost certain to resolve in favor of the bears. After all, the more convincing the initial break (4), the lower the chance of a successful re-break. Take into account as well that even if bulls manage to break back the barrier, there is still the 2-3 chop to push through too. Not unthinkable, but no easy task!

So when that bearish doji shows up in the top of the test (5), sticking above the barrier but *closing* below, we know what to do. A fine example of a one-step resolution.

Figure 8.12. As much as we love to exploit a three-stepper in the lows of a trend, not all such sequences are setup worthy (1-2-3). Just imagine a trade above bar 3 and note how quickly it can backfire.

But what's wrong with a trade above bar 4? Admittedly, it is fair to reason that at that stage not too many bears would still believe in lower prices anytime soon. But does that warrant an entry there. Personally I am not too convinced, but the excellent stop below bar 4 does compensate to some extent. Let's chalk it up to style.

Tip: The obvious risk of standing aside is that you might be left out. But don't let that be a factor. The dangers in trading never lie in missing a trade but in acting prematurely. And besides, there is always a good chance of a test!

Of course, a test is still no guarantee for a favorable resolution or a workable signal bar. Yet you'll be surprised to see how often that will be granted as well—as here in bar 5.

Moreover, note how bar 5 not only rounds off a three-stepper in the lows of the bear trend (1-2-5), but also in the third bottom itself (3-4-5). The tail of this doji allows for a fine stop as well, so no need to place our stop below bar 4.

If you will, a small damper is that there is no longer room for a full two-pointer on account of that halfway barrier (extended from the high of the first pullback). But recall that the proximity of a barrier can also prove an asset, courtesy of its magnet effect.

Figure 8.13. A healthy suspicion towards one-step reversals will go a long way even as a mere precautionary measure (2), but there is often a technical ground for it as well—a cluster nearby (dotted line). Yet like a bee that can only sting once, (small) clusters in a pullback rarely prove obstructive *second* time around. Such is the marvel of the trusted two-step principle (2-3). Hence our trade below bar 3.

If you find a standard stop a little too tight for your taste, the only real alternative is to opt for insurance above the pullback high and then shoot for the trend low. In that case, just to be safe, ignore that false dip in bar 1 and base your exit on the low just prior.

About a month later we have a cluster setup on the bull side (4-5). It is not the tight type as seen in earlier examples, but there is no mistaking the tension within, not to mention the trap bar on the right (5), which also rounds off a three-step variant (1-4-5). The tall span of the signal bar is a bit unfortunate, but there is still room for a decent reward towards the high of the pullback (nearest magnet).

Note: Since everything lines up for a break, why not place our stop closer by, say halfway the span of bar 5, or at least so that we can shoot for a two-pointer? Sounds like a smart idea, but is it really? Remember, a key reason for always placing our stops *beyond* a signal bar (or a swing point nearby), is that these are harder to run than "randomly" placed stops, because they sit beyond a *technical threshold*. Think of it this way: if it is your fate to get shaken out, at least have your opponents work for it a bit.

AUDNZD 2014–2017

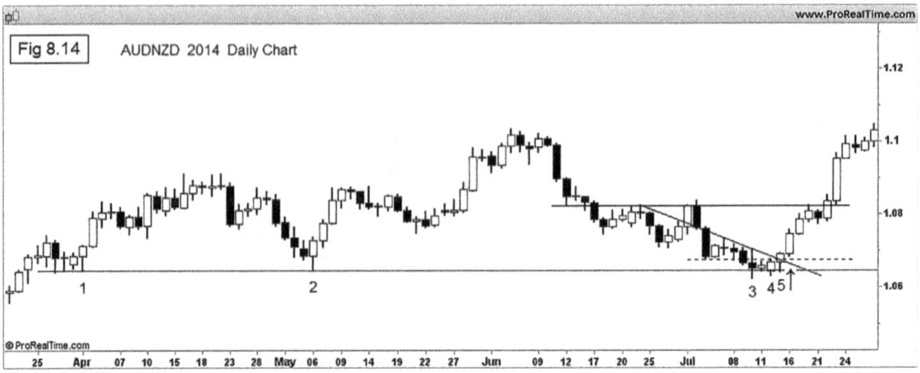

Figure 8.14. A great feature of a charting platform is that all barriers will automatically be saved. This not only speeds up our daily scans, it also keeps us on the alert. Take the bottom barrier here above. As it earned its place after bar 2 (lining up with bar 1), it is virtually impossible to overlook the *third* visit in bar 3, and as such the potential for a range reversal. (Do make it a habit to extend your range barriers at least a few months into the future.)

As for the setup, it would be premature to already plan a trade after bar 4 as the angular barrier still sits in the way; plus there is resistance from a cluster nearby (to the left of bar 3).

Note: As it is quite common for two clusters to *oppose one another* and even share a cluster line (dotted), we will look into this more deeply in Figure 10.9, but here's the basic idea: for this not to be a dealbreaker in a setup, we want "our" cluster (the buildup) to be at least equally "fat," or otherwise potent, as the opposing cluster.

So in that regard the 3-4 buildup is also a bit on the thin side (three bars against four, none of which very forcing).

But what a difference one extra session can make! After bar 5, our cluster has not only grown favorably, both the angular barrier and the cluster line are taken out in one fell swoop.

For protection, a stop below bar 5 could do, but more sensible is to opt for a stop below bar 4 (or even bar 3). We might have to tighten our target slightly (note the halfway barrier), but that's a small price to pay for the likely assistance of a powerful magnet.

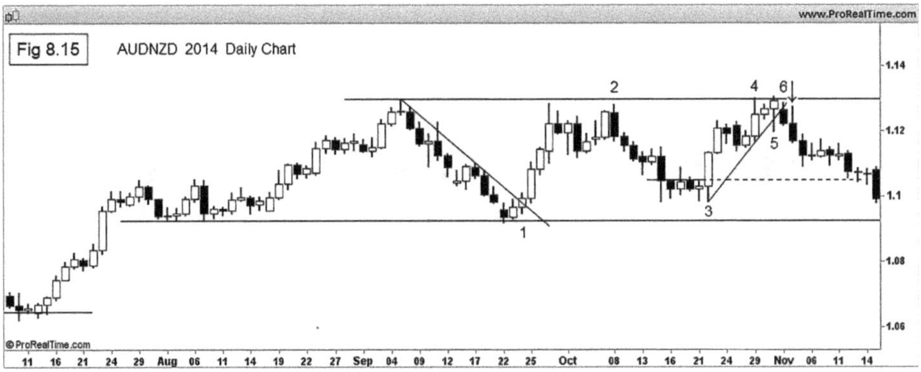

Figure 8.15. Here we see the full extent of the reversal from our previous chart. Should we feel bad for reaping only a small profit from such a fine trend? Not at all, we traded our plan. And besides, we are not done yet. If we are unable to catch the inevitable trend reversal, we may still have a shot at a pullback reversal. The latter in particular could be interesting since we can already spot a halfway barrier in which to look for a setup. Alas, in this case our fellow bulls beat us to the punch (1) and no test is offered.

As for a short below bar 2, I would advise against it because at that point the trend high on the left still counts as a magnet. Until that high is properly attacked (and ideally *broken falsely*), let's not be too keen on a reversal.

Bar 6, therefore, is more up our alley. Admittedly, a bit more fighting over the barrier would have been welcome given that rather aggressive runup (3-4), but we do have a triple top to compensate (Sep/Oct/Nov), plus a bearish resolution of a test (6). That cluster halfway the 3-4 rally is no longer a concern either because the earlier bounce in bar 5 already took the sting out of that support. We may see some counteraction still, but it is fair to reason that at this juncture *most* bulls would rather call it a day than venture out above the top barrier again.

Naturally, we should still place our stop above bar 5; and I do suggest that we short no further than the dotted barrier (for about 1.5 times our risk). Perhaps the magnet effect of the bottom barrier will pull prices through that support, but why take the risk.

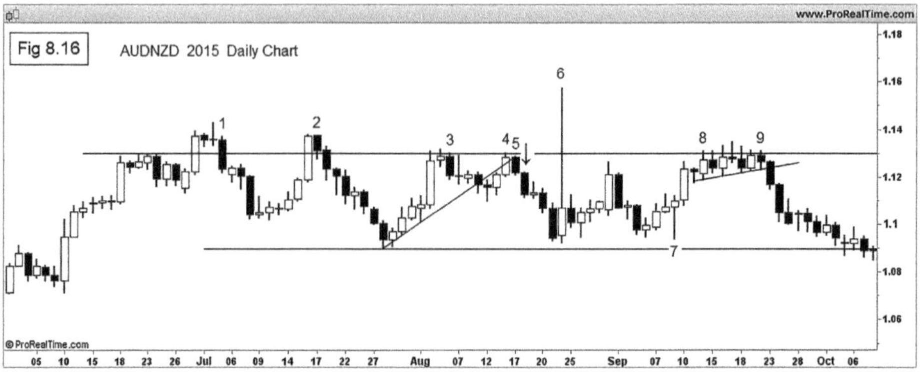

Figure 8.16. Despite repeated perforations, the initial swing top on the far left is never *convincingly* taken out. So no need to reposition the top barrier. (Note how several months later the 8-9 skirmish is still a function of the original barrier.)

Of the first four bear bars in or near the top barrier (1, 2, 3, and 5), bar 5 is the only one to meet our signal bar requirements (resolution of a test). While technically a “mere” inside bar, a standard entry here is perfectly fine. But the stop is best placed above bar 4. Small as this insurance may seem in pips, bulls then have to crack the range barrier to shake us out. After three earlier rejections, we can imagine some reluctance.

Freak bar 6 came about in what was later termed the August 24 flash crash, in which the Dow Jones Index sold off more than a 1,000 points in a few minutes time. The resulting spike on the AUDNZD, equally short-lived as the one on the Dow, is direct proof of how interconnected most markets have become, especially when the proverbial crap hits the fan. If you ever get caught on the wrong side of it, there is little you can do other than be thankful for your stop.

As for a short below bar 9, while we don’t necessarily need a *potent* signal bar to trade a cluster break, we do want the current session to at least modestly favor a breakout. As that is not the case with bar 9 (note that little bottom tail), and the powerbars in the 7-8 runup warrant caution as well, this is a rightful skip.

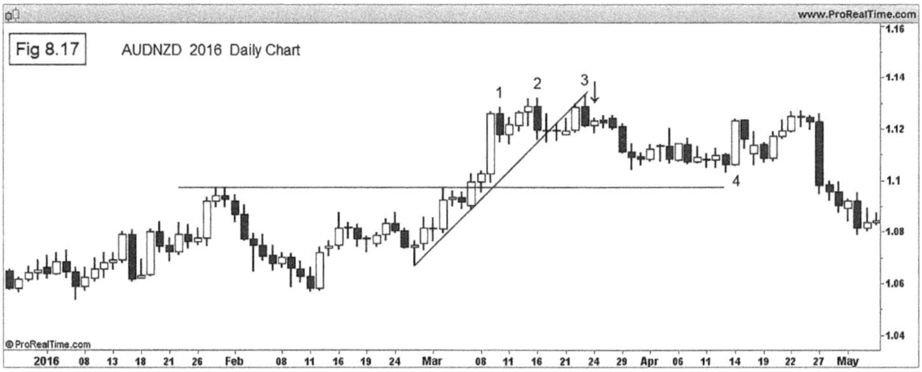

Figure 8.17. Here we have a three-stepper in the top of a breakout rally (1-2-3). As a fun fact, notice how bar 3 put a new high on the rally first prior to resolving a test: a classic bull trap.

Yet as we can see, even with a three-stepper as backup and a potent magnet for a target (the former range barrier), a win does not necessarily come easy. Not only does our short naggingly stall on the way to target, at some point it even faces an adverse powerbar (4). Not a pleasant prospect. Which brings up that all too common dilemma: should we stay in and hope for the best or bail out now that we still have a chance to do so cheaply?

Note: As much as it can be tempting to scratch a struggling trade, it may not be the best choice in *our* method. For example, there is little to be gained by exiting close to the initial stop, yet the potential penalty is almost three points (should the trade have worked out). An exit at break-even can perhaps be forgiven, but try not to freak out in a test! An ideal scratch would still pocket some decent profits, but let's face it, that will only rarely work for us because by the time we no longer believe in a win, any earlier gains will likely already have evaporated (see Figure 10.24 for a rare exception).

Tip: None of above is to suggest that we should never intervene, but if you find yourself scratching trades all over the place, it might be a sign you are too emotionally attached to your outcomes. If so, next time try this simple solution: ignore your gut and trust your stop. At the minimum you can feel proud of sticking to your plan. But odds are, your bottom line will prosper in the process.

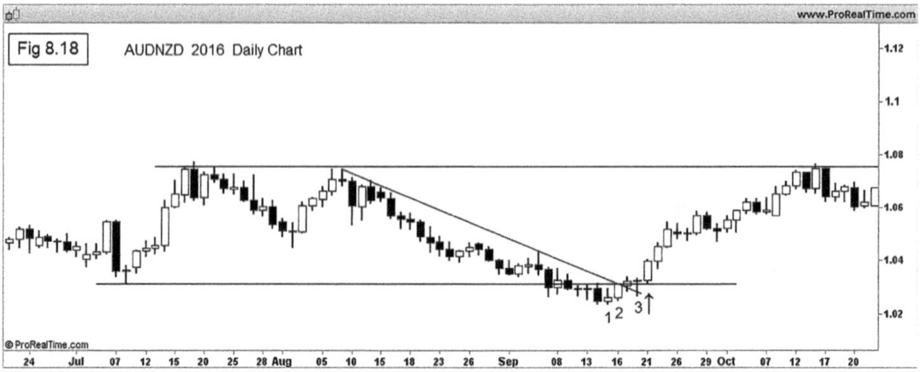

Figure 8.18. It's easy to justify a trade above bar 3 (resolution of a test), but why not already trade above bar 2? Looks a little premature at first glance, but there *is* some buildup in play, and both barriers are clearly under attack. And in the event of a test, a stop below bar 1 might still save the day. So all good if you like that setup.

Note: Here's a little food for thought. Say we take our chances on a re-break above bar 2. Could we then not trail our stop from below bar 1 to below bar 3, *after* bar 3 is taken out? After all, if that stop is good for the later trade, then why not use it for the earlier trade?

To answer that, first imagine the reversal to fail. In that scenario the trailing stop works perfectly and saves us about half a point compared to keeping the stop below bar 1.

But now imagine prices to shake that trailing stop only to reverse as originally anticipated. This time around we pay a serious penalty for lifting our stop: missing out on a two-pointer with a half-point loss to show for it. In other words, it takes *five* beneficial half-point scratches just to offset *one* that backfires. Food for thought indeed.

Note: The point of the above is not to discredit the use of a trailing stop, which in many strategies can be a highly effective tool for safeguarding profits (as in trend trading, for example). Yet I hope the above illustrates that there is a lot to be said for *not* meddling with our stops when trading for two-pointers. It may not always be the most productive approach, but it's hard to go "wrong" with it. And would you know of a more relaxed way to trade?

AUDUSD 2014–2017

Figure 8.19. You would think it takes at least three bars for an M-top to form, but it can actually be done in two, as in the up/down motions of two adjacent bearish dojis (1-2). When that shows up in a pullback, halfway a trend, with angular support on the verge of failure, the odds for a reversal could hardly be more favorable. But alas, that is still no guarantee for a win. Here the market reverses just shy of our two-point objective, and then goes on to shake our stop above bar 2.

Seeing a trade almost hit target only to fail in the end can be a little frustrating, especially if the original trade idea still stands. In that case, our first plan should be to reinstall the position—but not to mindlessly vindicate ourselves!

So, rather than reinstall below bar 3, we put the short back on below bar 4 (two-stepper). Even though this signal bar does not yet perforate the angular barrier (no confirmation break), the risk of a premature entry is quite small since the angle of support leaves little room for debate. (If you prefer, place the order with a bit more clearance, that's not likely to backfire at the target end.)

A standard stop above bar 4 looks fairly safe (outside of the barrier), but the more technical spot for protection is above the previous bar, the nearest swing point. Do check if that still leaves room for a two-pointer in regard to the dotted barrier.

By the way, if you missed this setup, it is not too late to short below bar 5, which effectively allows for a safer entry in a confirmation break (then you can probably make do with a stop above bar 4).

Figure 8.20. Here's the follow-up chart. The top barrier is now extended from the October high, but the bottom barrier is still projected from the bear trend low in the previous chart. Admittedly, that is a bit further back in time than what we normally scan for, but surely you can see merit in keeping an eye on such a prominent low (as all you have to do is plot a barrier and extend it well into the future).

As we learned early on, one of the strongest tipoffs to a nearing reversal is a faltering breakout (1-2). Yet allow me to once again stress the importance of waiting for a valid signal bar. Imagine the dismay of a bull who entered long in the top tail of bar 2, assuming a reversal—only to see prices drop to new lows again.

Equally illustrative is what a little patience can do. Just one session later, bar 3 bounces back from a false low, breaks back above the angular barrier too, and resolves a test to boot. What more to wish for. But let us not make the same mistake as our fellow bulls in bar 2. For a trade to be truly justified, this signal bar needs to be taken out first! Hence we arrange to enter a few pips above bar 3.

Note: In case you are wondering, that cluster to the left of bar 1 is no longer a real concern because the opposing pressure in the buildup is now about equal (1-3). True, bulls still need to overcome that block, but that goes for bears too, should they wish to shake our stops. From where we stand, though, their chances are not nearly as good as ours, because *we* have the conditions on our side.

* * *

This completes our evaluation of the five AUD pairs over the years 2014–2017. Not all setups may have struck you as textbook, or even valid, but hopefully you find that the majority are in accordance with the requirements discussed in Part One. You may have noticed also that we are offered about one good setup per chart per year. And surely it won't have escaped your attention that most of the setups follow through. Have we entered fantasy land?

First off, with 23 more pairs to look at, it is too early for conclusions. Keep in mind also that the method under review is specifically geared to finding *high-odds* setups. Yes, such setups do exist! They may not come in great numbers, but they are not exactly sparse either, as I am positive this backtest will show. In fact, assuming we have done our homework, spotting these setups is often more a matter of patience than of exceptional skill.

But let's not busy ourselves with statistics at this early stage. With the AUD pairs out of the way, it's time to find out what the CAD and CHF pairs have to say in all this.

chapter **9**

The CAD and CHF pairs

CADCHF, CADJPY, and CHFJPY

CADCHF 2014–2017

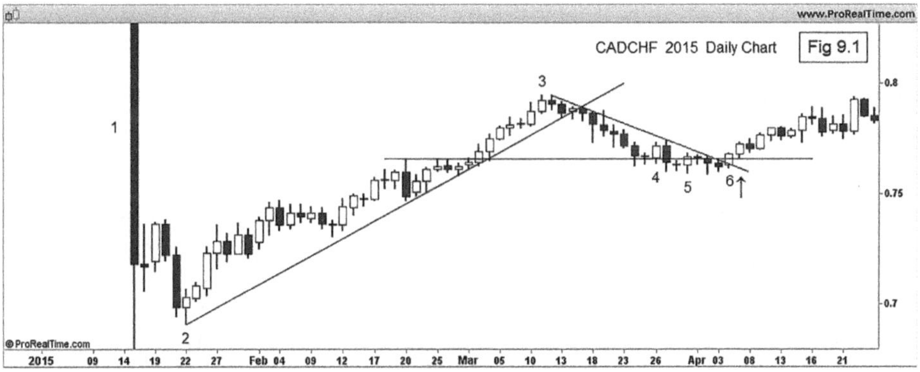

Figure 9.1. Remember that freak bar on the AUDCHF in Figure 8.7? Logically, a surprise intervention by the Swiss National Bank will affect *all* CHF crosses, hence the similar response on the CADCHF (1). This time around, however, the 2-3 pullback does not allow for a reversal setup, and so we leave it at that.

A few weeks later, though, we have a setup on the *bull* side (6). But is it wise to think long with that freak bar still fresh on the chart? Within reason, very much so. By no means should we discard the earlier selloff, but let us not dismiss the pullback either. As that is quite a trend in its own right, the 3-5 correction is technically a bull flag. And in the lows of it, we have a three-stepper (4-5-6).

Furthermore, an entry above bar 6 would not only confirm the perforation of the flagline but also the failure of that break below support. With such pleasant backup, a standard stop below bar 6 would have my preference. If you would rather put your stop below bar 5, all good, but the tradeoff is a higher risk of failure at the target end.

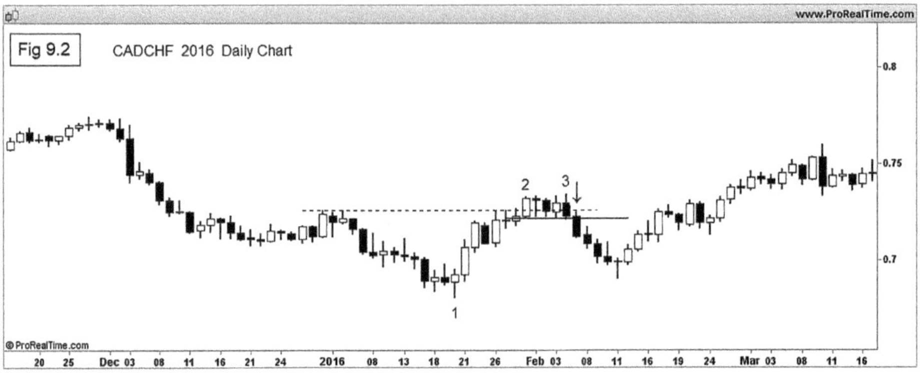

Figure 9.2. A good reason to at least study the very basics of price action is to be able to recognize the current theme in a chart as that will have a big say in what trade idea to pursue. One such theme is of course the pullback in a trend (1-2). We all know the plan with that. By learning to look a little deeper, however, we can often spot thematic action in our setups too, such as a cluster in the highs of a pullback (2-3). And should we care to dig a little deeper still, even the resolutions may start to stand out as thematic, as is often the case with trap bars (3). If all this can be figured out in any decent charting program, it makes you wonder why not *every trader* studies prices action.

As for luck, we basically have no need for it, but still it is nice to see the short below bar 3 hit target right before the market turns. That could have easily gone the other way.

Tip: So here's an idea. If ever you suffer a bad beat, rather than get all upset, just think of a time you lucked out. And don't forget, *one* lucky two-pointer already compensates for *two* earlier shakes.

Figure 9.3. Here we see the setup from our previous chart in another role (1). As bulls have broken above it, that cluster in the top of the pullback could now serve as a springboard for another runup—that is, if not for bears throwing a monkey wrench into the bullish plans (2).

As it would indeed be reckless to ignore such an ominous trap bar, bulls apparently decide on an alternative plan, and a clever one at that. Pop quiz: If a break into new territory isn't likely to come forth anytime soon, what else could possibly entice fresh bulls to buy in? That's right, a *false* break into old territory (3-4)!

Mind you, buying in on a re-break is not something to be considered lightly. Recall the similar break on the AUDCAD in Figure 8.2. There the re-break stood poor chance of success because the dominant mode was bearish (lower highs). In the chart above, however, the mode of the last few months is bullish (higher lows). That makes all the difference!

But let us pick our entry wisely. If proper buildup is key for a break, then so too for a re-break. Imagine bar 4 to have followed bar 3 straightaway; that could still be seen as a test. With two bars added, however, the buildup has not only doubled, the number of bears trapped below support will likely have doubled as well (all of which potential *buyers* in a re-break).

Note: For protection, a stop below the 3-4 buildup seems a fair call, but ask yourself first if you would still believe in your trade should prices drop back below bar 4. If that would already destroy all hope for a win (think re-break failure), then you might as well put your stop there, for the benefit of an easier two-pointer.

Figure 9.4. Of all the classic patterns believed to reverse a rally or trend, the head-and-shoulders is among the most respected. And for good reason, it is after all a three-step variant (highest top in the middle). Equally potent is the *inverse* type (1-2-3). As this one forms in a range, however, its reversal potential is limited. Yet as we have no intention to trade beyond a two-pointer, this may still do for us.

By the way, while our trade idea here is a range reversal, setup-wise we are looking for a breakout on account of that barrier across the head-and-shoulders. The push in bar 3 is not a setup for us, though, as there is no pressure on the barrier just prior. There is not enough room for our preferred risk-to-reward anyway.

Luck is on our side as not much later a two-stepper pops up (3-4). We could also call this a re-break failure setup or a resolution of a test. All fine, as long as we don't let it slip. An extra reason not to linger here is the looming magnet effect of the top barrier.

Note: Perhaps you may wonder why we don't try to exploit this magnet effect more often, even if only for a one-pointer. As the next magnet is never far away, it's hard to fault the idea. The problem, though, is that for such aggression not to backfire, one really needs to be able to tell the wheat from the chaff, which is rarely the case for those just starting out. Hence my advice to go the more selective route *first*—meaning to solely accept the setups that (a) indisputably stand out as valid, and (b) allow for a favorable risk-to-reward (ideally 1:2). Rest assured, finding even just 10 such setups per year would already make for a highly promising bottom line (more on that in Chapter 14).

Figure 9.5. Running the top barrier from bar 1 would be our first choice, but its relevance never gets confirmed by another visit. Hence we switch attention to a lower barrier later on.

This new barrier from bar 2 (ignoring the false push a few bars later) first comes into play after bar 3, nicely confirmed by the subsequent test (3-4). Interesting also is the angular support line, which already grants us a line in the sand beyond which to look for a short.

While that false dip in bar 4 may look good for the bulls, it is also a useful development for an eventual short. For we know that if a re-break fails, the follow-through potential is then even more potent. And there it is in bar 5.

While not strictly called for, here it makes sense to place our short below bar 4 instead, just to have that final hurdle out of the way. All the more so as it would hardly stretch our target.

Note: The choice for protection is a little more subtle because at first glance a standard stop above bar 5 looks too tight. Yet if bulls have it in them to attack the top barrier *again* (let's not rule it out), no stop in the magnet area, even above bar 3, can be seen as safe. And thus we might as well go for a standard stop as that comes with the tightest target.

FYI, the buildup on the far right is unsuited for a breakout because it regards a halfway barrier of an earlier bull run (not shown).

CADJPY 2014–2017

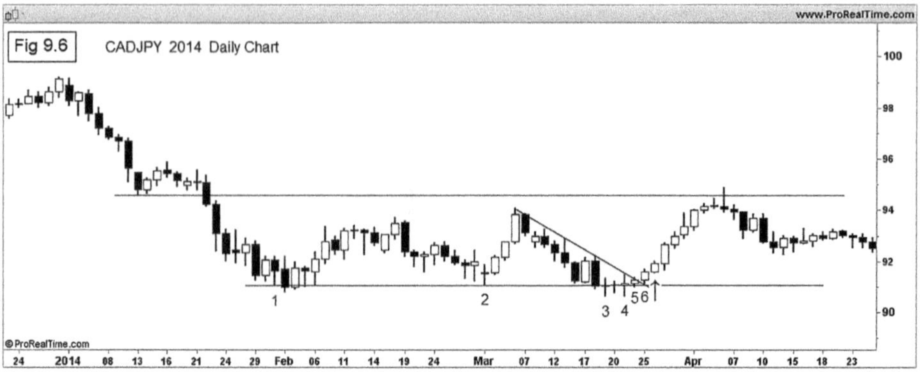

Figure 9.6. This chart shows a range reversal that could also be seen as a three-strep trend reversal. I chose to run the bottom barrier from the low of bar 1 because it lines up well with a few other bounces in the area and with the low of bar 2 later on.

Since the 3-4 fight is still inconclusive, bar 5 is the first to call for a decision: trade above this little inside bar or wait for a better offer. Personally I am not too keen on the fact that of the last five sessions, bar 5 is the only one to close *up*, and not too convincingly at that. The three-step backup is promising, but conditions alone are not enough to warrant a trade.

Next session we have a resolution, but this too puts us on the spot: can we still enter above bar 6 or should we now hope for a test?

It largely comes down to protection. Obviously, it wouldn't be wise to put our stop right below bar 6 or bar 5, and so the only real alternative is below bar 4. Luckily for us, that suits our purposes just fine because even with this insurance thrown in there is ample room for a two-pointer towards the nearest magnet (halfway barrier).

Tip: To *visually* check if there is room for a two-pointer, there is no need to count pips. Instead, use the box tool in your toolbar. First widen your chart a bit for a closer look. Then wrap a box around your entry and stop levels, hit copy, and place two boxes on top of the first. The high of the highest box then marks your target. If you visualize that box in half, that would point to a target of 1.5 times your risk. (Vice versa for a short position.)

Figure 9.7. The top barrier of this range is a no-brainer, but not so evident is that it sits a tad below the halfway barrier from our previous chart—a worthy reminder that even the most prominent barriers will lose their relevance at *some* point.

Looking at the action below the barrier, it is hard to find a better example of buildup in stages. So in no way would we look for a reversal. But remember, proper tension in the final buildup is still key for a setup, which is why we cannot trade above bar 1 just yet.

The buildup at bar 2 is more to our liking, but after all that pushing and pulling, wouldn't you also want to see a more convincing resolution, and ideally a perforation? Either way, as the next bar opens lower (Monday) and never trades above bar 2, our entry there would not have been hit anyway. We would then cancel and await new developments.

Two scans later we finally have our perforation (4). While the break itself is rejected, bar 4 is a valid signal bar as it closes bullishly for the day. It's small span is not an issue either because we can opt for a stop below bar 3, the nearest swing point, with excellent prospects for a two-pointer still (new territory).

Amazingly, bears once again manage to frustrate the long-awaited breakout. But as this time the barrier remains under attack (5), we can now leave all orders pending and hope for a fill next session. (Or perhaps cancel and reinstall with a stop below bar 5.)

Come on, bears, be a good sport and step aside.

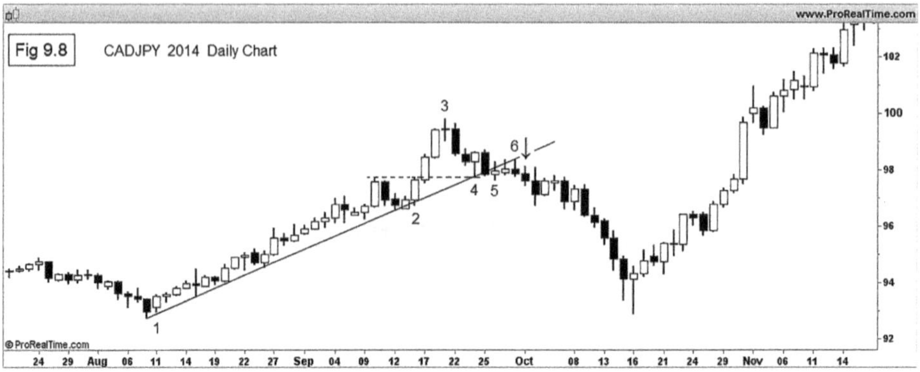

Figure 9.8. While it typically takes three notable attempts to turn a well-established trend, runaway rallies tend to reverse more swiftly (1-3), especially if they have yet to incur a pullback. Makes sense if you think about it.

Another reason for anticipating a sharper reversal than "normal" is the acceleration in the top of that bull run (2-3). Such enthusiasm rarely bodes well for these latecomers, and as such for the trend itself. Hence often referred to as a *blow-off stage.*

Not a promising sight either is the false break above bar 4. Instead of another push into new highs, the market responds with a dip below the trendline (5). It is only a first perforation, so nothing lost yet—but then bulls would do well to reclaim that broken support. If all they can muster is a test, such weakness will not likely go unnoticed. We should be looking to exploit that as well—but only after a convincing resolution. Does bar 6 fit that bill?

Note: Perhaps you would think that for trend reversal purposes, a more potent signal bar would be better suited, but that is not necessarily true. A benefit of a modest signal bar is that in many cases we can still shoot for a two-pointer and not worry much about overstaying our welcome in the pullback. And besides, bar 6 is actually of decent span when compared to the average bar earlier on, and is a trap bar to boot. So this resolution is by no means lacking. (The dotted support line is no longer an issue either thanks to the earlier hit in bar 4.)

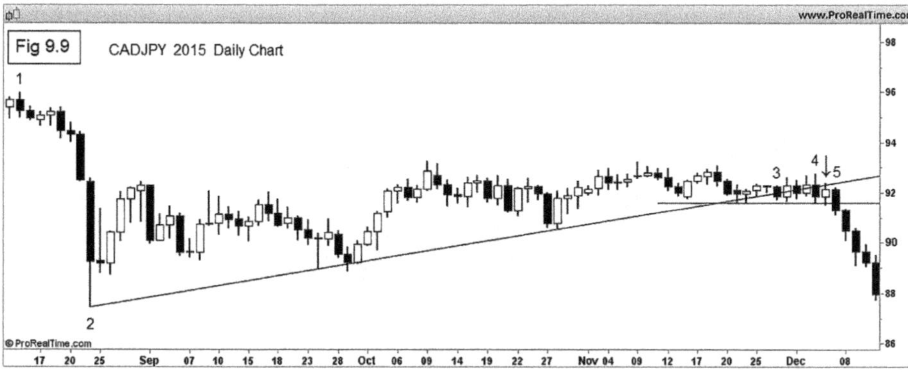

Figure 9.9. In the fall of 2015 the CADJPY prints a so-called *wedge* pattern (2-3)—effectively a giant bear flag, hanging from the 1-2 bear trend. Interesting to note is that the rallies from the angular line keep declining in span until prices can no longer bounce meaningfully and thus start to cling around that barrier: that's a big tipoff to now keep an eye out for a breakout.

Logically, we don't expect such a long-lasting barrier to crack after only a minor fight. But how do we know when the buildup is ripe for a break? The more bars the better, but ultimately it all comes down to the quality of the resolution.

Bar 3 is the first signal bar candidate (bear bar), but this resolution is questionable at best. (If you would rather take your chances, then at least opt for a stop above the current high of the buildup. And after your shake, stay alert for another try.)

Of the three bear bars in this barrier fight, bar 4 is clearly the most suitable signal bar. Note how this trap bar not only overpowers its direct neighbor, it overlaps all bars in the area, and challenges a buildup line while at it. Yet if for some reason you missed this setup, it's not too late to enter below bar 5. At that point a standard stop will likely suffice, but even a stop above bar 4 is still a viable option (as the low of the trend is likely up for a visit next).

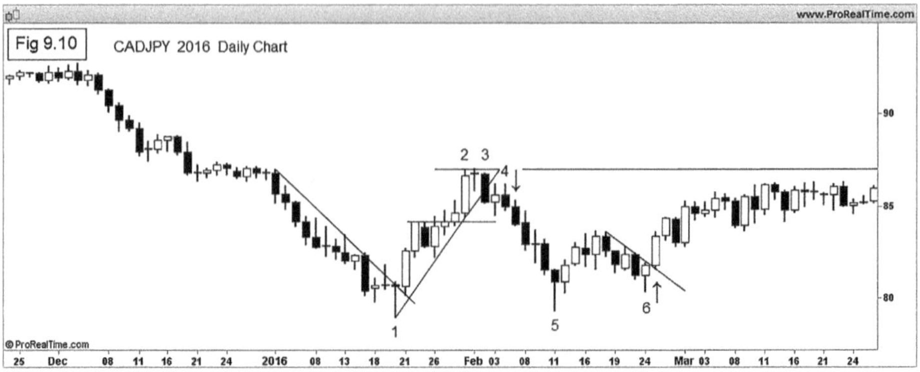

Figure 9.10. Of the many patterns believed to announce a reversal, the so-called *evening star* (2-3) is among those held in highest regard (right besides its M-top cousin). And it should be said, the implications of this three-bar pattern (bull bar, doji, bear bar) are very bearish indeed. Why then not short below bar 3 right away?

With prices in the halfway area of a bear trend, a reversal can be "expected", but let us not dismiss the aggression in the pullback (1-2). Another reason for caution is that a short below bar 3 would soon run into support of a cluster line. And since the perforation of the pullback line is also a first, the safer idea here is to hope for a test. It might leave us emptyhanded, but that's all in the game.

See what a little patience can do (4). With now an evening star *and* a two-stepper as backup (3-4), plus a test out of the way, there is little reason to hold back. Admittedly, we would have preferred an actual hit on the cluster line in the previous bar (as in Figure 8.13, for example), but given the bearish conditions at hand, I think this little shortcoming can be forgiven. If you prefer a safer stop, place it all the way above the evening star. For even with such insurance thrown in, there is still room for a two-pointer towards the trend low (magnet).

Not much later, the CADJPY calls for attention again, courtesy of a hard to miss three-stepper in the lows of the trend (1-5-6). This is one such setup best accepted right away. Even if met with a test, there is a good chance our stop below bar 6 will hold (prominent swing point).

Figure 9.11. Every now and then a catalyst comes along that has the power to disrupt countless markets worldwide, even those seemingly "nonrelated." The Brexit vote in June 2016 is one such event not easily forgotten (freak bar 1). Since polls and elections typically occur during weekdays there is no reason to shun such sessions as there is no real risk of a gap beyond your stop (unless of course you trade stocks). But keep in mind that the technical picture can still turn in an instant depending on how the count pans out. So if ever in position just prior, alternative tactics may be justified, such as scratching an already profitable trade. All this at your discretion.

In late September the generous CADJPY offers its third setup of the year, this time by means of a so-called *morning star* (2-3). As the name implies, this is the bullish mirror image of the bearish evening star, now comprising a bear bar, a doji, and a bull bar. The reversal implications are equally potent, but once again, the bar on the right is not necessarily a valid signal bar.

A key difference with the evening star from our previous chart, however, is that this time we can trade above bar 3 right away—because *both* barriers would be taken out. This is not to say that bears couldn't put up a fight still, but with a morning star as backup and a sound stop below bar 3 (*well below* support), a shake is not very likely (unless there follows an actual range break).

If for some reason we skipped this setup, or missed our scan, a trade above bar 4 is still doable (resolution of a test). That setup is then best traded with a standard stop.

Figure 9.12. No matter how strong a trend sits on the chart, at some point a pullback will retrace a big chunk of it. This could come about in all shapes and sizes, one of which is a range-type correction developing over several months, as seen here above. This is equally suited for reversal purposes, but the setup to scan for is then obviously more of the range reversal type.

After a false low in bar 4, it looks like we have three-stepper on our hands (1-2-5), but closer inspection reveals a dealbreaker. Did you spot it? Indeed, that little cluster in the 3-4 bear swing blocks the way.

Six scans later, bar 6 resolves a test (now effectively a four-stepper). That cluster is still there, of course, but as it already blocked the break above bar 5 (leading to the test), it is no longer a major obstacle. Just to be safe, though, let's put our stop below bar 4. If we then also opt for an entry above the bar prior to bar 6 (to have that little top tail out of the way), we have done everything in *our* power to get the odds on this trade in our favor.

Alas, all this to no avail.

Note: As the market clearly disagreed with our trade idea, could we not cleverly switch sides and bet on a breakout instead, say below bar 7? Frankly, that would be a terrible plan. Note that we are not dealing with a regular range barrier here but with one of the most resilient barriers in price action: the halfway barrier of a powerful trend. While these too at some point may fail, that usually requires a lot of prepwork. So rather than jump on a short below bar 7, a safer plan would be to wait for that break to fail, and then look to trade the re-break.

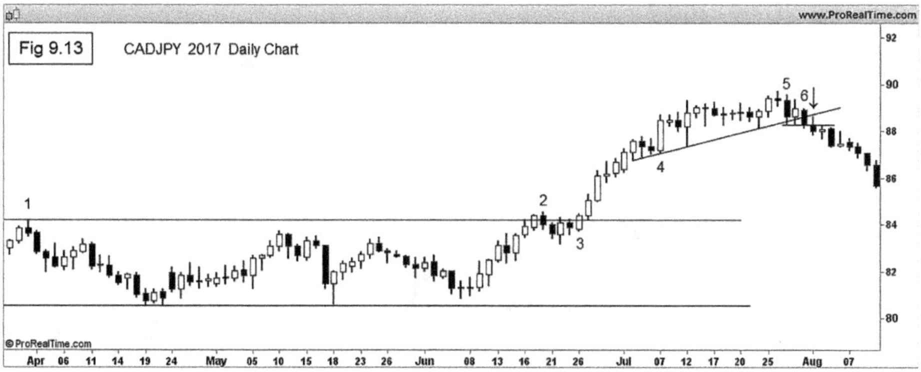

Figure 9.13. At first glance the 2-3 buildup sets up very nicely for a range break, if not for the fact that the top barrier is not yet confirmed (no touch or false break between bar 1 and 2). If we can't be sure of a barrier's relevance, the significance of its breakout is then equally doubtful. I am not saying this setup is a definite skip, but at least consider the missing element.

More textbook is the setup at bar 6, a two-step resolution with a re-break failure built in (5-6). Notice also how the buildup on the angular line resembles an elongated M-top (4-5), by itself already a bearish pattern. And as this regards a reversal of a breakout rally, the magnet effect of the broken range barrier could have a say in things as well.

Taking everything into account, placing our stop above bar 6 seems reasonable, but the more technical place for protection is above the previous bar as it marks the high point of a re-break. True, such insurance would call for a much wider two-pointer, but since we anticipate a selloff to the barrier below, that shouldn't be an issue. (Prices never made it to that barrier, but they did dip deep enough for a two-pointer.)

CHFJPY 2014–2017

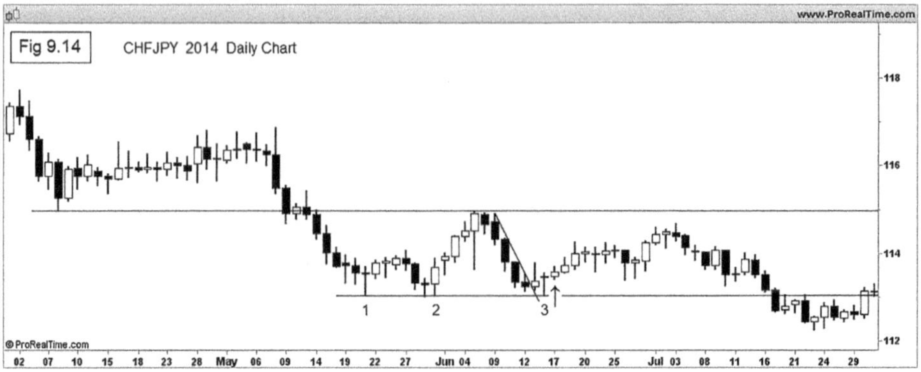

Figure 9.14. As much as all charts stand on their own, the themes within them are far from original, such is the repetitive nature of price action. For example, in the CHFJPY above we can spot the popular two-stepper in the lows of a bear swing (1-2). Surely we have seen such action before. Which is not to say that it is also a valid *setup*.

Whatever pattern or sequence shows up, by itself it can only provide an indication as to where prices are headed next. Hence we always wait for the so-called resolution. And that is why bar 2 won't do for us. Partly because there is not much room for a trade towards the halfway barrier, but consider also the tricky spot for a stop. And by the way, the conditions for a reversal are not great to begin with due to the bearish aggression in the foregoing selloff.

Fair enough; but why then trade above bar 3?

At that point the risk of bearish counterplay is no longer as prevalent because we now have a three-stepper as backup, plus a test out of the way (resolved in bar 3). The span of our signal bar is also more suitable. True, we still would have liked a more technical stop (below a false dip), but the odds on the whole are good enough to accept.

Note: On paper, this trade hit target just before the market reversed. But recall that if it truly hinges on a few pips, there is a chance our exit may not have been filled in the live market due to an unfortunate spread (or maybe we wrapped our orders around the signal bar a tad wider than required). As we cannot be sure of the outcome, we book this trade as a loss.

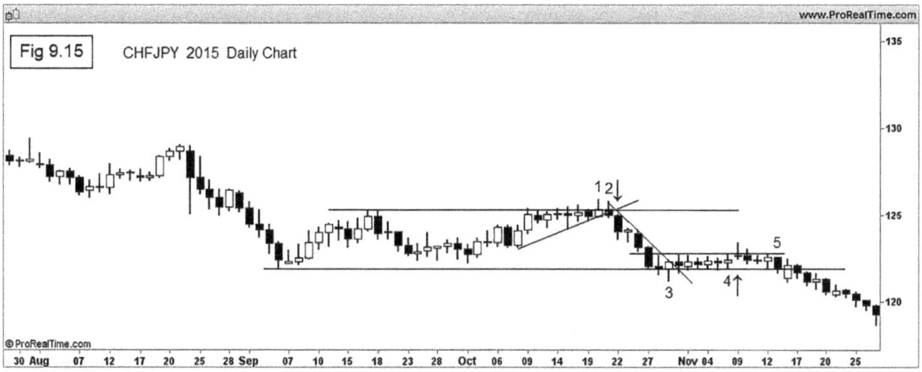

Figure 9.15. It doesn't take a charting expert to see merit in a short below bar 2 (with a stop above bar 1). The rejected perforation of the halfway barrier and the looming failure of support are clear signs that bears are still very much in control. But then we might ask: who in their right mind would want to take the other side of our short?

Frankly, that is a cocky question. Surely we will often do business with less educated traders, but for all we know we might be dealing with a savvy party who simply views things differently—be it from the same chart, another time frame, a hedging plan, or what have you. Let's just be thankful for knowing that there is always someone willing to take the other side of our bets—which at some point may even pay off for *them*, as our next trade nicely illustrates (4).

Note: As a sidenote, have you ever been tempted to purchase one of these so-called secret indicators? I'm sure there are those who fall for it. Yet if you think about it, what good is a signal that only a select few can see. If you want to get the market on your side, a smarter idea would be to look for an indicator that *everyone* uses. And here's the best part: we already have such an indicator in our own charting program, at no extra cost. That's right, the bars in our charts!

As for that cluster setup (3-4), let us assume our stop is already hit in bar 5. Would that have called for a short? Personally, I am not a fan of switching directions right after a shake, but in fairness, it's hard to fault the idea. Why dare short *here* and not in, say, Figure 9.12 earlier on? Check the conditions.

Figure 9.16. Before we head over to the EUR pairs, here's one last trade on the CHFJPY. At first glance the 2-3 setup bears strong resemblance to what we have seen on the CADJPY in Figure 9.13. A noteworthy distinction, however, is that the barrier in the earlier chart was not yet confirmed prior to the setup (hence invalid). Here above the barrier *is* confirmed (at 1).

The prospect of a pop into new territory will have many traders on the alert for a setup. But not solely from the bullish camp! After all, each and every short from within the range would show a loss in a breakout. And the only way out for these unfortunate bears is to help that break along—as in *buy* back or perish. Is it shameful of us to look to exploit such predicament? Sure it is, in the welfare business.

In the markets, however, one trader's pain is simply another trader's edge. And that is why it pays to study price action: to understand *when* the odds are favorable. True, small mistakes may still slip in, but there is no reason to ever fall for an obvious skip, such as the attack in bar 2. There is simply not enough buildup below the barrier to back up a break at *that* point.

Let's stay sharp, though, because it would not be uncommon for the attackers to come back for another try. And as that would not only add to the buildup but also weaken the opponent's morale, the chances of a second perforation to follow through are usually already quite promising (two-step principle). Of course, for any of that to call for action, a proper resolution is a must. And that is where bar 3 comes into play. A perfectly suitable trap bar.

Note: There's one thing worthy of mention. Does November 8, 2016 ring a bell? It is the date of the US presidential elections, the outcome of which pretty much rocked the entire financial system (4). With that on the agenda just a few days out, is it wise to accept that trade above bar 3? In principle, very much so. As the elections are held during the week, there is no real risk of a gap. True, there is the fair risk of a freak session, which could screw up our trade just the same. So perhaps there is something to be said for letting it all blow over. I wouldn't worry too much about it, though. Major elections and other tricky polls are rare occurrences anyway, and most will probably pass you by without exposure. Yet if by any chance you have a position on and for some reason the outcome of the poll is postponed to over the weekend, be wise and just close out. You don't want to risk a gap beyond your stop.

chapter 10

The EUR pairs

EURAUD, EURCAD, EURCHF, EURGBP, EURJPY, EURNZD, and EURUSD

EURAUD 2014–2017

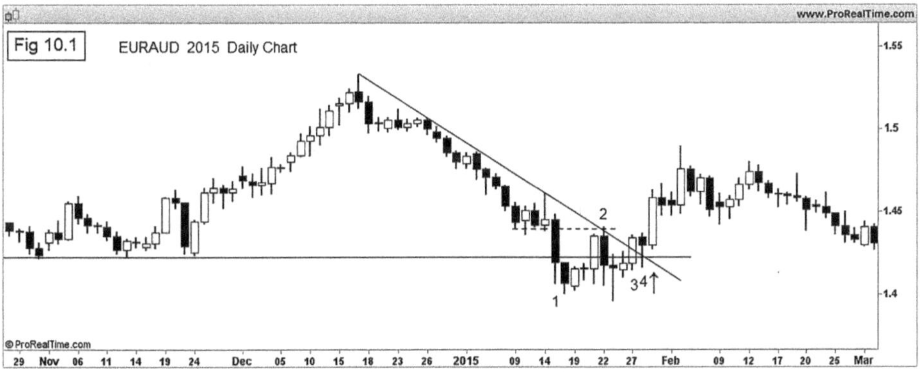

Figure 10.1. It is hard to say which idea has the least chance of success: pushing for a break right after a strong rally (1) or for a reversal straight into resistance (2). Mind you, these are traps we too could fall for when looking at some faster time frames. But not on the dailies!

The attempt in bar 3 looks premature still, if only for the absence of a safe stop nearby, but we may have something going after a test.

While most tests and resolutions take at least a few bars to play out, not uncommon is the "one-bar sequence," as seen in bar 4 (the bearish close is not an issue as it regards a *bullish* doji). To be honest, this setup is still only so-so, but if you wish to take your chances, at least you can now do so with a standard stop (test out of the way).

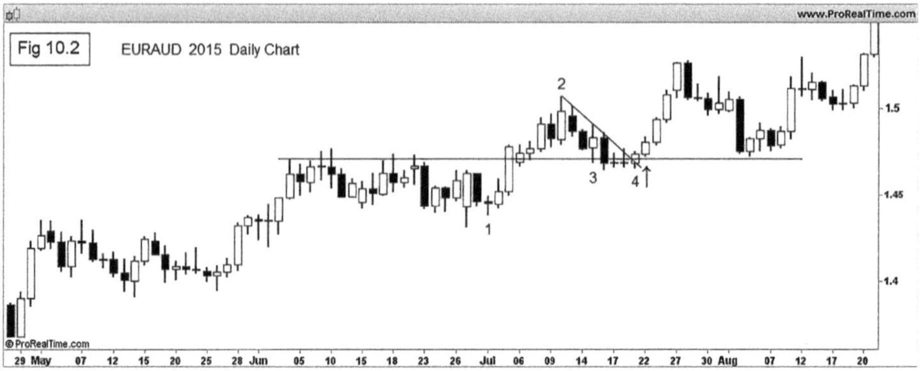

Figure 10.2. Take a moment to test your chart reading skills and see how many cues you can detect in favor of a trade above bar 4.

Here's what I count. Starting with the basic conditions, as the chart is predominantly bullish (trading higher throughout), bulls already have the better papers to resolve the 2-3 test in their favor. Additionally, there is backup not only of the broken range barrier but also of the halfway area of the latest bull swing (1-2). The 3-4 action confirms this support and at the same time builds up to the resolution in bar 4. A bonus is that this signal bar not merely perforates the pullback line but *closes* above it, thus setting up an even stronger entry in a confirmation break. Its modest span is another welcome feature as it allows for a fairly easy two-pointer. And to top it off, there is a cute little bear trap in the low of bar 4 (did you also spot that false dip?).

Tip: In principle we could even afford to miss a few of these features and still justify that trade. That's the power of *favorable* conditions. But let us not be so lenient regarding *adverse* conditions, if at all present. For one weak feature (say a tricky stop) could already suffice to postpone a trade idea or even kill it.

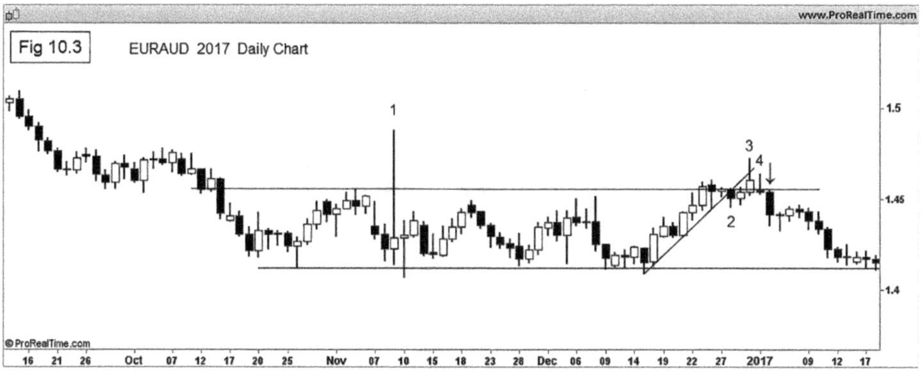

Figure 10.3. If you set up your charts to show about four or five months as they load, there is rarely need to scroll back to understand what's going on. But don't go any tighter than that. So if your charts only show a few months of bars (say on a mobile device), always check the recommended period. It would be handy to know, for example, that the range on the EURAUD here above is hanging from a trend. Not only would you be less tempted to trade the break in bar 3 (against the halfway area), you would instantly recognize the reversal potential.

There is actually another reason for why the break in bar 3 stands poor chance of following through: it comes about in what is technically still a test of the angular barrier, broken two days prior (2-3).

When then bar 4 shows up, with its close back inside the range, we know we are not just dealing with a "lowly" inside bar. On the contrary, this is a perfectly valid resolution bar as it allows for a sharp entry right below the top barrier and a fine stop above a bearish top tail.

Note: Bar 1 is a grim reminder of the total mayhem that went on during the counting of the US presidential votes on November 9, 2016. Quite a few markets that day were hit in similar fashion. Do such panicky sessions have any technical meaning? If they sit at a crucial spot in the price action, perhaps we shouldn't totally ignore them, but on the whole I wouldn't grant them too much credit. In any event, no freak bar could ever serve as a signal bar.

Figure 10.4. The nice thing about trading the dailies is that you never have to wonder about the bigger picture—you're already looking at it. Is the chart trending up, then that is what the market is doing and so your trades are best chosen in line with this pressure. Abide by this simple yet time-tested premise and you'll find yourself on the right side of the market more often than not.

As always, though, only a proper setup will do for a trade, which is why the break in bar 1 is a skip. The break in bar 2 is equally premature (still no buildup), but as this one follows through, it will be interesting to see what happens next.

In a perfect world a break is tested in a lackluster, almost obligatory manner. Aggression in a test is not a dealbreaker per se (2-3), but then we like to see an extra step or some other form of buildup in the barrier before engaging in a reversal. For this reason, an entry above bar 4 looks somewhat premature. (An order there wouldn't be filled anyway.)

Note: Of the four signal bar candidates in the 4-5 cluster (bull bars), bar 5 is clearly the most persuasive. While we may have preferred a close outside of the range, a perforation is always a great feature too because that also allows for an entry in a confirmation break. Of course, the tail of the perforation bar should not stick out too much or stand too tall compared to its body, as then we would be dealing with an *adverse* doji. I guess that speaks for itself.

EURCAD 2014–2017

Figure 10.5. It might appear ironic that we see no problem in acting on a minor perforation (such as above bar 5 in our previous chart), yet shy away from an indisputable break, as in bar 1 here above, stemming from a bear flag to boot. Yet if you think about it, postponing the trade makes perfect sense. Because if we immediately take position below bar 1, not only would we risk a terrible start, we might not even survive an otherwise harmless test.

Bar 2 is already more up our alley (bearish doji), but a valid concern regarding this resolution is that the flagline has yet to be hit from below. In fact, we would actually prefer a modest re-break—as then we may see chance to exploit its failure.

If the above scenario is so preferable, why then short below bar 3? The simple answer is that we now have a little M-top for a setup (2-3). Admittedly, it is not the most exemplary variant, yet with a stop above bar 2 and a broken bear flag as backup, I think we can take our chances on that short.

Should you see it differently, it is not too late to opt for a short below bar 4. You might have to tighten your exit a bit, but in return you stand to benefit from a highly favorable magnet (as the bottom barrier is now almost certainly up for a visit next).

By the way, if the 2-3 setup appears vaguely familiar, have a look at Figure 5.2 in our introductory chapter on trend reversals. Pretty much the same *theme*, wouldn't you say.

Figure 10.6. Technically regarded, the 2-4 situation isn't that far removed from what we have seen in Figure 10.3 earlier on. Once again bulls defy the conditions by challenging the halfway barrier of a bear rally. And again their break comes about in what is essentially still a test of broken support (2-3). And equally similar is the notable rejection by means of an inside bar (4).

All this sounds good for a short, if not for one little issue: the downward potential. Indeed, even if we set this up with a standard stop above bar 4, there is too little room in the range for our minimum reward of 1.5 times our risk.

Yet if shooting for smaller targets fits your style, this is a very valid setup. You could even place your stop above bar 3 and still have room for a one-pointer. (Keep in mind that the bottom barrier is best derived from the original low of the bear rally, not that false dip in bar 1.)

Tip: If ever on the fence about whether to apply insurance on a trade of which the target is the same either way (say a range barrier), consider the safest option first because the premium is only a smaller *profit* (relative to the risk). The situation is different when there are no obstacles in sight. Then you have to weigh the pros and cons of insurance more carefully because the safer stop will put your target further out.

Figure 10.7. Given the habitual resilience of ranges, it is safe to say that reversals are far more common than breakouts. Yet as all barriers eventually get broken, it is important to keep an open mind. Initial perforations, however, are rarely built up properly and as such tend to fail more often than not (1). One would almost think that these probes are solely meant to test the waters. Subsequent perforations stand a better chance of following through, but these too require proper planning or are just as prone to get rejected (2).

After two failed attempts to break out, the attacking parties usually become demoralized or at least take a step back, which automatically raises the chances of a range reversal (two-step principle). Still, for any of that to warrant action, a proper resolution is a must.

And there it is in bar 3. With now *three* false breakouts on the chart, it is safe to state that bulls have won this barrier fight. Which then leaves us with two options: place our entry above bar 3 right away or take our chances on a test.

It is not a hard call. The mere fact that we have a three-stepper on our hands (1-2-3) already lowers the chance of a test substantially. Add to that the *close* above resistance (stronger than a mere perforation) and we have even more reason not to linger at this crucial juncture.

For protection, a standard stop would have my preference here, but a safer stop below bar 2 is also fine. If that's your call, do check if there is still room for a two-pointer. Even if your exit would only sit a tad above the top barrier, do *not* bank on a perforation. You might get away with it, but why risk a good trade for a few extra pips.

Figure 10.8. Two reasons not to hop on a break after poor buildup (1) are (a) the high chance of failure and (b) the high chance of a test. As to the latter, if tests are already commonplace for breakouts that *are* properly built up, then arguably even more so for those that are not. If such a break follows through, however, then we would welcome a test—as long as we pay attention to its nature. Remember, the last thing to look for after an aggressive pullback (2-3) is a swift resolution (4).

So bar 4 is a rightful skip, but what's wrong with bar 5; isn't that a trap bar? While it could be viewed as such, thanks to its tiny neighbor, the bar itself still stands quite weak in the buildup, and offers a tricky entry in the midst of a cluster to boot. (And for what it's worth, the high of the bar isn't even taken out).

Yet if we had to choose, we would much rather buy above bar 5 than short below bar 6 (halfway area of a bull trend). And sure enough, it isn't long before this bearish foolery is called out—by a morning star no less (6-7). Now *that* is a proper resolution!

Note: As for the outcome, we can't tell from this chart whether our entry above bar 7 is triggered before or after the dip in bar 8. If before, our stop below bar 7 may already have been hit on the day of entry (hard to tell as well). Rather than consult a smaller time frame (or conveniently assume we would have chosen a safer stop), let's simply book this trade as a loss. But not without staying alert for another try! Consider also that *if* a new signal bar is granted, the extra step in the buildup would imply a setup even stronger than the original (9).

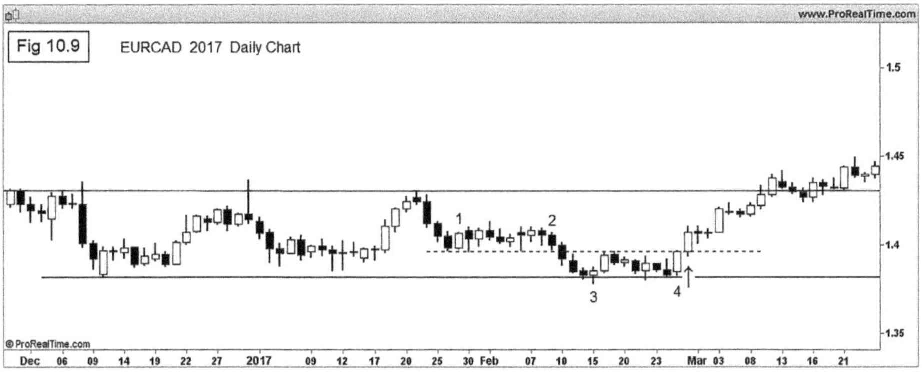

Figure 10.9. One of the first things to do when planning for reversals is to check the distance to the nearest obstacle, to see if there is room for a trade to begin with. Clusters in particular are best not taken lightly. But what if there already sits a cluster directly to the left of the setup, as in 1-2 vs 3-4? Would that ruin the trade idea?

Not necessarily. Let's first discuss the above scenario in which the two clusters share a cluster line. In principle we can treat this like a regular cluster setup (entry above bar 4, stop below bar 3), yet a key distinction for validity is that our cluster is at least of similar strength as the opposing one. Imagine bar 4 to have attacked the cluster line a week earlier; that would be a skip since at that point the pressure in our cluster (buildup) is not pent-up enough to hope for a push through the opposing block. One thing, though, this is not solely a matter of counting bars. If one cluster shows fewer but stronger bars, that could still be seen as equal pressure.

In situations where the two opposing clusters sit a bit apart (Figure 10.17), the above still applies, but we need to be very mindful of where the opposing line is located as we don't want that to sit in the way of an entry (even if our own line is broken). If neither cluster allows for a trustworthy cluster line, then we either wait for more info or go by the pressure element alone (Figure 10.15).

Of course, all the above only serves as a guideline on how to handle double-cluster situations. Rest assured, we will have ample opportunity to look a little deeper into the concept going forward. In fact, our next chart already shows an interesting variant.

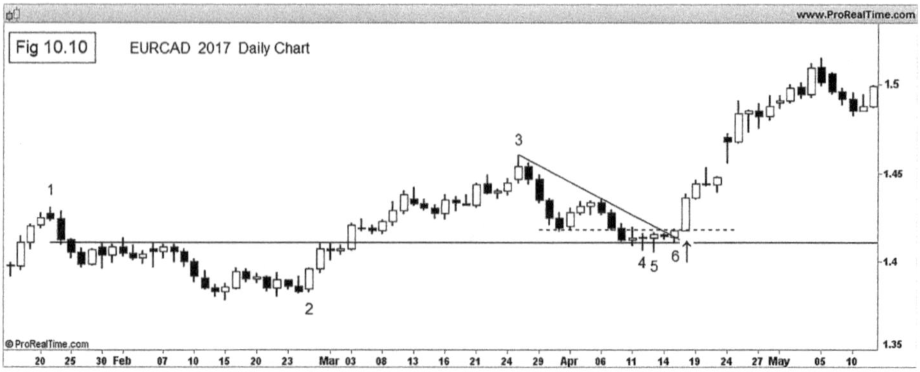

Figure 10.10. Before we discuss the setup, first note that swing point on the far left (1). In our previous chart this marked the top of a range. Yet the 2-3 rally, the 3-4 pullback, and the new support barrier clearly call for a different perspective.

Tip: Always extend your range barriers at least a few months into the future (or even invisibly past the price axis) as that will keep you in touch with important levels as time goes by. But as this chart shows, it is important not to get complacent with whatever you plotted earlier on. If not in every scan, make it a habit to check all your range barriers for relevance at least once a week.

Since our trade idea is a pullback reversal, we can begin by looking for a pullback line; then we can look for obstacles in the pullback itself, like that little bear flag about halfway the 3-4 swing.

While not as hard as clusters, flags can hinder a reversal just the same as illustrated by the dotted line. This is actually a *favorable* feature from a setup perspective as it grants us a line in the sand beyond which to look for an entry. But remember, we may only consider a trade if we deem the buildup potent enough to take on that flag.

I would say that when bar 6 shows up the pressures are about even. If you agree, then this is already a valid setup because both the pullback line and the cluster line are perforated. While the resolution is relatively modest, the tiny span of this trap bar is actually a bonus here because it allows us to opt for the most technical stop in the area (below bar 5), with excellent odds for a two-pointer still.

EURCHF 2014–2017

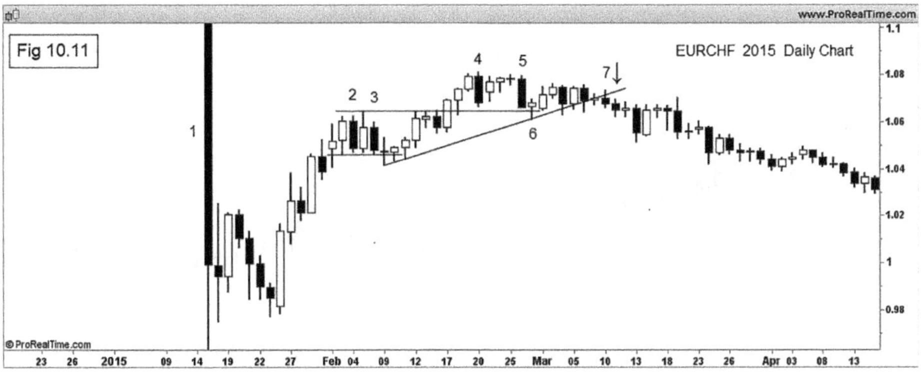

Figure 10.11. It's hard to recall a bigger shocker to the markets than that infamous SNB decision on January 15, 2015 (1). What was it all about? For quite some time the Swiss authorities had pegged the CHF to the EUR at a steady rate of 1.20—meaning they intervened each time that threshold came under attack. Then out of the blue they let go of this policy, which hugely appreciated the CHF against all prominent currencies (hence the EURCHF selling off).

With such a fat freak bar on the chart, the only logical response at *some* point is a pullback. And odds are it will not be a modest one either. Should the pullback indeed come in hard, then be extra wary of reversal traps. For example, the 2-3 two-stepper (or M-top, if you will), should be an easy skip because the powerbars leading up to that setup clearly let on that it is too early for a bet against the bulls.

The second M-top looks more shortable (4-5), but now there is support underfoot (nicely confirmed in bar 6). In the subsequent buildup, however, the support situation appears to have switched from horizontal to angular. Which then brings us to bar 7. Do we finally have a resolution worthy of a short?

To its defense, it is a trap bar with a close below support. It can also boast of powerful backup in the shape of an Mm-variant (4-5 plus 6-7). A valid concern, though, is that the support situation *could* be seen as horizontal still. Since we agreed to pass up on all dubious winners, we have little choice but to skip this one as well. (Off the record, place your stop above the 6-7 cluster.)

EURGBP 2014–2017

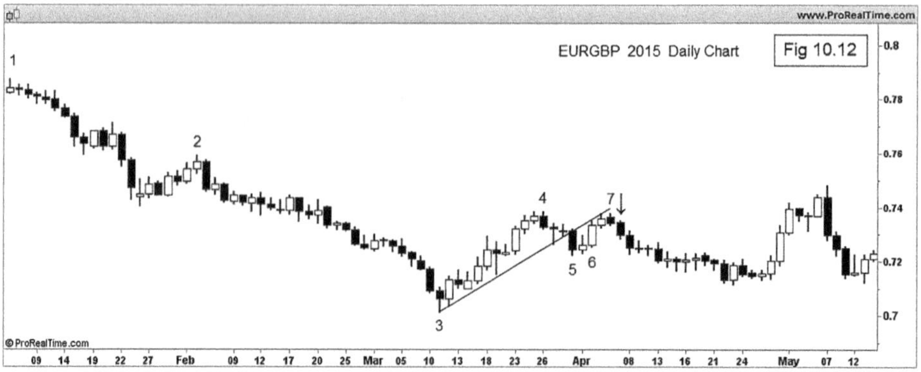

Figure 10.12. If a trend is any good, the inevitable pullbacks rarely make it past the halfway area of the *latest* rallies, as in 3-4 vs 2-3. So that's where we typically look for a setup first. Should prices push on, then we can always see how that would sit with the bigger trend (say 1-3).

A benefit of diagonal pullbacks, as opposed to the choppy varieties, is that they usually allow for a straightforward barrier. Then it is largely a matter of waiting for that line to fall under pressure. Not all perforations immediately warrant an entry, however, as with bar 5, so there we switch to Plan B and hope for a test of some sort—and of course for that test to resolve to our liking. Is that the case with bar 7?

While not the most pressing resolution, I see no reason not to trust this signal bar, especially if we take into account the powerful bear trend and the looming M-pattern in the 3-7 sequence (the right leg of which hopefully forms in our short). That is serious backup. Plus we can opt for a stop above the pullback high (4). Such insurance may seem almost negligible in pips, but don't underestimate its *technical* merit.

Note: As for the bullish morning star (5-6), recall that these patterns are far more potent in lows of a pullback because there they have something to *reverse.* This one shows up well away from the lows, and pushes up resistance to boot. If anything, we should look upon it as a favorable development. For in the face of a faltering morning star, bulls basically have two options: hope for a miracle or bail out. Since the trend is down, odds are quite a few will choose the latter. And any bull that sells out is an extra bear in the orderbook.

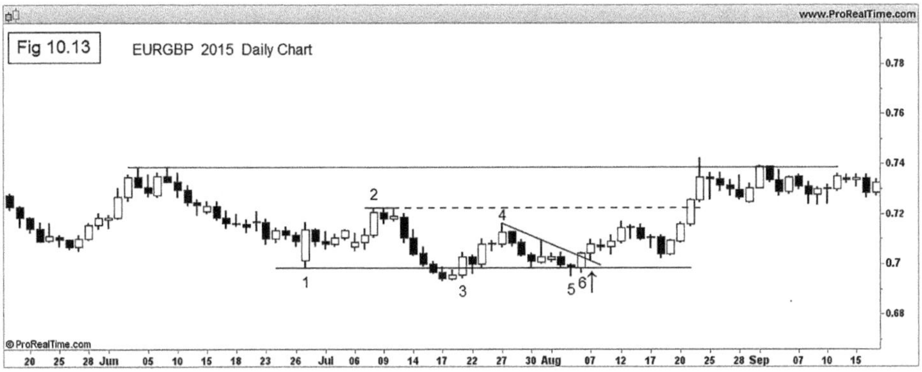

Figure 10.13. A few months later the EURGBP shows all the makings of a reversal on the bull side (1-3-6). If on the fence about whether to act on bar 6 right away, recall that the risk of a test is quite low for three-steppers. And if you can find a good spot for a stop (below bar 5), all the more reason not to linger.

Once we have decided on our stop (one point from entry), we know our preferred target (two points from entry). Then we can see if there is room for it. As not *all* obstacles in a range call for a tighter target, below you find a few pointers to help decide on the matter.

Tip: For starters, shun all clusters within a two-point distance from entry (base your exit on their barriers). Swing points, on the other hand, can be viewed as either hard or relatively harmless. The harmless type usually sits quite close to the setup, likely to get overrun by the pressure from the buildup. The tricky type tends to sit further out, often near the midrange area. As that is already an obstructive zone in and of itself, any swing point there should not be taken lightly.

Translating the above to the trade above bar 6, we may ignore that swing point at 4, but not the one at 2. Given the fairly tight range, perhaps you *could* bank on the magnet effect of the top barrier to grant you a full two-pointer, but then you might as well shoot for the magnet itself. My advice would be to simply play it safely and be content with a decent profit of about 1.5 times the risk on the trade.

Figure 10.14. In early May 2016, the EURGBP has us on the alert for a pullback reversal in the halfway area of a bear swing (2-3 vs 1-2). The customary setups for this purpose are of the two-step variety, like an M-top or any close variant. Less common, but no less promising, are the setups of the clustering type, as with 3-4. This is basically a stretched-out version of an M-top. Do note that as a consequence of the sideways action, the support situation has switched from angular to horizontal. And so we must wait for a signal bar to either attack, perforate, or close below this cluster line.

Bar 4 is the first to break that barrier, but that doesn't automatically make for a signal bar. Note the rather "bullish" bottom tail. Even though the perforation allows for a confirmation break, we cannot yet trust this resolution. And thus we hope for a better offer.

Luck is on our side as two bars later the barrier is perforated again; this time the culprit is a trap bar with a close below support (5). Surely we can have no issues with that. And telling by how quickly the magnet effect of the bottom barrier kicks in, we are not the only ones looking to short this re-break failure.

Note: Coming back to our discussion on potential obstacles (see previous chart), that swing point at 2 is not an issue as our two-point target would already be hit. But even if it sat closer by, the magnet effect of the bottom barrier will likely push prices through (given how close the barrier sits). Not that it is recommended to bet on that for a few extra pips, but it is to some degree defensible.

Figure 10.15. Remember our discussion on the concept of two opposing clusters in Figure 10.9. Here we see another variant (1-2 vs 3-4). As neither cluster allows for a straightforward barrier, this time we can only go by the opposing pressures. It is not hard to do, though, as both clusters appear well matched, and bar 4 clearly favors a short.

Just in case, let's draw some lines to see if we are not missing anything. Starting with the 3-4 cluster, regardless of where we place a line, an entry below bar 4 would *always* sit beneath it (as it is the lowest bar). So no problem there. As for the opposing cluster line, if we run that from the high of bar 1, then once again we're good to go as it couldn't obstruct our intended entry. In sum, the only barrier that could possibly sit in the way of a short would run from the middle part of the 1-2 cluster. Is that worrisome enough to stand aside?

I would argue that this is one such setup in which the cluster line situation can be ignored for the benefit of the greater good. The excellent conditions play a big role in this call and so too the quality of the resolution in bar 4. For let's face it, bulls would have to be quite suicidal to even *oppose* such an ominous trap bar.

Note: Freak bar 5 shows the response to the infamous Brexit vote on June 23, 2016. Since our setup is offered well before the vote, this is not a hindrance for acceptance (if push comes to shove we can always scratch a good profit beforehand). It is nice to know also that the outcome of the poll will be known on a Friday (the 24th), so little chance of our stop getting hit in a gap over the weekend (if still in the trade).

Figure 10.16. Once we have a good view on a range, a little experimenting with the line tool will usually reveal some matching swing points from which to run the barriers (1-4 and 2-8). These levels may still change as times goes by, but don't be misguided by false perforations (3 and 5). As these *validate* rather than invalidate a current barrier, it is not for nothing that they often lead to reversals.

All true, yet practice shows that it typically takes two failures for the attackers to become demoralized (if at all, of course). For that reason it wouldn't be wise to trade above bar 5. Even though the conditions for a breakout are not particularly favorable (note that cluster on the far left), that doesn't necessarily mean they are ripe for a reversal.

Let's stay attentive, though, because not much is needed to change a setup for the better. And indeed, when just two scans later bar 7 shows up, we not only have a two-stepper as backup (5-7) but also a break and test out of the way (6-7). That's a pretty powerful setup.

Note: Given that clustering obstacle in the midrange area, our target on this trade is a no-brainer. The stop and entry, on the other hand, are more a matter of taste. The most aggressive option is to wrap both orders around signal bar 7. You could also place your stop below bar 5 (nearest swing point) or your entry above bar 6 (high of the test); or even opt for *both* insurances if still content with the risk-to-reward. It's all good.

As for a short below bar 9, looks nice in hindsight, but that would be in disrespect of the 7-8 bull run. And since the subsequent test doesn't offer a tradable resolution either, we leave it alone.

EURJPY 2014–2017

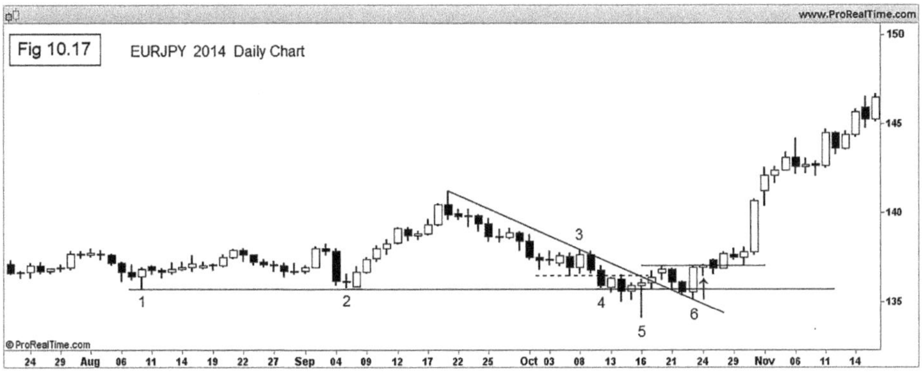

Figure 10.17. In the fall of 2014, bar 5 has us on the alert for a range reversal. A first glance, an entry above this bar would clearly be invalid (below angular resistance). At *that* point, though, chances are we would have opted for a sharper barrier (excluding the perforation in bar 3), in which case bar 5 would have stuck through. Why then skip?

For starters, we are not big fans of tall signal bars. Should that leave room for debate, an indisputable dealbreaker is that little cluster to the left of bar 4. The issue is not that the pressure in the 4-5 buildup isn't potent enough to take on that block (fairly equal), but the fact that an entry above bar 5 would still sit *beneath* the dotted cluster line (whichever way we run that barrier).

It is no big surprise, then, to see the break above bar 5 tested first. Examine also how this test neatly respects the angular barrier, a textbook case of former resistance now acting as support. So if not done so already, this is a good time to replace the sharper line mentioned earlier with the one as depicted.

Admittedly, the tall span of bar 6 is again not ideal, but at least now we have a test as backup, the high of which would be cleared on entry as well (solving the cluster line situation). It is nice to see also that there is still room for a two-pointer towards the high of the chart (might even prove a magnet). Consider also the two-step element (5-6), the trap bar resolution (6), and the fact that this regards a three-step reversal from a ranging perspective (1-2-6).

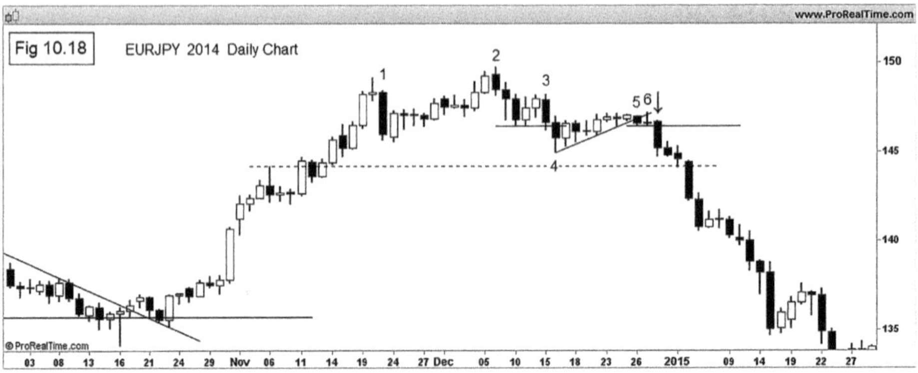

Figure 10.18. The first half of this chart shows the full extent of the range reversal from our previous chart. Pretty impressive. The problem with such one-sided rallies, however, is that they are hard to keep up. Moreover, it would not be uncommon for such trends to turn with little preparation. In this case, however, we do get ample warning thanks to one of the most respected three-step variants in all of price action: the popular head-and-shoulders (1-2-3).

Even so, it wouldn't be wise to short below bar 3 just yet as there is support not far below (extended from a bump in the trend). And indeed, bulls don't waste time testing that break. Whether that will do them any favors remains to be seen, though, because what we now have on the chart is yet another classic pattern: the equally popular bear flag (4-5). Couple that to the head-and-shoulders already on display, and it's not hard to guess which side the axe will fall.

In fact, we would have happily shorted below bar 5 if only bar 6 had stuck below that tiny signal bar. All for the better it turns out because thanks to bar 6 we now have a test of the flagline out of the way, plus a more enticing signal bar to short from (bearish doji).

Tip: Truth be told, as the spread in the low of bar 6 may have been just wide enough to trigger our entry below bar 5, it is only fair to report *that* trade as a loss (assuming a shake above the high of the flag). If such mishap is ever your fate, always see if you can reposition—because it is quite common for a shakeout bar to double as a new signal bar, as happens in bar 6. That's a chance to quickly recoup your loss and even bag a point to the good.

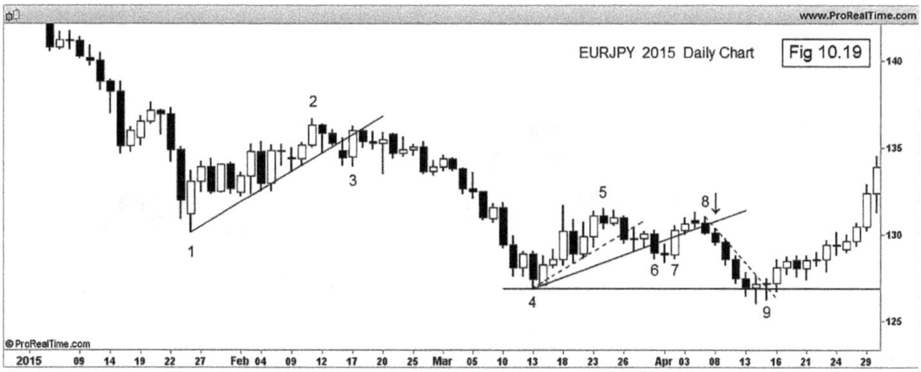

Figure 10.19. One of the first things to check when contemplating a pullback reversal is the *nature* of the correction. In general, the choppier the pullback (1-2), the harder it is for a reversal to succeed (note the riposte in bar 3 and the scruffy test afterwards). While not necessarily off-limits, choppy pullbacks rarely make for interesting setups.

The 4-5 reversal is also quite choppy, but this time the action cleans up shortly after. Note in particular the new pullback line and the way it is broken and tested (6-7). And we couldn't have wished for a more suitable resolution either, a textbook re-break failure (8). Of course, the stop on this short is best placed above the previous bar, the high point of the re-break. That should be a no-brainer.

Note: If worried about that morning star (6-7), recall that these patterns rarely live up to their promise when positioned *well away* from the lows (see Figure 10.12). Consider also that our trade would only get triggered below bar 8, which by itself would already indicate a failing morning star. And let us not forget our powerful ally on this short: the trend low. If you were a bull, would *you* dare buy in front of such a logical magnet or would you rather wait for that low to be hit and take it from there.

As for a reversal above bar 9, there is perhaps something to be said for it, but strictly seen it is only a two-stepper (4-9). While that may at times do for a runaway rally, here we are dealing with a well-established trend; hence a three-stepper would be more appropriate.

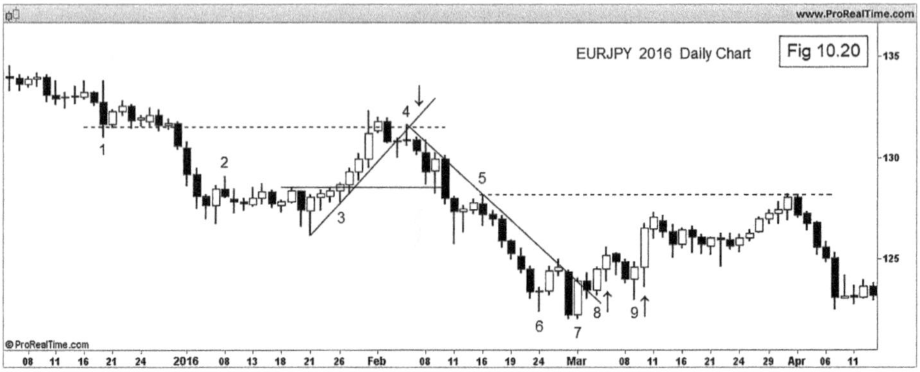

Figure 10.20. This is a great chart to discuss a few subtleties on how to exit into an obstacle. For starters, imagine to be long above bar 3 (not a setup) and your plan is to target the nearest resistance. Where exactly would you get out? While you could do so below bar 1, a more technical idea is to shoot for the nearest magnet (dotted cluster line). Makes sense if you think about it.

The same goes for our short below bar 4. There we ignore the high of bar 2 and shoot for the lower cluster line. It is not even that relevant where exactly we perceive the barrier to sit. For the goal is not to squeeze every last pip out of a trade but to avoid exiting prematurely.

A single bar can also prove a magnet. The high of bar 5, for example, a trap bar in the halfway area of the 4-6 trend, is once such swing point likely to function as a target for a trend reversal.

Even though the harmony element of the 6-7-8 three-stepper leaves room for debate (in view of the strong downtrend), let's say we take our chances. If we do so with a stop below bar 8, there is no need to tighten our exit just yet as there is room enough for a two-pointer.

This trade quickly fails, but note that we can reposition above bar 9 (as the shakeout bar is also a new signal bar). But now there is no longer room for a two-pointer below the high of bar 5. So on this trade we plan to exit just below that magnet—and for good reason!

Note: I hope this last example shows that greed plays no role when aiming for a magnet. It is purely a technical consideration, that we can use to either *extend* our profits or to *safeguard* them, whichever of the two is required in the situation at hand.

Figure 10.21. When a range hangs from a trend, as is quite common, it makes sense to first look for a setup in line with that trend. In the chart above, for example, we would love to trade a range reversal in the bottom barrier as that is also a halfway barrier.

Not so favorable is that this halfway barrier stems from a freak bar (1) and also "lacks" an extra bounce between bar 1 and 3 (to confirm its relevance). But is that reason to skip the setup at bar 4?

It's debatable. This resolution is certainly not without merit if only for the backup of the trend. The dip below the halfway barrier allows for a fine stop as well. The close of bar 4, above resistance, is a potent feature too (stronger than a mere perforation). That little cluster at 2 is not a real concern either as it already proved obstructive to the bounce in bar 3. Yet there is no denying the somewhat uncomfortable support situation. I guess it is a personal call.

As it turns out, bar 4 is not taken out anyway as the next bar is an inside bar (5). That clears things up for us because with a test out of the way (one-bar sequence), the support situation is now more established. However, I don't think we should go so far as to trade this with a stop below bar 5, even though its bottom tail technically counts as a swing point. So if not done so already, I would advise to wrap both the stop and entry around bar 4 as that is still the dominant bar in the setup. The target on this range reversal is the midrange barrier.

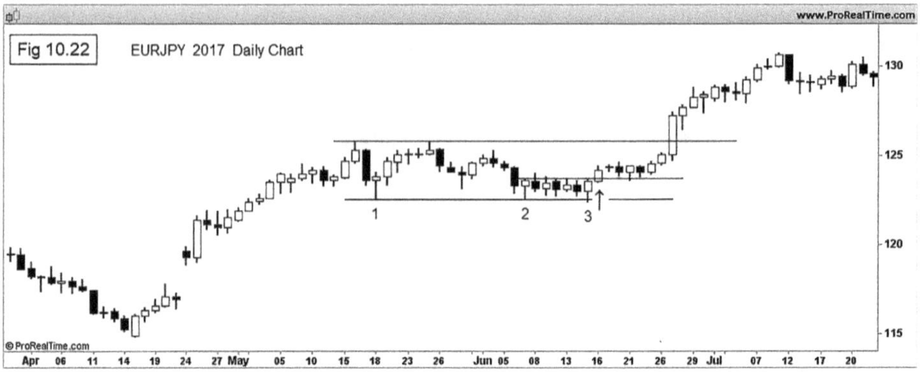

Figure 10.22. If there is such a thing as an infallible setup (please tell), our next wager on the EURJPY in 2017 definitely comes close to earning that magical label.

First off, with the chart in trending mode, it isn't hard to come up with a trade idea: a pullback reversal. Nor is it hard to guess in which barrier to look for a setup. The shallowness of the pullback, normally a reason for caution, is actually an asset here, due to its *range-type* nature (testament of trendside dominance); and note in particular the quality of support: a three-stepper with even a cluster thrown in (1-2-3), nicely resolved in trap bar fashion (3).

If you will, a small bummer is that we cannot shoot for a two-pointer due to the proximity of the top barrier; yet even that can be seen as an asset; after all, the closer a magnet, the stronger its pull.

Note: Should the position of the cluster line leave room for debate, you could place your entry order a few pips wider (on top of the spread), as is customary, but personally I see little need for such insurance here. So that is more a matter of style.

Perhaps you might wonder: if the chart is so bullish, could we not bet on a break through the highs or even let the trade run with a trailing stop? In all fairness, I *heartily* encourage you to try out such ideas for yourself. In a backtest, though, it is best stick to standard policy as that will yield the most reliable results. (That said, let's not split hairs should our reward on this beauty fall a little shy of 1.5 times our risk. That would truly be a waste.)

EURNZD 2014–2017

Figure 10.23. Here's another example of a trending chart that corrects in *time* rather than in *price*. In our previous chart, the correction was still deep enough to look for a reversal in the lows. Here above nearly every dip is picked up at higher levels, leaving us no choice but to scan for a break into new highs.

As we learned in Chapter 3 on range breakouts, if there is too little tension on a barrier prior to perforation, we skip and wait for a test (1). Tests are a common occurrence anyway, even after proper buildup, so all the more reason not to do anything rash.

In the event of a test, however, similar caution regards the resolution. Not just *any* bounce will do. Bar 2, for example, is a tricky offer at best. Just think of where our stop would sit.

Tip: All else equal, the ideal test slips back in the range first, by a noticeable degree, and then resolves back out. This not only allows for a safer stop (*away* from the barrier), it often allows for a safer entry too (*closer* to the barrier). The resolution in bar 3 perfectly illustrates this advantage: note how we can now enter much closer to the barrier and put our stop a little deeper inside the range (advisably below the previous bar, the nearest swing point).

For your information, freak bar 4 marks a brief crash on the Dow Jones Index, the panic of which quickly spread to countless markets worldwide, including many Forex pairs. It worked out favorably for *our* trade, yet if there is one thing to learn from such incidents, rare as they may be, is to always have a stop in place.

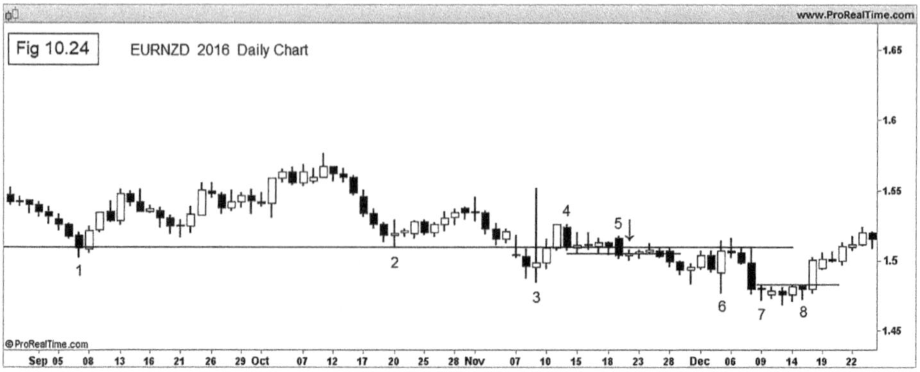

Figure 10.24. Since bar 4 appears to resolve a test of a range breakout, why not bet on a short right there? Partly because the presence of that freak bar still warrants caution (3), but consider also the two following bull bars (both taller than the average bar in the chart). Remember, aggression in a test is a warning not to look for a *swift* resolution.

After a few bars of pushing and pulling, however, bears have shown to stand their ground well. And due to this prepwork we now have a two-stepper in the buildup (4-5), plus a trap bar resolution (5). The perforation of the buildup line is of course a nice feature too.

By the way, the dip in bar 1 is excluded for barrier purposes because bar 2 lines up better with a trend low in July (not shown).

All looks good for this short until all of a sudden a bullish powerbar throws a spanner in the works (6). Not a pleasant sight, but let's not do anything silly, like quickly bailing out for only a negligible loss. For one, the bottom barrier could still save the trade (former support, now resistance). But why fear a loss to begin with when we have stop in place just for that occasion.

Tip: If you ever consider a scratch, at least wait for your trade idea to be *technically* invalidated. Exiting the short above the 7-8 cluster, for example, is to some degree defensible and would even pocket some profits. Such situations, however, will not often occur when trading for two-pointers as we do in our method; because by the time we no longer like our position, most likely the adverse development will have already confiscated any earlier gains and even put us in the red.

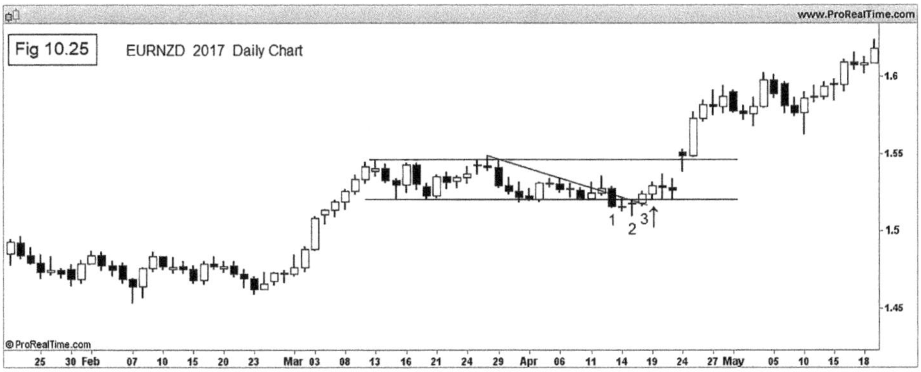

Figure 10.25. The dominant theme in this chart strongly resembles that of Figure 10.22. This time, however, bears are the first to break out (1). Yet as we have seen many times over, this is actually a favorable feature from a reversal perspective because if that break fails (as can almost be expected given the trend), these bears may soon have no choice but to buy back their shorts in a re-break.

That said, an immediate entry above bar 2 will not do for us as this bar does not yet hit the bottom barrier (in the absence of a perforation, you may have to widen your chart a bit for a closer look).

True, we could ignore this element and place our entry a few pips above the bottom barrier; we might even get away with it. But why learn such bad habits. Which then brings us to bar 3. Can we still trade above this bar, or would it be better to now hope for a test?

I think this can be accepted still, but in principle only with a standard stop because a safer stop below bar 2 would hardly leave room for a one-pointer. So unless your plan allows for such deviations, either go for that standard stop or skip.

Tip: If ever on the fence on whether to trade or skip, know that there is always a simple solution: stand aside. Sure, it's all very praiseworthy to "step out of your comfort zone" but save that for the local bootcamp. After all, the great prerogative of trading, unlike many games and sports, is that you are never forced to make a move. Why then not simply wait for an offer where the odds are *fully* to your liking.

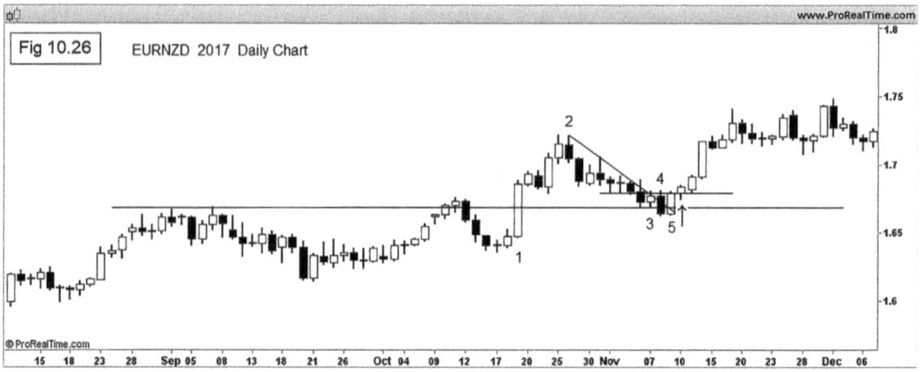

Figure 10.26. When you have your hopes set on a test of a breakout, yet the market marches on without looking back, it can seem like the opportunity is lost (and perhaps it is), but don't give up on the trade idea just yet—on the contrary. The further a break trades away from a barrier, the bigger the chance an *eventual* test will resolve in its favor. That's worth a little patience.

In the above chart, it's nice to see also that a test of the range barrier would coincide with a pullback to the halfway area of the breakout rally (1-2). Any extra support is welcome.

While the bounce in bar 3 is too weak for a setup, it is still a useful feature as it paves the way for a later two-stepper. The dip below support in bar 4 adds to the prospects of a reversal as it allows for a re-break failure scenario and already offers a nice swing point for a stop. When then bar 5 shows up, that cluster in the 2-3 pullback is no longer a real concern either because *our* cluster (below the shared cluster line) is now of similar strength. And to top it off, the perforation in the high of this signal bar sets up an ideal entry in a confirmation break.

The stop on this trade is best set below bar 4 (nearest swing point). As bar 5 is an inside bar, you could also opt for a more technical entry above bar 4, but if you were to choose only *one* insurance, the safer stop is generally the more beneficial.

EURUSD 2014–2017

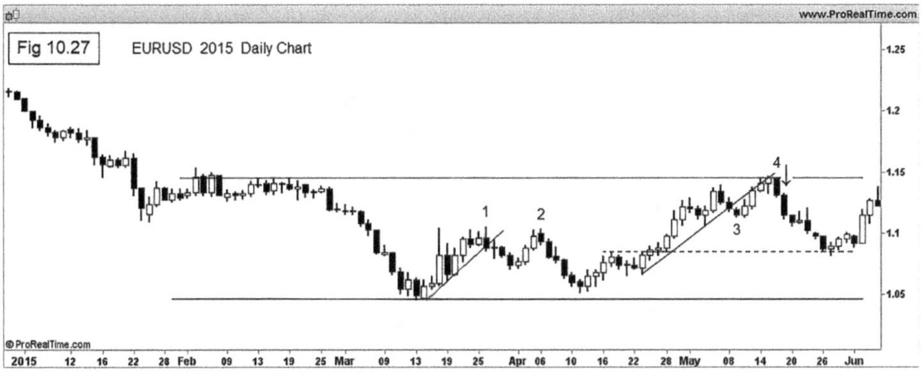

Figure 10.27. There is no question about it: the EURUSD is the king of all Forex pairs and few markets, if any, can rival its popularity as a vehicle for all kinds of daytrading strategies. On the dailies, however, it is just a pair like any other in our list of 28, and not particularly generous at that. At least not in the tested period (2014–2017).

Given the prominent bear trend on the left of this chart, a trade idea is easily found: a pullback reversal in the halfway area of the *latest* rally. A short below bar 1, however, technically a trap bar, is not a safe bet for us yet due to choppiness of that pullback.

As for bar 2, while this *could* be interpreted as a two-stepper (1-2), this setup too has its drawbacks. Take a moment to compare this resolution to the one in Figure 10.12. There the signal bar was also relatively weak, but at least the test pushed nicely up the broken pullback line. There is an M-pattern in play, potentially completed below bar 2, but is that enough to take our chances on a short? It's debatable.

No such concerns regard our short below bar 4, now situated in the halfway area of the bigger bear trend. Not only is this test more textbook (3-4), it's hard to wish for a more suitable resolution.

The stop on this trade is still best placed above the previous bar, so that bulls have to venture out *above* the halfway barrier first to shake us out. We could probably go for a standard stop too, but if the premium for a safer stop is only a marginally wider two-pointer, it is usually wise to go for that (unless you really see no reason).

Figure 10.28. Whether dealing with a long-lasting range barrier or a brief cluster line, the setup requirements for a break are technically the same. Meaning we need to see a barrier fight first, and also some pre-breakout tension right before the resolution. That is why the perforation in bar 1 is a skip from where we stand.

Since the trend is clearly up, a first failure to break out is not likely to keep the bulls away. Should they indeed come back for another try, we might even tag along. But remember, we will not do any of the dirty work ourselves! Our plan is as simple as it is effective: we always wait for the barrier fights to resolve first—as here in bar 2.

As this regards a break into new territory, we can put our stop below the low of the buildup (1-2) and still shoot for a reasonable two-pointer. So that's a good call. Whether to opt for a safer entry too (above the false high two days prior) is more a matter of style.

Interestingly, the theme of the second setup strongly resembles that of the first (3-4 vs 1-2). The barrier is now slanted, but the break and test play out very similarly. A bonus feature in this two-stepper is that the bars line up more neatly (no issues about where to get in).

Note: Although our entry above bar 4 is not hit next session, we can leave all orders pending because the position of that inside bar still favors a breakout. Not advised, though, is to reposition with a tighter stop below the inside bar, for the purpose of a tighter two-pointer. If a shake is our fate, we humbly accept, but let us not be so cooperative as to pose ourselves as low-hanging fruit.

chapter **11**

The GBP pairs

GBPAUD, GBPCAD, GBPCHF, GBPJPY, GBPNZD, and GBPUSD

GBPAUD 2014–2017

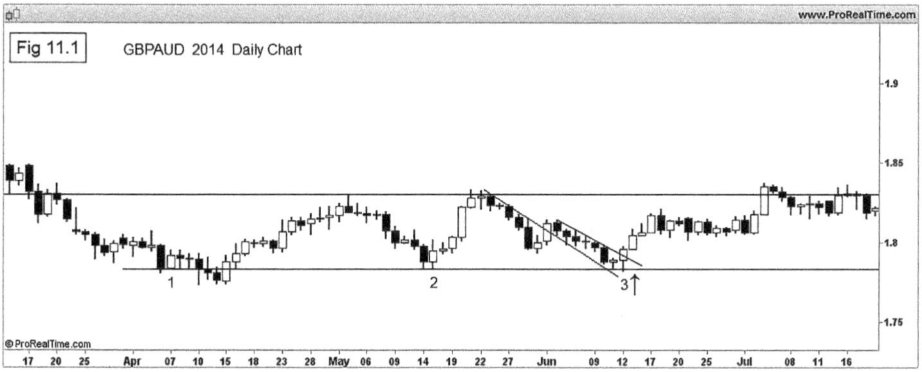

Figure 11.1. A great feature of ranges is that if we run their barriers at least a few months out, we can rest assured that at some point one of them will come into play again, be it for a break or a reversal. That won't necessarily lead to a setup, but if the market proves kind, as here above, we are not likely to miss the offer (1-2-3).

Tip: Don't be discouraged if on occasion it seems like an eternity for a setup to show. Macro-economic uncertainties and geopolitical turmoil can really mess up your charts, but sooner or later all that will subside. As a swing trader, try not to get too wrapped up in the moment. Look at things from a *yearly* perspective and you'd be hard-pressed not to make it worth your while.

Figure 11.2. Should you ever spot a "silly" trend on a chart (meaning of the runaway type, with no pullbacks to speak of), before you do anything silly yourself, keep in mind that old saying that is still as true today as it ever was: a market can stay irrational much longer than a pigheaded contrarian can stay solvent.

As we learned in Chapter 5, standard policy for trend reversals is to wait for a three-stepper of some sort (1-2-3). But not all three-steppers are setup worthy. Ideally the pattern forms sideways (over weeks rather than days), and the signal bar should not sit too close to the high or low. There are indeed exceptions (as in Figures 5.5 and 6.5), but only in conjunction with a topnotch resolution. Is that the case with bar 3? Personally, I am not too convinced, and by the looks of it, neither are our fellow bears.

Can one extra session make a difference? Absolutely! Note how that false high in the top tail of bar 4 now unmistakably betrays the struggle of the bulls. While not a trap bar in the literal sense (the low of bar 3 is still not broken), we might as well regard it as such.

As for our target, there looks to be room for a two-pointer (twice the span of bar 4), but of course we doublecheck. Silly trend or not, we don't want to accidently plan our exit *below* that halfway barrier.

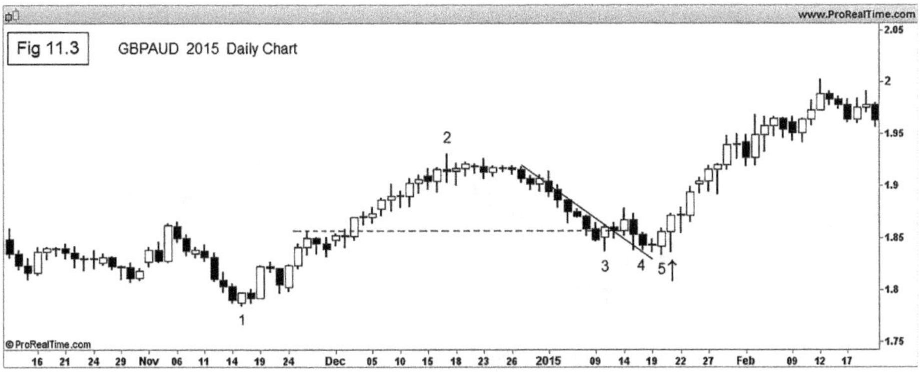

Figure 11.3. Few rallies push on without any pausing along the way. If there are no meaningful corrections in *price*, there are usually some in *time*, as in that cluster halfway the 1-2 bull run (from which the dotted line is drawn). The interesting part is that such sideways action is not merely useful as buildup for a breakout; that cluster could easily come into play again as a magnet for a pullback. And equally common is for it to then serve as a springboard for a reversal. All the more reason to keep a close watch on this chart.

Since bar 3 already offers an entry back above the dotted line, why not bet on a reversal right there? We all know the answer, but it bears repeating: one-steppers tend to fare poorly against aggressive or otherwise impressive pullbacks.

Note the difference with the setup at bar 5. There we not only have a two-stepper as backup (3-5), this signal bar also resolves a test in trap bar fashion. Add to that the morning star in the lows of the pullback (4-5) and it is safe to conclude that at *this* point the odds for a reversal are well worth accepting.

Tip: As a brief reminder, suppose we got tricked into a trade above bar 3, with a quick shake to show for it. What's the first thing we do? That's right, we stay alert for another try. For if we already liked that one-stepper, we will like a two-stepper even more.

Figure 11.4. Three-step reversals are even more potent than the two-step varieties (1-2-3) but not necessarily more *tradable*. Bar 3, for example, dips too deep below support for a safe entry; hence we switch to Plan B: a test. If that isn't granted, or its resolution fails to set up, there is always Plan C: a pullback reversal. For that purpose, we can already spot a nice barrier in the halfway area (dotted).

Tip: Don't be put off if prices do not immediately bounce in support (4-5). On the contrary, regard it as a boon as such action typically allows for a safer stop. Think also of the bears in that break. Should they come to regret their shorts, as can almost be expected given the halfway area, they may soon be forced to *buy* back out, which can only help a reversal. The bottom tails below the barrier already hint at what's coming. In fact, the only thing missing for a setup is a proper resolution.

And there it is in bar 6. Challenging all barriers in one fell swoop, this bar definitely puts the question to the bears: fight back or buy out. Our bet is on the latter.

For protection, a standard stop below bar 6 would have my preference, but below bar 5 is also fine.

Note: That big selloff in bar 7 marks the outcome of the infamous Brexit vote on June 23, 2016. Since our target was not yet hit, we book this trade as a loss in the backtest. In a live environment, however, I am sure we would have all been aware of that poll, so this is one such rare occasion where it would have been totally justified to pocket the current profits on the trade (*before* the 24th) rather than take a chance on what could easily prove a freak session.

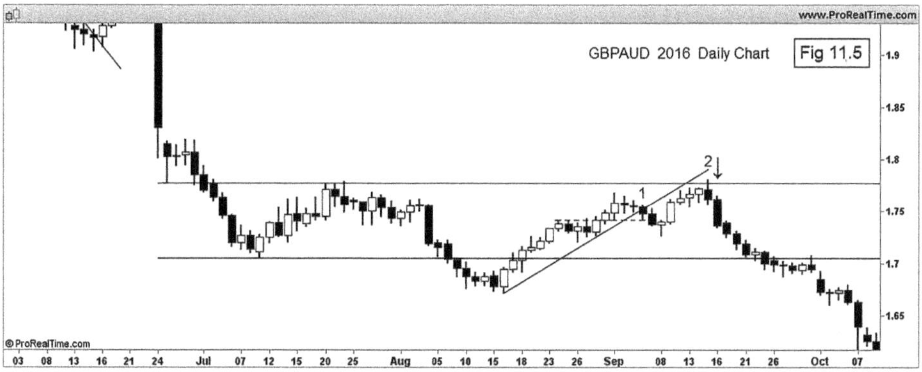

Figure 11.5. Here's the follow-up chart. To say the vote turned out bad for the GBP would be putting it mildly. Not a pullback worthy of mention until that bull run in August. In such bearish conditions, a plan is easily found: wait for the correction to fizzle out and then look for its reversal.

In the meantime we can scan for a pullback line, but keep in mind that we may have to tweak this barrier along the way depending on how the correction plays out. (There is usually ample time to figure out the angle before a setup comes to pass.)

A short below bar 1 is of course out of the question: while first perforations are not necessarily premature, they always call for caution; so surely we would have spotted that cluster to the left of bar 1. Notice also the terrible options for protection. As it is not hard to imagine the pullback to push on towards the halfway barrier (magnet), even a stop above the current pullback high would not be safe in a test.

Examine the difference with a short below bar 2. There we not only have a test out of the way, we couldn't have wished for a more suitable resolution either (trap bar). Note also the false perforation above the halfway magnet. It doesn't take a price action specialist to see that this is a good time for bears to take over (and for bulls to sell out). And that is why the *bottom* barrier is now the more likely magnet.

GBPCAD 2014–2017

Figure 11.6. Since relatively calm trends are more likely to push on than reverse, a looming break into new-territory should always have our full attention. An entry above bar 1 looks a little premature, though, as there is no pressure on the barrier in the previous session.

An entry above bar 2 has more going for it (confirmation break), but now there is a problem with protection because the only safe place for a stop is all the way below bar 1. Even though the target in a new-territory breakout is generally not our biggest concern, there is of course a limit. This particular setting is perhaps still playable, but as there is room for debate, let's simply skip and hope for a test.

The fact that it takes a while for a test to come in lends credit to the breakout but is also a warning not to fall for a *swift* resolution (3); because the path for a reversal is not as "open" as it would be after a more diagonal pullback.

Yet after *four* false dips below support and even a W-bottom in that buildup (3-4), everything points towards a reversal. If we linger now, we may not get another chance.

While a standard entry above bar 4 is principally valid, more logical is to place the order above the previous bar, the high point of the buildup (in which case bar 5 looks to be a standoff, awaiting a fill next session). Insurance below bar 3 is more a matter of taste as bar 4 already marks a notable swing point. If that stop has your preference, do check if there is still room for a two-pointer as now the territory is no longer "new." So if called for, plan your exit a few pips below the dotted barrier.

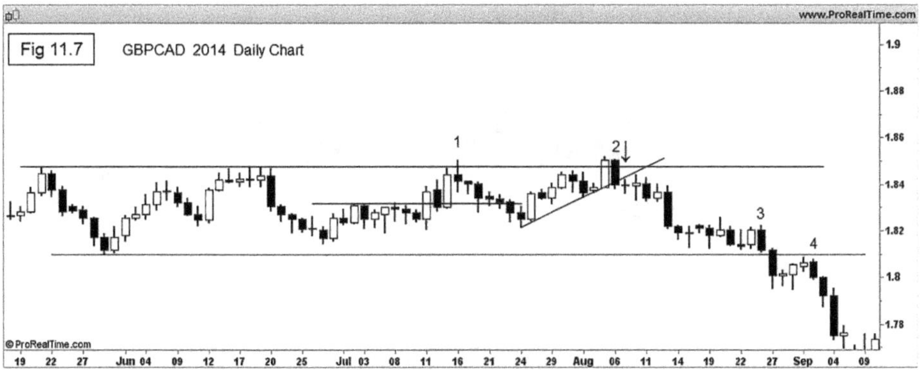

Figure 11.7. Does this range look familiar? Good job. It is Figure 2.1 from Chapter 2. Although the other charts in Part One were specifically selected from the years 2012–2013 (as a prequel to our backtest), we started out with this one from 2014 simply because it lends itself well for introducing some basic range reversal concepts.

Here's a quick recap. With horizontal support directly underfoot, a short below bar 1 is not even an option. A short below bar 2, on the other hand, is pretty much a no-brainer. Not only are there now *two* false breaks as backup, angular support is about to fail as well. A dip below bar 2 would confirm it. So that's where we place our entry. What we didn't yet discuss earlier on is where to place our stop.

Tip: There are two options for protection: above bar 2 or the previous bar. In cases like this, where the target is the same either way (bottom barrier), it makes sense to simply opt for the safest stop because its only downside is a lesser *reward.*

While in principle the relevance of the bottom barrier is not yet confirmed (no clear matches after the original swing point), it would be reckless to ignore such a likely obstacle for a few extra pips. So let's not even go there.

As for the later range break, there is something to be said for it, but technically it is a skip as bar 3 is the only bar in the buildup to actually challenge the bottom barrier with a hit. Similar reservations regard a short below bar 4. As there the test has yet to challenge the barrier, we cannot trust that resolution either.

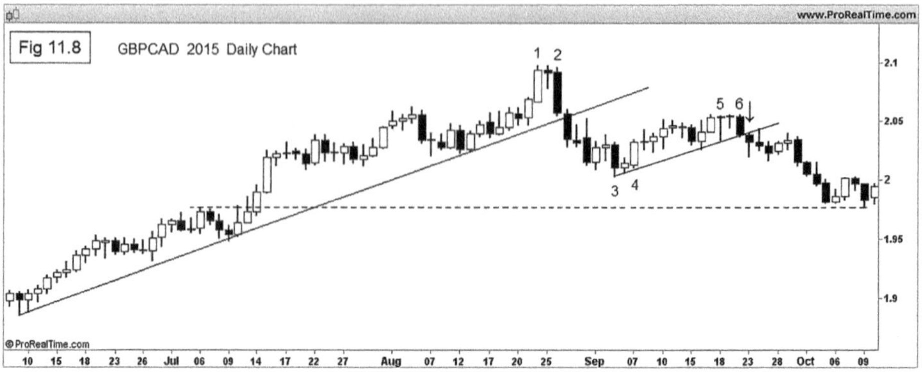

Figure 11.8. As you will have noticed, there is ample overlap between our price action studies and what is commonly referred to as *Technical Analysis*. And for good reason as we should not be too proud to stand on the shoulders of all those clever giants who figured out the popular patterns. Where mainstream TA falls short, however, with all due respect, is that not much is offered in terms of *timing* a trade. While it is one thing to be guided in the right direction, to actually use a pattern for *entry* purposes is quite another. And that's exactly where price action shines!

In the trend above, for instance, anyone can spot that evening star sticking out like a sore thumb (1-2). Yet it couldn't possibly be a setup. For one thing, the trendline is still intact. Consider also the sideways action of the weeks prior, potentially blocking the way down.

A bit surprising, therefore, is to see bulls make no real effort to reclaim their broken trendline. It is only after a morning star, well below support, that they finally step up (3-4). But what they have to show for themselves does not look particularly promising for a re-break. Quite the contrary, the 3-6 test harbors all the characteristics of a bear flag. But does that justify an immediate short below bar 6?

Admittedly, this lacks the preferable hit on the flagline just prior to bar 6, but in return we enjoy the backup from yet another evening star (5-6), which also allows for a sound stop (not easily hit in the event of a test). Remember, a minor shortcoming in a setup is not a dealbreaker if the conditions and the setup as a whole are still to our liking. Take into account as well the looming magnet effect of the halfway barrier below, waiting to kick in as soon as the flagline is broken.

Figure 11.9. In this follow-up chart, prices very typically find support in the halfway barrier of the bull trend (dotted line in Figure 11.8). Telling by the lackluster buying, however, bulls have not yet forgotten the illustrious evening star which caused their trend to reverse, or the bear flag shortly after (still visible on the left of this chart).

To their credit, bulls do push on and even manage to set up a range break in trap bar fashion (1). If we look a little deeper, however, the odds for that break to follow through at this point are poor at best. One concern is that the push in bar 1 comes about in what can still be seen as a test of the broken angular barrier. But more importantly, the path for a breakout is simply not free (due to the flag on the left).

So more logical is to look for a reversal. An immediate short below bar 2 looks premature, though, as we can imagine bulls not to give up so easily. Bar 2 also stands relatively weak against its trap bar neighbor. Plus there might be a buildup line in play as well.

Bulls indeed give it another try, but again their attempt is thwarted, and this time more convincingly (3). While *their* hope is now set on that buildup line to hold, *our* hope is for that support to crack. We are already happy to see the perforation in bar 3, which allows for an ideal entry in a confirmation break.

Note: While this looks like a nice win, on closer inspection it is best reported as a loss as it is fair to reason that we would have played this with a stop above bar 2—in which case we would have *just* missed our target in the low of bar 4.

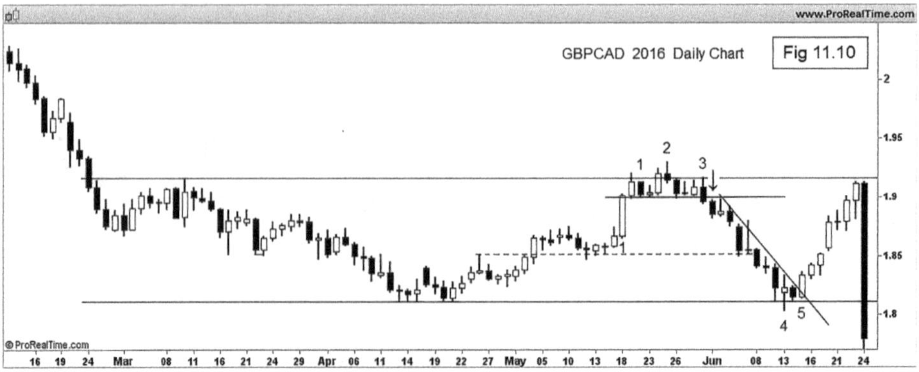

Figure 11.10. The great thing about price action is that it works on all time frames. A major advantage of the daily chart, however, is that it is almost impossible to lose track of the conditions. For example, when that head-and-shoulders popped up (1-2-3), traders on the 4-hr chart may have already lost sight of the bear trend. And those on the 1-hr chart might even think the trend is *bullish*.

Yet for us on the dailies, it is highly unlikely to misread the conditions. Nor we would we easily miss a three-stepper in a halfway barrier, or the fact that the so-called *neckline* is perforated by a trap bar (3). Quite the opposite, this is a setup of dreams. The only thing to do now is see if there is room for a worthy reward.

Tip: Don't be misled by the relative width of a range as that is no guarantee for a two-pointer. Often the contrary is true because the further away the opposite range barrier, the more likely the *midrange area* will have a foot in the door first. So if there is any action in this tricky area, grab your line tool and scan for a barrier—and if necessary plan your exit in front. (For instance, a good idea would be to exit a few pips above the dotted barrier.)

As for a range reversal above bar 5, that would be premature given the obvious aggression in the 3-4 selloff.

FYI, the freak bar on the far right is yet another response to the Brexit vote on June 23, 2016. Many major indices took a hit that fateful day (the 24th), yet none as badly as the pound itself.

GBPCHF 2014–2017

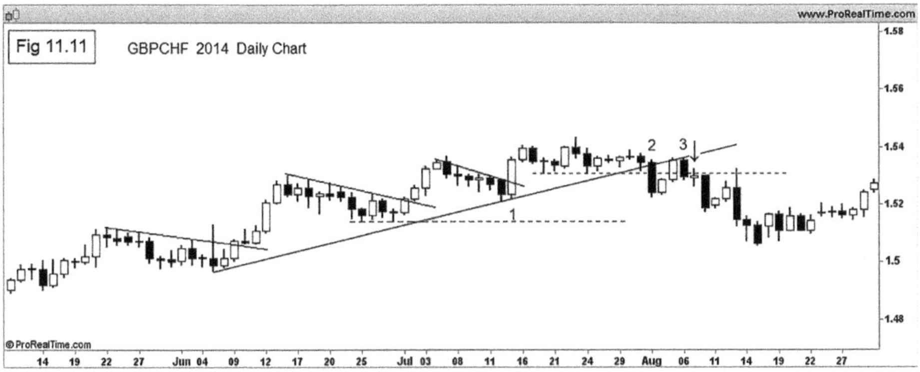

Figure 11.11. Flags, pennants, diamonds, head-and-shoulders, wedges, cup-and-handles, double tops, triple bottoms—these are but a handful of the many colorful formations that form the bread and butter of the typical technical analyst. Studying these patterns will benefit our perspective too, but remember, they only serve as *guidance*. In effect, all technical formations fall into one of two categories: reversal patterns or continuation patterns.

The three bull flags in the GBPCHF above are well-known continuation patterns (not really playable for us). The head-and-shoulders in the top of the trend is a reversal pattern. This one *is* playable, but not right away as that would call for a terrible entry (below bar 2). And thus we hope for a test.

As it turns out, bar 2 is not even taken out as the break is immediately tested—which not much later resolves as desired (3). Looks like a perfect setup, but one thing to keep in mind is that the flags in the trend could prove obstructive on the way down. So let's check if there is room for a trade to begin with.

The first support to consider is the low of the highest flag. This can be discarded as it sits quite close to the setup and is already tested by the break in bar 2. Next up is the break level of the middle flag: not a biggie either as the low of the higher flag already hit upon it (1). And so the first real obstacle in sight is the low of the middle flag (lower dotted line). All good for us as that leaves just enough room for an acceptable target (about 1.5 times our risk).

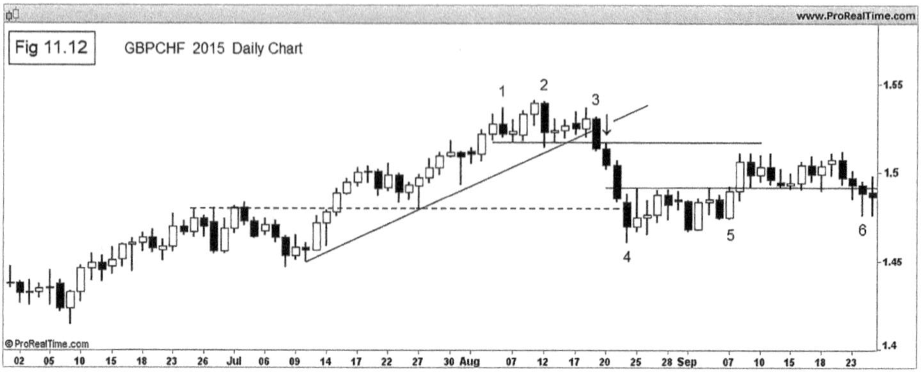

Figure 11.12. Here's another three-stepper of the head-and-shoulders type (1-2-3). Shape-wise it is almost a copy of the one in Figure 11.10. Setup-wise it is more similar to Figure 11.11, in that the trendline and neckline are perforated simultaneously.

Do note that we are practically forced to trade this with a standard stop given the proximity of the halfway barrier (dotted line). That's fine, though, because with a three-stepper as backup and both the neckline and trendline taken out, there is no real need for insurance.

After a trend reversal, the new trade idea is typically a pullback reversal in the halfway area. The 4-5 cluster builds up nicely for this purpose, but alas, even if we opt for a stop below bar 5, there is not enough room for our minimum reward.

Note: Assume for a moment we do enter above bar 5 and a number of days later we start to suspect a re-break. Should we just sit still and let it happen or could we perhaps lift our stop to just below that cluster line, to keep us in the race for a win while preventing a *full* loss? Frankly, if we resort to such tactics, we might as well scratch right away as even the slightest dip would surely shake us out. However, there is an alternative idea worthy of mention—and that is to wait for a *serious* adverse break and then hope to scratch in a bounce. For instance, if not already shaken out in the low of bar 6, we could exit in the close of that bar (when we run our daily scan). While not necessarily advised, this bail-out option is more sound because the trade idea is now *technically* no longer valid due to the adverse break. Apply at your discretion.

GBPJPY 2014–2017

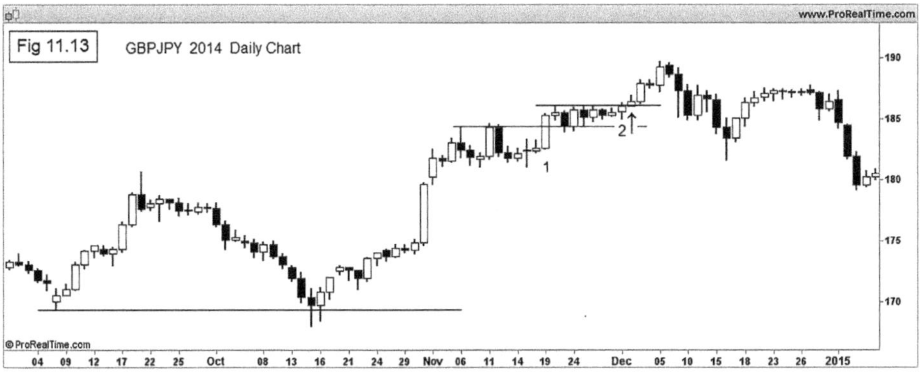

Figure 11.13. If you have been trading Forex for a while, you may have noticed that the GBP pairs can be quite volatile, often showing swings that far exceed the average swing on most other pairs. This is mainly because they are priced relatively high—because it takes more pips to make the same percentage move on a higher priced pair than a lower priced pair.

Note: It might appear that the typical volatility of the GBP pairs allows for a better risk-to-reward, say 1:3. Keep in mind, though, that the span of the average stop will usually be wider as well. While it is certainly not unthinkable to ever trade for a bigger target than the standard two-pointer (for example to make use of a potent magnet), for the most part we should be happy if we don't have to tighten!

Just like ranges are more likely to hold than crack, so too are trends more likely to trend on than reverse. With that in mind, there is perhaps something to be said for the setup at bar 2: a trap bar that breaks away from a cluster and at the same times resolves a test of a break in bar 1. But let us not ignore the elephant in the room: would we really have the guts to put real funds on the line at *this* stage in the trend? Now that is a question we all best answer for ourselves.

Figure 11.14. It can't be stressed enough: a setup is only as sound as the quality of protection. Hence the common need for insurance. But a safer stop is only useful if it can boast of *technical* merit. To illustrate, assume we wish to trade above bar 2 but we are not too keen on a standard stop; it wouldn't do to merely lower this stop with say 15 pips as it would just be floating in "midair."

A trade above bar 2 looks premature anyway, but let's discuss what to do if we took our chances there and not much later suffer a shake (4). Of course, we accept the loss gracefully—but not without a fight! Recall that whenever we get taken out by a *trap bar*, our trade idea usually still stands; moreover, thanks to the extra step, the odds for follow-through may even be higher than on the initial setup (1-2-4). We may even be so fortunate as to have a morning star thrown in (3-4), plus a more technical place for our stop (below bar 4).

Speaking of luck, it so happens that the market reverses just high enough to hit our two-point target, which grants us a chance to quickly double our winnings on the subsequent two-stepper (5-6). All good for us, but what to do if the first target was *missed*? Should we reverse our position below bar 6 anyway, or just stay in?

Note: From a technical viewpoint we should probably lean towards reversing, yet there is still a lot to be said for not interfering. At least two benefits come to mind: (a) by leaving *all* trades as originally set up, we can never be tempted to do anything silly, like scratching an eventual winner in the face of a little setback. And (b) even if faced with a loss we can still feel proud of sticking to our plan.

GBPNZD 2014–2017

Figure 11.15. If we set up our charts to show about 100 bars (four or five months), there is rarely need to scroll back to see if anything is brewing; or perhaps only to briefly check the relevance of a barrier plotted earlier on. By the way, rather than experiment with a new barrier, pick the old one and see if you can find a better place for it. Or simply use a crosshair cursor to check for matching swing points.

A first failure to break a range barrier is often taken in stride by the attacking parties. A second failure too may not yet kill their morale, but then they would do well not to let the defenders take over *too* much, as happens after bar 1. The problem is that a new attack on the top barrier will now most likely be viewed as a mere test (2-3), meaning most traders would then rather look for a *bearish* resolution. And so should we.

But let us pick our entry wisely. An immediate short below bar 3, for example, looks awfully premature. One concern is the relative proximity of powerbar 2, but consider also the lousy spot for a stop, right above the range barrier (easy prey if bulls are not done yet). And as for a short below bar 4, that doesn't look too appealing either, in the halfway area of that fairly aggressive test.

Tip: Whenever it looks like a trade idea has blown over, keep a half eye on the action still because you never know what the next few bars will bring. After bar 5, for example, all of a sudden we have a two-stepper and a re-break failure to back up a short (4-5). And as we are surely not the only ones to dig this resolution, the magnet effect of the bottom barrier is now also more likely to kick in.

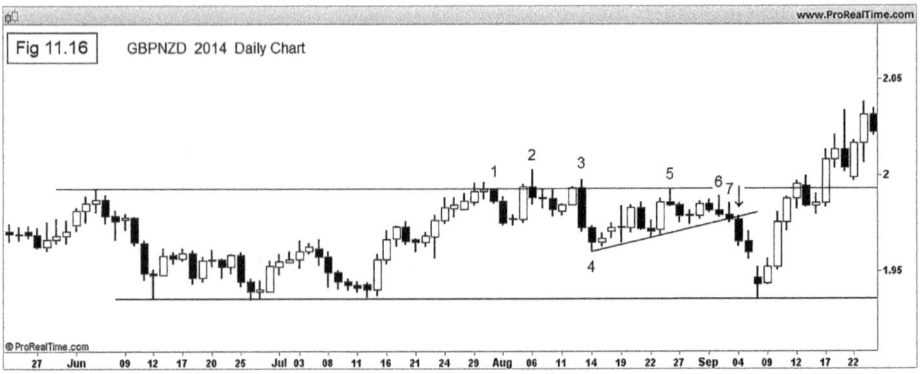

Figure 11.16. Not every pair on our watchlist will grant us a trade in any given year, but there are always a few that set up more than once. In 2014, the GBPNZD offers two range reversal opportunities, the second of which is shown here above (the first on the previous page).

Why go for the test and not the three-stepper earlier on (1-2-3)? The simple answer is that bar 3 stands too tall for signal bar purposes.

The initial test is not suitable either (4-5), but then the action slowly morphs into a bear flag (4-6).

We can already guess where things are going after bar 6, but let us not be so foolish as to front-run the failure of a flagline! For all we know the next bar could bounce hard on support and then we would be stuck with a terrible trade.

There is indeed a bounce in bar 7, but its close is back on the flag-line—and its low already sticks through. So this time we can opt for an ideal entry in a confirmation break.

Tip: For protection, a standard stop would have my preference here. Partly because of the conditions at hand but also because the benefit of insurance is questionable at best. After all, should bulls have it in them to defy the flag break and push prices back above bar 7 (no small feat), the top barrier is almost certainly next. So it can be argued that a stop above bar 6, or even above bar 5, would be just as vulnerable as a stop above bar 7. Admittedly, the price for extra safety (wider target) is not really a problem in this chart, so in that respect there is perhaps *some* merit in a wider stop, if only for mere luck. Yet it still begs the question: if insurance isn't likely to pay out, why pay the premium?

Figure 11.17. If we were to guess which trade idea is most popular among investors, stock traders in particular, the trusted pullback reversal in a bull trend quickly springs to mind. And for good reason. We would gladly trade such setups ourselves, even if only for a two-pointer. Yet where we as swing traders clearly have one up on those bullishly orientated is that we are equally willing to trade the bear side (1-2). But more importantly, we have no need for a trend. The smallest of pullbacks can set up reversals just the same, and are more abundant to boot! In principle, any old test could do—as in 3-4 and 7-8.

Extra potent are the setups that harbor a re-break failure, as is the case with both these tests as well. Strictly seen, though, the setup at 4 is a skip because the max reward is under 1.5 times our risk. Yet if ever you fancy a quick scalp in front of a magnet...

A short below bar 8 is definitely playable as it regards a break into new territory (no issues with the target). The stop is of course best placed above the high of the test.

Note: Why not already short below bar 6 (with a stop above the 5-6 buildup)? To some degree this resembles the situation in Figure 11.16 where we opted for a short below bar 7 despite the absence of pressure on the flagline in the previous bar. But there is a notable distinction. In that chart we simply had everything going for that flag break. In such cases, a small imperfection in the setup can often be forgiven. When it comes to cracking the barrier of a range, however, my advice would be to sooner wait for extra buildup than act on too little of it.

GBPUSD 2014–2017

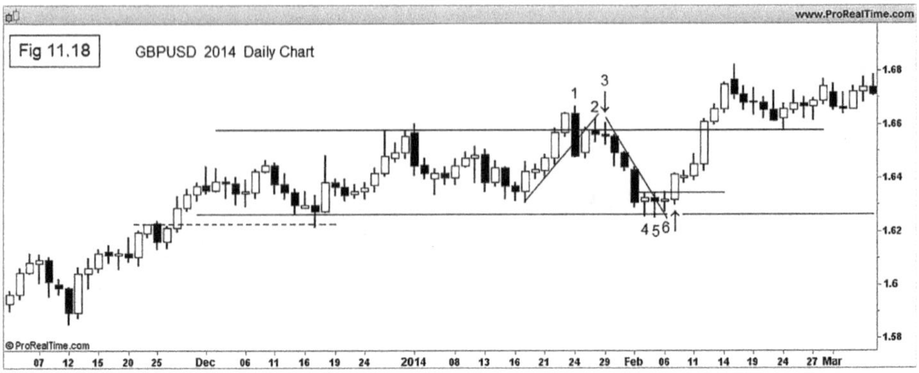

Figure 11.18. If a mere perforation into new territory would instantly trigger follow-through, few traders would be so reckless as to stand in the way. But as we can see in bar 1, there is no shortage of bears on the other side of that break. And the reason is not hard to guess: the break is set without buildup.

As is typical, bulls are not deterred so easily. Yet it remains to be seen if they truly have the guts to refute that ominous trap bar, not to mention the failure of angular support. If all they can muster is a test, that should definitely have our attention.

Well then, how about bar 2? While this second rejection is not nearly as prominent as the first, now we have a two-stepper on the chart (1-2) plus a valid resolution of a test. That's a short setup.

If for some reason you find this resolution too weak, or perhaps you missed your daily scan, it is not too late to short below bar 3 (advisably with a stop above bar 2).

The conditions for a reversal at the other side of the range are even better because there we have the ever-potent halfway barrier of a trend to back us up. (Initially we may have opted for the dotted line, but after the 4-6 cluster it makes sense to plot the barrier as depicted.)

Even though we can look upon the bounces in bar 4 and 5 as a two-stepper (two adjacent dojis), this reversal setup looks a bit too weak to already challenge the foregoing selloff. But when then a third doji shows up, we have a three-stepper at our disposal (4-5-6) plus a test out of the way (one bar-sequence). Time to bite the bullet.

Figure 11.19. When first introduced to price action, it can be tempting to think that this type of trading is all about *setups*. Yet focusing on setups alone with little regard for *conditions* is an instant recipe for failure—like that builder with all the right tools but no sense of construction.

Take bar 3, at first glance a trap bar resolution. Why skip? Because the foregoing runup is way too aggressive (1-2). Meaning the conditions speak against the trade idea.

After a few weeks of sideways chop, however, in which prices never made it back to the top barrier, it becomes more and more apparent that bears have taken over. Still, let us be mindful of the tricky support situation, which could even be seen as horizontal or angular. In that light, the resolution in bar 4 is still not very convincing.

No such concerns regard the resolution in bar 7. Examine how this setup effectively starts with that failed reversal attempt in bar 5, which of course will not sit well with the bulls. For a brief moment they may have had their hopes set on that re-break in bar 6, only to see that fail in bar 7. You never know, but it is a fair guess that bulls at *this* point would rather sell out than hope to withstand the looming magnet effect of the bottom barrier.

And there you have it. With the AUD, CAD, CHF, EUR, and GBP pairs out of the way, we have reached the final quarter of our backtest. Next up are the four NZD pairs. Then we close up shop with the three USD pairs.

chapter **12**

The NZD pairs

NZDCAD, NZDCHF, NZDJPY, and NZDUSD

NZDCAD 2014–2017

Figure 12.1. Since all breakout situations are inherently unique, it is hard to generalize on the amount of buildup needed for a setup. Yet it is easy to understand when buildup is *lacking*, and that is already half the work done. For example, it is not hard to decline the break in bar 1 as it comes about too swiftly after a runup; nor are we tempted by the perforation in bar 2 as it lacks the preferable pre-breakout tension.

Rest assured, though, the more examples you study, the easier it becomes to tell the wheat from the chaff. And so it is with signal bar 3, which singlehandedly resolves a test, refutes a re-break attempt, challenges a buildup line, and leaves behind a nice swing point for a stop. What's not to like.

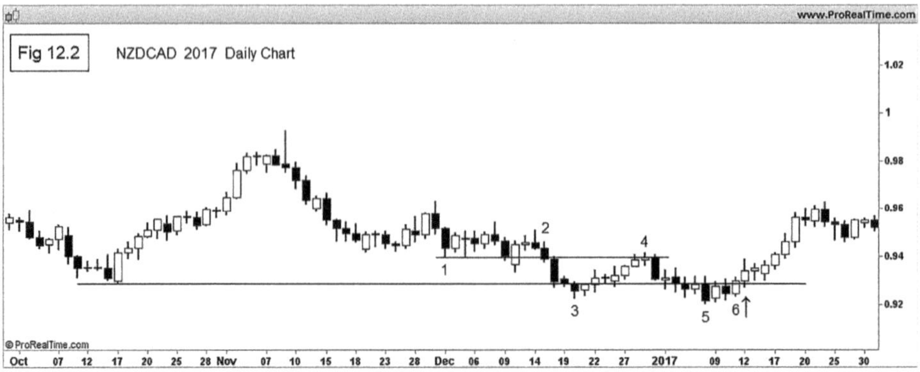

Figure 12.2. As we have already seen here and there, it is quite common for a cluster to sit in the way of a reversal. This need not rule out a trade, as long as we have a cluster of *similar strength* as buildup. As that is clearly not the case with 3-4 versus 1-2, there is no point in looking for a setup just yet.

Two weeks later, though, the barrier fight is still in full swing. Note how bears almost got the upper hand in bar 5, but then were forced to back off (5-6). Seeing bar 6 push back above the range barrier, and even close above it, do we have a setup now?

The buildup has clearly grown favorably (3-6), so no issues there. But what about that earlier cluster line; it that still a worthy obstacle at *this* point in the chart or can we simply go by the re-break of the bottom barrier?

If we think of that line as an obstacle, the only rightful call is to skip. However, there are a few arguments for not being *too* concerned. A first is that the line already blocked an earlier attack (4). This is not to say it couldn't prove obstructive again, but now we have more buildup to help us through. And since we can play this with the best stop in the entire chart (below bar 5), some opposition after entry would not be the end of the world. Take into account also that a break above bar 6 would technically confirm the failure of a range break. A final consideration is that this setup regards a three-step reversal of the ranging type (first step in October). Isn't it reasonable to conclude then that *most* traders would rather be long than short above bar 6?

NZDCHF

Figure 12.3. Imagine to be part of a military regiment sitting tight at the frontline. There is some shooting back and forth but nothing decisive. Finally there comes the call to advance, and lo and behold, you and your buddies make it through. But something doesn't feel right. Why are things so quiet? Where's the opponent? Where's the backup? And just when you realize the glaring trap, enemy fire springs up out of nowhere, forcing you all to flee for dear life, back to where you came from!

How is this little story relevant to our studies? Well, it pretty much reflects the predicament of the bears who ventured out behind enemy lines in bar 3. And note that they didn't just break *any* barrier, they boldly forced themselves through halfway support (of the 1-2 rally). That is a tricky proposition in and of itself, and even more so when it regards a *first* perforation.

The point is, if the break in bar 3 is a failure candidate, it naturally follows that the re-break in bar 4 stands good chance of following through. I must stress, though, this is an exceptional setup; after all, with all that chop to the left, standard policy would be to wait for more buildup (still a valid call).

Tip: If ever on the fence on whether to accept a *one-step* re-break, look specifically for two crucial features: (a) it must regard a setup in a halfway barrier, and (b) your stop should stand good chance to survive a test (which can almost be expected). As to the latter, note the harmless hit on the barrier in bar 5, well away from our stop below bar 4.

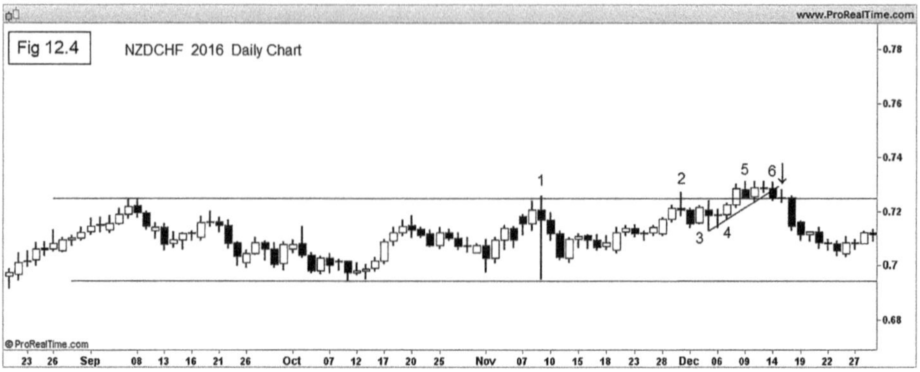

Figure 12.4. If we ignore the fluke perforation in freak bar 1 (US presidential elections, 2016), the rejected break in bar 2 is only a first failure for the bulls. Seldom a biggie. Their troubles start when their subsequent attempt also fails to follow through.

Given the series of higher lows in the second half of the range, the odds for a breakout are actually quite good. The 3-4 buildup isn't half bad either but lacks the preferred pressure on the barrier to have our full approval. It does sit close enough to the barrier to offer support in the event of a test, so that is something to keep in mind.

A week into the break, however, bears have put up a cluster of their own (5-6). Now we have a situation of two opposing clusters, with the range barrier acting as a shared cluster line.

While in principle this could resolve either way, the odds for either outcome are not even. Think about it. To come out victoriously, bulls would have to push prices back through the 5-6 cluster. Bears, on the other hand, only need to crack the low of bar 6 to "confirm" the failure of support, and as such the failure of the range break. And that is why we deem a reversal more likely.

Tip: Rather than opt for a stop above bar 6, a more logical place for protection is above the 5-6 cluster. Even though this stop would only sit a few pips higher, don't dismiss its technical benefit: only a break into new territory could now shake us out. When the premium for insurance is only a marginally wider two-pointer, opting for a safer stop (or entry) is usually our best bet because the chance of it backfiring at the target end is really small.

NZDJPY

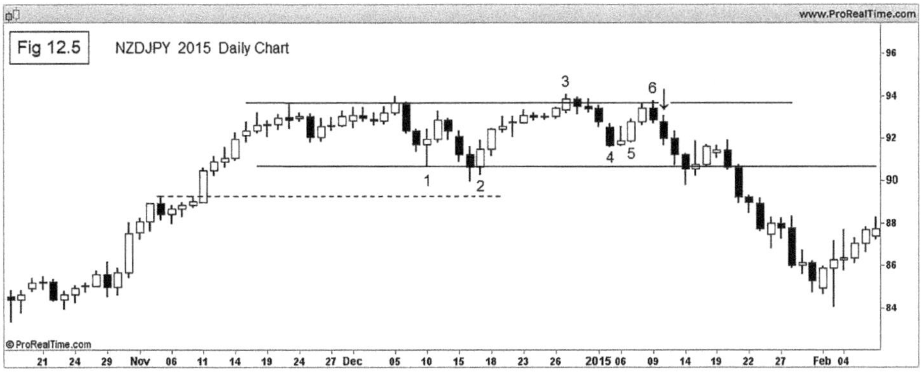

Figure 12.5. At a casual glance, the re-break in bar 2 looks similar to the one discussed in Figure 12.3. Yet the conditions are not nearly as attractive. First off, the support situation is less evident (solely based on bar 1). Consider also the potential magnet effect of the halfway barrier of the bull trend (dotted). And if that isn't enough to skip, take into account the limited room in the range above bar 2.

Kudos to the bulls for reasoning otherwise, but they should have known better than to immediately push their luck in bar 3. True, it is only a first rejection, so nothing lost yet, but then they would do well to show their resilience and not let prices slide back too much.

Clearly, there is no sign of such enthusiasm in the 3-4 action. This is not to say that a range break is now no longer possible, but it will be harder to pull off: because any new attack on the top barrier will now most likely be viewed as a test of a reversal attempt. And that is exactly why we love the sight of bar 6 (bearish resolution).

Note: Don't be put off by that morning star in the test (4-5). Recall that such a pattern is only bullish in the right conditions. With a barrier right above it, that morning star looks more like a bull trap.

Even though there is now a good chance of a pullback to the halfway barrier (dotted), our target on the short is still best based on the low of bar 1 (just shy of a two-pointer). After all, there is no point in risking a good profit for a few extra pips.

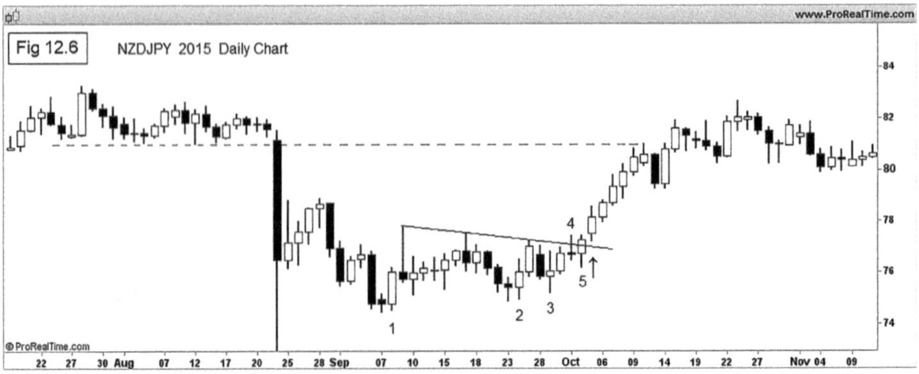

Figure 12.6. Whenever a chart suddenly crashes, as on August 24, 2015, a natural response is to want to know why. Yet if you think about it, such knowledge would do more harm than good. Since all we need for our assessments are the bars in the chart, no headline or pundit could ever enlighten us—but they might just lead us astray.

In the weeks following the crash, the market chops back and forth and little is to make of it. The bounces in the lows favor a trend reversal more than a pullback reversal, but if it weren't for a barrier across all that chop, a scruffy chart like this is best left alone.

Note: What's the benefit of a barrier? For starters, it offers all interested parties a clear line in the sand beyond which to do business. Plus it limits our options regarding the resolution: we would solely look for a signal bar to either hit the barrier or push a bit through.

As only bar 4 and 5 meet this requirement, it is not hard to pick the rightful signal bar. (By the way, should the high of bar 5 sit a tad below the high of bar 4, we can always place our entry above the latter.) So a decent setup after all, effectively a four-stepper of some sort (1-2-3-5). Note also the dotted magnet looming above.

Tip: As for the target, while there looks to be room for a two-pointer, distances in a chart can be deceiving, so always take a moment to verify. Remember the box trick? First widen the chart a bit vertically for a closer look. Then wrap a box around bar 5 (a few pips wide on both sides to account for the spread), hit copy and place two boxes on top of the first. If the top of the highest box sits below the dotted line, all good. If above, arrange to exit a few pips below.

Figure 12.7. In this follow-up chart the trend reversal holds up well, but there is obvious resistance from the action just prior to the August crash (the action on the dotted line in our previous chart).

As that forms a range, a logical idea is to keep an eye out for a range reversal in the top barrier. As always, though, let's not do anything rash. Bar 1, for example, is only a one-stepper, and bar 3 sits too deep for a pleasant entry; plus there is an adverse powerbar in play (2).

A short below bar 4 looks more interesting, if only for the three-step element (1-3-4), but the proximity of that powerbar remains disturbing. Recall that the ideal situation for a short is always when bulls have little to lean on, as then they are more likely to dump their longs (and become bears in the orderbook).

Of all the signal bar candidates in the top barrier, bar 6 is the only one to tick the right boxes. Don't let its size deceive you. Next to thwarting yet another breakout, this small session also challenges a bear flag (5-6). In fact, the close of bar 6 already sits below the flagline.

Note: Small signal bars are not necessarily a liability and may even prove an *asset*. Because due to their tight span we can often opt for the best stop in the area without compromising the feasibility of a two-point target. For example, rather than opt for protection above the false high prior to bar 6, still a bit tight, we can place our stop more safely above the false high prior to bar 4.

In case we missed this setup, it is not too late to short below bar 7. Our entry is now less favorable, but that by itself is irrelevant. All that matters is whether we still like our odds.

NZDUSD

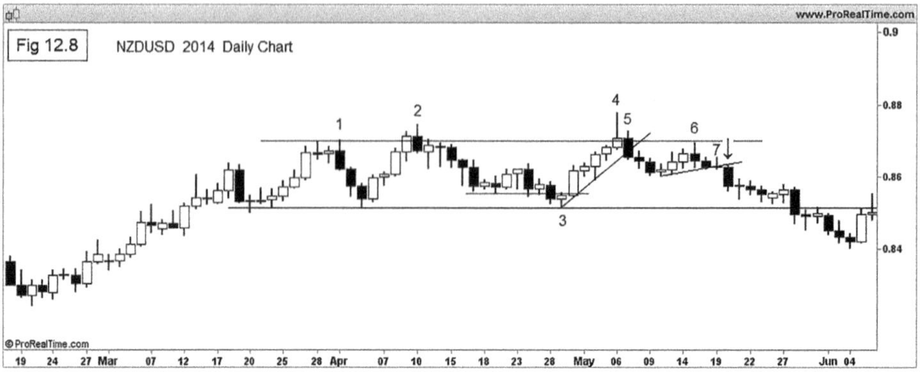

Figure 12.8. If a trend is any good, the first trade idea that usually comes to mind is a pullback reversal about halfway the latest rally. Yet next to these common corrections in *price*, equally interesting are the so-called corrections in *time*, which occur when a trend only pulls back modestly and then forms a range. That too favors trend continuation, but the set-ups to look for will be more of the range reversal type.

In the NZDUSD above the best setup is actually *against* the trend, but before we get to that, why not trade above bar 3? The simple answer is that there sits a cluster in the way. Recall that in cases of opposing clusters, we want our block to be at least equally fat or otherwise potent as the enemy block. That is obviously not the case at bar 3.

After three failures to break out (1-2-5), it's safe to say that a range reversal is now more likely. Nonetheless, let us not ignore the aggression in the latest runup (3-4). So rather than immediately short below bar 5, here we take a chance on a test.

A test is granted but unfortunately the resolution is not to our liking (6). Let's stay sharp, though, because you never know what the next few bars will bring. And indeed, just two bars later we suddenly have a bear flag on the chart, plus a resolution in trap bar fashion (7). Another feature worthy of mention here is the potential magnet effect of the bottom barrier (aka halfway barrier).

Tip: Always be extra attentive when you spot some buildup near the *midrange area*, because once that resolves there is usually an excellent chance to exploit the magnet effect of the nearest range barrier.

Figure 12.9. One of the worst things you can do as a trader is chase a runaway trend. Your chances of success are particularly grim if you take position after a late bout of enthusiasm (1). Don't fall for it. Better to be left emptyhanded than holding the bag.

A smarter idea is to try to hop on after a pullback. Yet always be mindful of the *type of correction* you are dealing with because that will have a big say in the *type of setup* to scan for. Choppy pullbacks, for example, rarely allow for a swift reversal (2-3). It is not surprising, therefore, to see the 3-4 cluster broken at the bottom first. At that point there is simply too much resistance overhead.

A good time to start watching things more closely is after bar 5 and the subsequent attack on the cluster line. As it is reasonable to assume that the low of the pullback is set, we now have something go by.

Note that it still takes more than a week, and about three weeks in total, for the correction to fully bottom out. But once completed there is no mistaking the three-stepper now on display (3-5-6). A sequence like this is often referred to as an *inverse head-and-shoulders*, one of the oldest and arguably most respected reversal patterns in technical trading. So surely we are not the only ones to have spotted it. Hence we are happy to see that the trap bar on the right is perfectly suited for signal bar purposes (6).

Lest you forget, let me stress again that we can prepare our entry above bar 6 with *zero* risk of an overnight gap—such is the marvel of end-of-day Forex. Eat your heart out, stock traders.

Figure 12.10. Did anyone say price action is random? They must be either diehard skeptics or simply too lazy to study the evidence to the contrary. How often have we not seen a range hanging from a trend, as above, or discussed a reversal setup in a halfway barrier.

As for a short below bar 1, there is perhaps something to be said for it, but the conditions are far from optimal. One concern is that the chart as a whole is still quite bullish (higher lows throughout). Consider also the unfavorable entry (well away from the top barrier), or that a stop at the other end of this signal bar would be easy prey in a test. Insurance is not really an option either, as then there would hardly be room for a decent reward towards the bottom barrier.

No such concerns apply to our setup at the other end (3-4). There we not only have the trend on *our* side, the risk of a bad start is also much smaller (test already out of the way). Admittedly, the aggression in the 1-2 selloff might keep some bulls at bay, but bears in turn would do well not to ignore a *cluster* in halfway support. The tight span of that cluster is also more a positive than a negative as even a modest reversal to the midrange area would do for a two-pointer.

As for bar 5 later on, while there is no mistaking the bearish message of this powerbar, the foregoing action is way too choppy for a safe short (the bar stands too tall anyway). Mind you, this is not to say that we aren't surprised by the outcome. Indeed, seeing bulls shake off that trap bar as if nonexistent, and then push on to trap the bears instead, is quite a remarkable sight. Hats off.

chapter 13

The USD pairs

USDCAD, USDCHF, and USDJPY

USDCAD 2014–2017

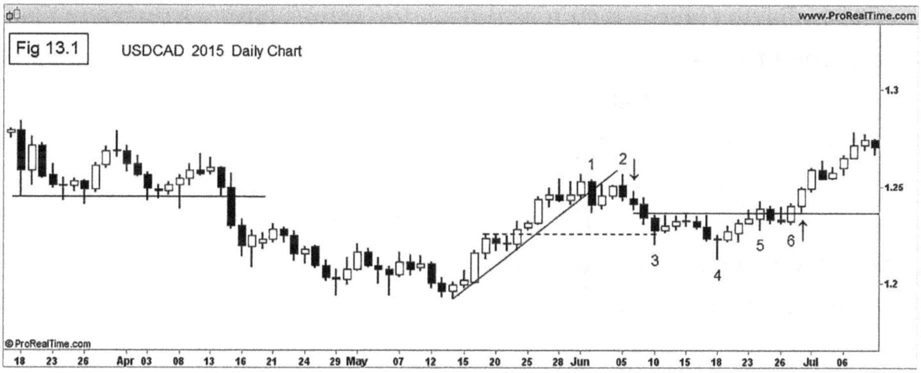

Figure 13.1. With now only three more pairs to go, I am sure you will have noticed, and hopefully taken to heart, at least one simple fact: to succeed as a price action trader there is only a limited number of popular themes to get your head around. Take the two-stepper here above (1-2). Even the trap bar resolution of the test couldn't be more thematic. (Alas, this one is only good for a one-pointer.)

A few weeks later, we have another common pattern on the chart, a so-called inverse head-and-shoulders (3-4-6). If this looks familiar, it is indeed a near-copy of the one in Figure 12.9. The main distinction regards the final buildup, now revolving around the barrier (5-6). Yet once again the resolution is easy to spot (trap bar).

Figure 13.2. Strictly seen the bounce in bar 1 resolves a test of the bottom barrier. Looks nice in hindsight, but ask yourself: would you have entered above this session, with all that chop to the left? If not fully sure, report it as a skip.

As bulls do come out victoriously, a few weeks later a new trade idea forms when the 2-3 rally starts to pull back. Of course, we are well aware of that adverse powerbar (4) and the fact that the dotted line will likely prove a magnet. Bar 5, therefore, is an easy skip.

Call me a nit, but I am not too keen on bar 6 either. Notwithstanding the two-step element (5-6), it is still hard to speak of a convincing resolution. Plus the adverse magnet still lurks.

Doesn't that also apply to bar 7? To some degree perhaps, but with now a three-stepper as backup (5-6-7), plus a false break below support (which almost hit that magnet anyway), the prospects for a reversal have notably improved.

Note: Assuming we would now take our chances, note that our entry above bar 7 is not hit in the following session. No need to cancel, though, because nothing has changed for the worse. The same goes for the situation after bar 8, although you *could* now opt for a tighter stop. But don't push your luck and opt for a tighter entry too! Since bar 8 is effectively still an inside bar to bar 7, the latter remains the dominant bar in this setup, above which the reversal is likely to take off in earnest. Hence it is advised to just keep the entry above bar 7. The stop is more a matter of style.

USDCHF

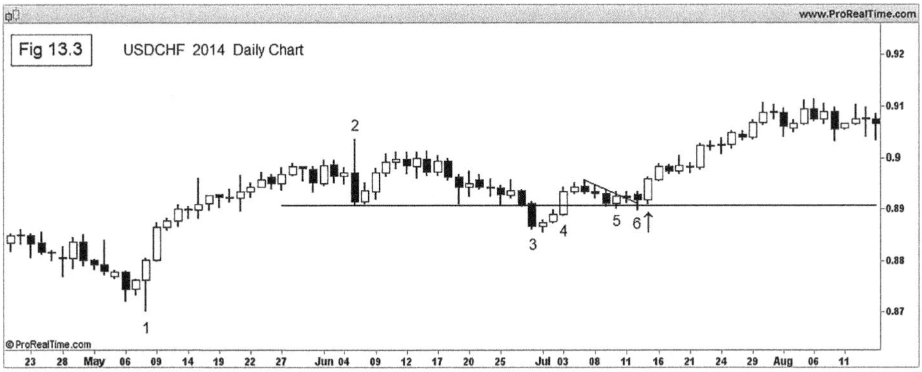

Figure 13.3. A fun fact of the 1-2 rally is that it both starts and ends with a freak bar. The bar in the top, however, turned out to be a fluke, which will surely have contributed to the clever plan with which bulls managed to revive their trend—allow bears to crack support first (3) and then trap them shortly after (4). That one never gets old.

We would love to trade that re-break ourselves, but as it fails to set up, our attention goes out to the test. Which brings us to bar 5. Forming a two-stepper with bar 4, we effectively have our resolution, yet the place for a stop is a bit tricky (right below support). Ideally we would opt for protection below the false break earlier on, but that is not really an option (unless you see no problem in shooting for an awkwardly wide two-pointer). As there is no real reason to decline, though, we must assume to have played this with a standard stop.

Although it looks like the next bar never trades above bar 5, a brief spike in the spread may have hit our entry anyway. Hence we have no choice but to book this trade as a loss.

Yet not all is bad as this turns out to be one such situation in which the shakeout bar is also a new signal bar (6). That's a chance to quickly recoup our loss and even come out a point to the good. Don't be put off by the bearish close of bar 6. Remember, on a small-bodied doji, the tail is usually more determinant than the close. That false dip below support further adds to the likelihood of a reversal and allows for a fine stop to boot.

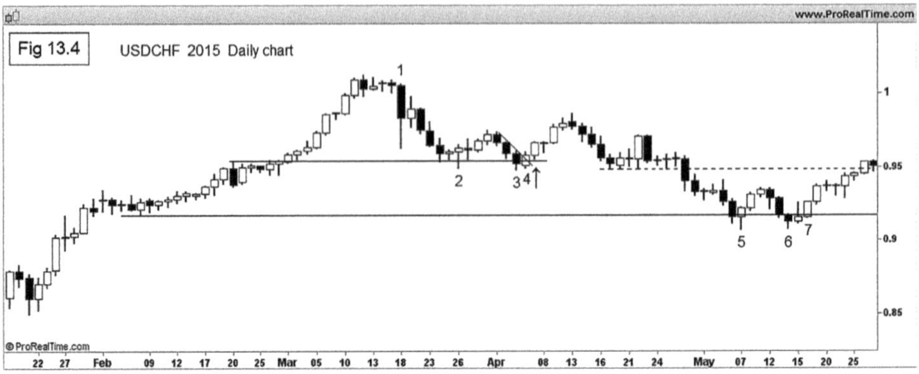

Figure 13.4. Most commonly a pullback in a trend will aim for an obstacle in the halfway area of the latest rally. That's already handy to know, yet the best part is that once that magnet is reached, it can then be used as a springboard for a reversal. So that's our trade idea here.

Of course, for a setup to be valid, a proper resolution is still a must, which is why we generally prefer a two-stepper (2-4) over a one-stepper (2). One-step resolutions should not be ruled out, but then the last thing we want to see in a pullback is a powerbar (1).

As we can be fairly sure to have played this with a stop below bar 3 (a no-brainer, really), it is unfortunate that this very insurance causes the trade to fail at the target end whereas a standard stop would have just worked out. If this ever happens to you, don't let it spoil your day. You played it well, feel proud.

Not much later the USDCHF sets up another two-stepper, this time in the halfway area of the bigger rally (5-7). As this calls for a stop below bar 6, however, there is hardly any room left to make it worth our while (in view of that overhanging cluster). And so we let it go.

Tip: Let me stress again that there is nothing wrong in shooting for an occasional one-pointer. Yet if you're the type that aims to aggressively exploit every little magnet, do verify whether such ventures truly benefit your bottom line. In fact, it's good practice to periodically review *all* your wagers by category, to see if there are any hidden flaws in your game. For even if profitable across the board, a particular type of trade or management idea could still perform quite poorly. If so, it may not sink your boat, but why not fix that leak.

USDJPY

Figure 13.5. Open any charting platform for the first time and it is easy to feel overwhelmed by the countless bells and whistles, not to mention the endless list of indicators available at the click of a mouse. Yet soon you will discover that all you really need as a price action trader is the *line tool*. You could even start with the crosshair cursor; simply by moving it up or down you will quickly spot the matching highs and lows. The one thing to master, if you will, is which perforations to exclude (1). Nothing a little practice can't solve.

After bar 3, we know we have the right barrier in place, but it is only after bar 4 that we can begin to look more seriously for a range reversal. Do note that bulls still have a potent swing point nearby as backup (2).

Since the low of bar 4 is not taken out anyway, we focus on the test. When doing so, it is always nice to see a buildup line come into view as then we know exactly what to look for: a bar that either attacks this line or sticks a bit through—and there we have it in bar 5. With now a three-stepper as backup for a short (3-4-5), that swing point at 2 is no longer a major concern.

Note: As for our stop, at first glance there is little point in insurance because a re-break above bar 5 is almost guaranteed to revive the top barrier magnet (recall a similar situation in Figure 11.16). That said, there is perhaps some merit in putting the stop above the bar following bar 4; that is after all the nearest swing point and still allows for a very doable two-pointer. Might as well go for that then.

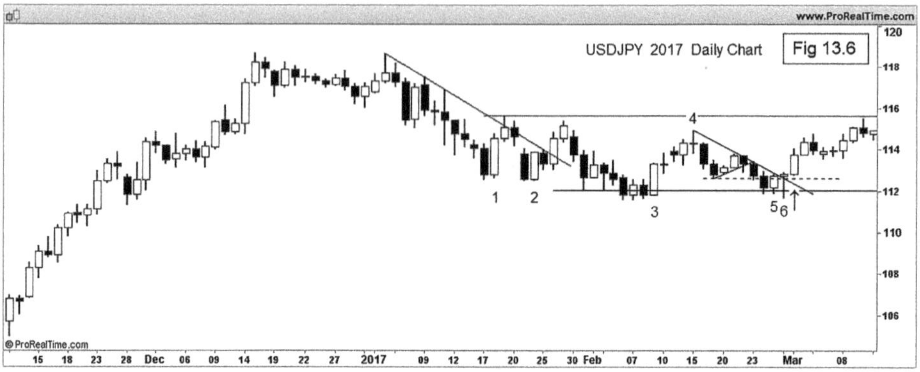

Figure 13.6. A great prerogative of purely trading price action, as opposed to looking at things more fundamentally, is that all the necessary info is already displayed in the chart. Moreover, once accustomed to the typical themes and principles, a single glance will often suffice to see if anything is brewing. And no need to sift through thousands of markets after the close. As hopefully this backtest has shown, there will be ample trading opportunities even on a small list of just 28 charts, which takes no more than a few minutes to scan.

Just to illustrate, take the pullback in the bull trend on the USDJPY above—why tire ourselves with pointless scrutiny when it is plain to see that things will only get interesting (for us) when this correction bottoms out. And even then we may not find a setup anytime soon.

For example, the two-stepper in the low of the pullback (1-2) can be quickly brushed aside in view of the overhanging pullback line. An entry above bar 3 is not really an option either given the limited room towards resistance (note the halfway barrier). A trade above bar 5 would also be premature because there is resistance from a little bear flag (halfway the 4-5 test). Wouldn't you agree that with a little help of our line tool, these adverse features can all be assessed in a matter of seconds?

So all in all it shouldn't be too hard to pick bar 6 as the only rightful signal bar. What are its credentials? In one fell swoop this powerful doji fattens up our buildup, resolves a cluster line situation, and even *closes* above angular resistance—and does all that in trap bar fashion.

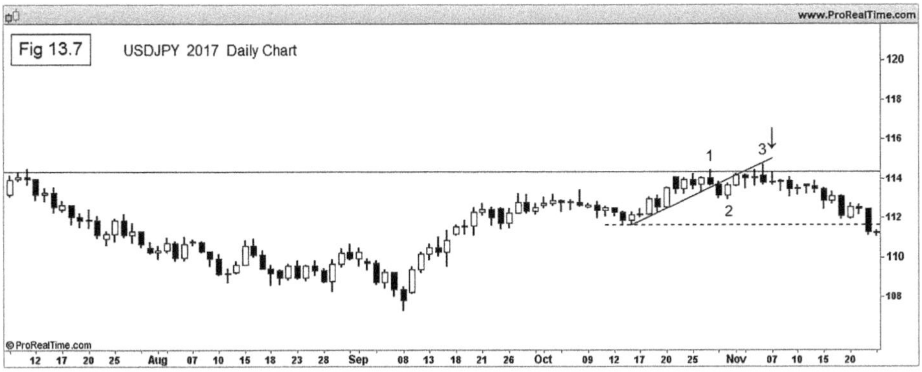

Figure 13.7. Let's wrap up with one last example of our trusted range reversal setup. While we shouldn't dismiss the possibility of a range break, practice has it that when prices run from one end of a range to the other, we typically see a reversal first, if only due to profit-taking. Another thing worthy of mention is that the top barrier is quite solid, originating from a swing high in May (not shown).

But let us not be *too* bearish here. As the latest action is unmistakably bullish, the most we can aim for is the nearest support (dotted line). And only when the chart is ripe for it. An immediate short below bar 1, for example, would be asking for trouble (note the chop to the left).

Bulls indeed step in for another try and for a moment even manage to break out. From our perspective, though, this still counts as a test of the broken support barrier (2-3). Hence we are happy to see that resolve bearishly (3).

Note: And there you have it! This completes our backtest of the 28 currency pairs over the years 2014–2017. If you are not already a fan of price action, I hope to have at least sparked your interest. The good part is that there isn't all that much to study. Once you boil it all down, there are only a handful of setups to know about, and the situations in which they occur are incredibly repetitive. Prove yourself an avid student and before long you will start to notice this amazing consistency for yourself. And here's the best part: once you see it, there is no way to *un*see it.

chapter **14**

Backtest Results

plus a few pointers on how to start trading live

Here is where you might expect a detailed account of all the setups we found in the tested period, the types that proved most profitable, or the pairs and years that yielded the highest scores, but is such data really useful? I mean, don't we all know that the best picks of one year often underperform in the next? Rather than focus on such fleeting statistics, allow me to break it down in a more practical way, as follows:

Based on what we have seen after examining 28 currency pairs over a four-year period (or six if we include the study material in Part One), this method of ours averages about one good setup per market per year. Now that is good info! And more importantly, even without keeping score we can safely state that the winners outperformed the losers, which underpins our original thesis that there *do* exist such things as *high-odds* setups. (For those who learn how to find them!)

Perhaps you might wonder if you would ever be able to find enough of these setups to make it worth your while. Let me alleviate these concerns. For this is where the high-odds moniker comes in—or if you will, quality over quantity. As we will discuss below, finding just 10 high-odds setups per year could already make for an amazing bottom line, let alone more than 20!

Granted, we still have to keep our wits about us to make it all work in the actual markets, but there is no reason to be negative about our prospects. For if you think about it, even a *random* trade with an equal stop and target already has a 50/50 chance of success (excluding fees).

Imagine then what can be accomplished if we place our trades with a little more precision.

Here's where we currently are: we studied price action, learned all about setups, built ourselves a fine method, tested it on a good number of years, and proved it sound. So far we couldn't have asked for more. But one thing we have yet to do is prove ourselves as *traders*.

The logical next step is to start trading on low volume, say by risking just half a percent of funds per trade. You could even trade on negligible volume, but I think it will be more useful to at least make it count a bit. Needless to mention, this is always a personal call. So if need be, spend a whole year just getting a feel for trading live. There is no rush, you are in it for the long haul anyway.

While no bell will ring to tell you when to trade up, be wary of signs that clearly indicate the opposite, such as feeling miserable after a shake or euphoric after a win; or getting impatient, feeling vindicative, or trying to prove yourself to some imaginary bystander. These are all signs that a trader has yet to grasp the true nature of trading, which in the end is a simple game of chance.

Yet if we purely look at things from an accounting perspective, there is little reason to hold back once we start to average one winner for every one loser (thanks to our favorable risk-to-reward). But that still begs the question: what percentage of risk per trade should we strive for?

I am sure we've all heard the advice not to risk more than 2 percent of capital on any one trade. That is sound advice indeed, for daytraders. For just think of what could happen on bad day if such individuals keep firing off trades in sheer frustration at, say, 4 or 5 percent capital risk. Their accounts could be decimated in no time.

As end-of-day traders, however, we are already in a fresher frame of mind, if only because we never sit locked in terror, glued to our screens. And even if at some point we do incur that dreaded string of losses, we are still not likely to tilt because we have a whole 24 hours to internalize that the current setback is just a cost of business. Hence I would argue, with some caution, that we might go so far as to risk 3 percent of capital on any one trade.

To be honest, you could also limit yourself to a certain amount or even base your risk on the quality of the setup in question. All that can work equally well. But more practical at this point is to discuss a risk model as a set percentage and for all trades the same.

So let's do just that and first see what that would bring on an equal number of two-point wins and one-point losses.

Assuming 28 setups (one for every pair), risking 3 percent on each trade would amount to a highly respectable 42 percent on a yearly basis (14 x 6 minus 14 x 3). Make that 15 wins and 13 losses, why not, and we're already talking 51 percent.

As not all our targets will be two-pointers, the end results will likely be lower, but not necessarily by a whole lot if we take into account the subtle art of compounding. (More on that in the next chapter.)

Either way, all the above is just for illustrational purposes, so don't get too hung up on percentages. Yet I hope the message is clear: it is not hard to do well on a 3 percent model! For example, imagine a lackluster year in which you only find 10 worthy two-pointers. Even if only half of these work out, that would still amount to 15 percent! Make that 6 wins and 4 losses, and you're already up 24 percent.

Again, the above is not to gloat over illusionary percentages but to show that there is little point in putting strain on yourself by targeting, or worse *expecting*, a certain percentage. Just take it as it comes; you have all the time in the world to work on your game. The one thing to promise yourself, or make that a rule, is to solely accept the quality setups and leave all the rest be. Stick to this simple philosophy and you're already well on your way to becoming a swing trading master.

*　　*　　*

chapter 15

Questions and Answers

tips, pointers, reflections, and other practical info

With all the technical lessons out of the way, this chapter is devoted to the more practical side of trading, geared specifically to traders new to Forex, and in particular to swing trading. Seasoned daytraders may also find a few pointers on how to transition to the end-of-day Forex. And for the stock traders out there who may have picked up this guide mainly out of curiosity, a number of tips will be offered on how to minimize or even fully mitigate the risk of opening gaps for their swing trading purposes. Much of the following has already been discussed along the way, but it's handy to have some practical tips and pointers listed together in a frequently-asked-questions format.

What are the capital requirements to start out with?

A big advantage of the Forex markets is that the broker fees are usually a function of the volume you trade with. Meaning you can trade as small as you like and not have some standard fees wipe you out. Of course, this low-risk phase is solely meant to get a feel for trading and to find out where you stand ability-wise. It needs no explaining that to make it worth your while at some point you need to trade up. Yet the key is to start. So if you have only a small sum to spare, use that. The experience you gain along the way is still a marvelous asset and will set you up for later. Just keep this one rule in mind: never trade bigger than you can afford to lose. That speaks for itself.

How to calculate the volume for a Forex trade?

This process is perhaps a little less straightforward than for most other instruments, but the principle is the same. Let's look at a stock trade first. Assume our account currently holds $10,000 and we wish to risk 3 percent per trade ($300). To find out how many shares to buy or sell, we need to know the distance from entry to stop in cents. For example, if we enter long at $12 with a stop at $11, that would be 100 cents. So if we trade only one share, a loss would cost us $1. Hence this trade allows for 300 shares (discarding fees).

This works the same for Forex trades, but there are a few more factors to take into account. One is that the distance from entry to stop is now measured in pips. The currency pair in question also has a say in things, and so too the currency of our account. As it is nearly impossible to figure out the necessary volume by head, most platforms have a built-in tool that does the thinking for us, based on our risk-model and what we type in for stop and entry on the order ticket. If this function is absent, look for a *Forex Position Size Calculator*, freely available on many Forex websites (I found a nice one on myfxbook.com).

Depending on your platform, your order ticket may ask for volume either in *units* or *lots*. One lot is equivalent to 100,000 units (a mini lot is a tenth of a standard lot). It works the same either way. For example, if the calculator comes up with 120,643 units for a particular trade, that would be equivalent to 1.2 lots (let's not split hairs).

A standalone calculator may also require you to fill in the ask price of certain currency pairs to factor in a conversion to the currency of your account. On the one from myfxbook.com, however, there is no need for this as this calculator is hooked up to live prices.

Lastly, while most platforms will probably block a trade if something is seriously off on the order ticket (so as not to exceed margin), it is still a good idea to experiment with some dummy trades on the demo version of your particular platform, just to get the hang of it.

Any further tips on how to use the order ticket?

Always use a so-called bracket order for stop and target, so that if one side is hit, the order at the other side is automatically canceled. On most platforms this will be a standard feature in the order ticket, commonly referred to as an OCO (one cancels other) or an SL/TP (stop loss/take profit). Besides managing your trades, a big advantage of a bracket order is that it will only be activated *if* the entry order is filled.

Rather than place orders as "Good for a Day," place them as "Good 'til Canceled," so that you don't have to reinstall if your entry is not hit next session—assuming the setup is still valid (otherwise cancel). If the new bar calls for a different stop, however, that *will* affect the volume for the trade and possibly the target level too (if not capped by an obstacle). Then just cancel and reinstall as if it regards a new setup. And needless to mention, always check all orders first before you click send.

What's the idea behind compounding profits?

In essence it is purely an accounting trick to speed up the growth of an account. As it demands no extra effort and can even work protectively, it would be silly not to apply it.

Here's how it works. Say your account currently holds $10,000 and your risk model is 3 percent. That means you would now risk $300 on your next trade. If the trade ends up a two-point winner, your account will then stand at $10,600 (excluding fees). So now you will risk 3 percent of that. And so on. In the event of a loss, however, the risk on your next trade would be 3 percent of $9,700. And after another loss, you reduce your volume once more, which is how compounding works protectively. (Technically you couldn't even blow up.)

The growing factor will quickly kick in once you start to average more winners than losers. You can verify this phenomenon with the use of a *Compound Interest Calculator*, freely available online. If unfamiliar with this tool, I think you'll be surprised to see how fast an account can grow tenfold even on "modest" percentages.

While most calculators are designed to compound profits per year, you can also interpret the year box as a quarterly box, or whatever increment you wish to check.

For all intents and purposes, the fastest way to make *any* account grow is to let it build and not take anything out. So make sure to always trade with funds that you have no need for in the near future.

What about overnight fees?

The great advantage of a leveraged product such as Forex is that we can trade on margin, meaning we have more funds at our disposal than we actually have in the account. If we trade overnight, however, we do need to factor in the so-called swap fees, which are calculated on the full value of our position. This fee is dependent on the volume for the trade, the currency pair in question, whether we are long or short, and on whatever our broker takes as a cut (a small additional fee as specified in their terms of service). We may even be credited a small amount.

Here's an example: say we go long the EURUSD and the interest rate currently stands at 2 percent on the euro and 3 percent on the dollar. Since we are effectively buying euros and selling dollars, we *earn* 2 percent and *pay* 3 percent, resulting in a daily debit of 1 percent/365 days. Plus we pay the broker's cut. If on the other hand we would short the EURUSD, we would be credited the 1 percent difference minus our broker's cut. (For more examples, look for a *Forex Swap Calculator.*)

On the whole these fees are quite manageable for positions lasting only a few days to a few weeks. If at any time you have to incur a bigger fee, just see it as a cost of business. The good part is that by diligently working on your trade *selection*, you automatically lower the chances of getting stuck in the dreaded stallers.

Which broker to use?

This is always a personal choice, plus much of it depends on where your live and the rules and laws in place. You can start with a "Forex Broker Comparison" website. There you will find a long list of brokers, with info on their fees, commissions, and spreads. Some sites even compare the spreads in realtime. The tightest spreads are typically offered during the EU/UK and US sessions; so it is normal for them to be a little wider during the Asian sessions. (Consider also that not all brokers offer equal spreads to all clients, so always check a little deeper.)

While tight spreads are nice, they shouldn't be a first priority when trading the dailies. More important is to look for a broker of good reputation with *decent* spreads and a platform that is pleasant to work with. To speed up this process of broker selection, a handy idea is to apply for several trial accounts simultaneously and check them out for a week or so to see which one you like best. All this requires some research, but once done, you're good to go.

Which charting software to use?

It is irrelevant which software you use as long as your charts are customizable and the prices in them correspond with the quotes on your trading platform (if not one and the same). Personally, I am a big fan of the Prorealtime platform and have been using their charts for as long as I can remember. You can also use Prorealtime as your broker.

Most brokers will offer charts in their trading platforms, but these are not always pleasant to work with. If that is your experience, consider a proper charting service for a small monthly fee.

As for free charts online, steer clear. Firstly because you cannot trust their prices to be accurate. And most likely you will not be able to work in templates, save your barriers, or set the close of the daily bars to preference (see "Which closing time to use?" later in this chapter). As the saying goes, with proper tools, half the work is done.

By the way, since the Forex markets are not centralized, the quotes on our order tickets may differ slightly from one platform to the next, but they will be very close to the "global average," or some brokers would lose business pretty fast (or risk getting taken advantage of).

Which closing time to use for the daily bars on Forex?

Since the Forex markets don't actually close during the week, the way to set up the daily bars leaves room for debate. Many traders argue that the session is over when the US stock markets close for the day, while others prefer to let the bar trade on for a few more hours to either 00:00 CET or 01:00 CET (the EU and UK close respectively).

A solid argument for the US close is that there is rarely much activity afterwards. Yet you could also argue that *if* there is still some activity, it's best to see that reflected in the current bar.

The good part is that it doesn't really matter which close we use. As the highs and lows of a session are typically set earlier in the day, most bars will look very similar. The closing prices may differ slightly, but that rarely affects setup validity. And if it does, the pros and cons of each setting will probably balance out over time.

So here's an idea: unless you have a specific preference, simply pick the close that corresponds best with your scanning routine. Traders in Europe, for example, may prefer the US close so that they can run their scans well before midnight. US based traders, on the other hand, may prefer the UK close. As a middle ground option, I have used the EU close for all charts in this guide.

As the closing prices in most platforms are to be set in UTC, which can be a little confusing, always verify whether your bars get printed as you prefer. Since it is hard to tell *during* a session if that is the case, it is best to check this shortly after the intended close; you should already see a small dash once a transaction is printed in the new session. If your chart instead stays on the current bar, something is off.

As a final note, if you set your bars to the EU close in order to run a comparing backtest on the years covered in this guide, you may still see small differences due to daylight savings time (DST). While you could account for that in your backtest, it is rather cumbersome to do and only rarely will it make a difference regarding the validity of a setup or the outcome of a trade. Of course, for *trading* purposes it is always wise to adjust the charts for DST when applicable.

What is the best way to handle a Friday setup?

I wouldn't advise to set up a trade over the weekend, the reason being that most brokers already allow for trading to trickle in on Sunday, so *before* the Monday open (which due to all the different time zones isn't set in stone to begin with). You may only see a few random quotes, but most likely with shamelessly wide spreads. These spikes may not even show up on the charts afterwards, yet they can hit your order just the same, with nasty slippage as a result. (Tip: If your charts show *six* bars per week instead of five, uncheck the "show weekend data" box in your chart settings.) To avoid the above, it is best to watch the Monday open in realtime and only place your trades once the spreads have normalized a bit (at least for the pair in question).

Since it's hard to generalize on the subtleties and intricacies of the Monday open, it might be a good idea to watch at least a few opens first, just to see how your broker typically handles the action. For example, if you find that only a few pairs are hit by excessively wide spreads, that's handy info. Either way, don't let this spread business put you off. While statistically one in five signal bars is a Friday session, most can still be traded like any other weekday.

What to do when late for the daily scan?

First of all, don't fret. Since good quality setups only rarely come about, most likely you can even miss a few scans in a row, or perhaps even go on holiday, and not miss any setups. If you are a little late or even a few hours late, check your charts as soon as you can. For even if there was a trade to set up, prices may not have broken your signal bar yet (Asian sessions are notoriously slow) or have done so only modestly. If the latter, you can often accept a slightly worse entry (as if dealing with a taller signal bar), or place the trade with a limit order in the hope of a tighter fill later on. You may also find that the market broke your signal bar falsely. As that can happen even to the best of setups, your trade idea may still be valid. Then either enjoy the "discount" and enter right away or place an order at the original entry level so that the market has to turn favorably first. Or if you want to play it even more safely, arrange to enter beyond the false break. Do check whether that still allows for a feasible two-pointer (or a worthy reward in case of an obstacle).

How to adapt the *Forex Daily* method to stocks?

The amazing thing about price action is that all the themes and principles we have come to appreciate in Forex are equally common in other markets. In fact, strip away the names of all charts, and it is hard to tell whether you are looking at a stock, an index, a commodity, or a currency pair. The time frame too will likely be a mystery to the casual eye.

However, this is not to say that a method specifically designed for one type of market can be put into effect elsewhere *as is*. If you prefer to trade stocks, for example, it is imperative to at least take into account the higher risk of opening gaps. As there are many ways to go about it, the following ideas might help to decide on the matter.

As always, your first task is to create a watchlist. While you could simply pick one of the many indices in your platform, more practical is to create a list of say 50 or 100 highly popular stocks (the stocks with most liquidity usually have the tightest spreads).

If it suits your schedule, one way to handle opening gaps is to avoid them altogether. For example, you could run your scans *before* the open, but place your trades shortly *after* (if still valid). If a stock gaps modestly, you could even factor that in as if dealing with a taller signal bar. Should a stock gap too wide for a safe entry, you could then place a limit order above or below the signal bar (whether long or short), in the hopes of a fill later on (plenty of opening gaps close the same day).

If trading the open does not fit your schedule, some more advanced platforms allow you to place your orders with a restriction in the order ticket that specifies the maximum gap you are willing to accept, referred to as *stop limit orders*.

If that won't do either, another idea is to only scan the markets that are rarely seen to gap. There are plenty of ETFs, indices, and even individual stocks that almost behave like currencies. You could even trade these alongside your Forex account.

If you are up for it, there is actually a clever way to take advantage of gaps. For this you need to keep track of all stocks that according to your analysis are likely to set up in the near future. The idea is to scan these markets in the *final hour* of the session, and if indeed a signal bar forms, to then place a trade right before the markets close.

The upside of this tactic is that if the market gaps favorably, the position will already be pleasantly in the plus. The obvious downside is the risk of a premature entry, or even an adverse gap (not very likely if the setup is sound, but don't rule it out). This tactic might also work for an occasional Friday setup on Forex, but don't use it for regular weekday setups. Your only benefit would be a slightly sharper fill. That's not worth the risk of a premature entry.

Besides the larger number of markets to choose from, another reason you might prefer stocks over Forex is when your heart goes out to trend trending more than swing trading. This is not to say that currencies won't trend, but they rarely do so as extensively as stocks in a bull or bear market. The ranging tendency of currency pairs is exactly why they are highly suited for *swing* trading—pun intended! Just think of the countless reversals we spotted in our backtest.

As a final tip, there is even a "lazy-man's approach" to all this and that is to trade the *weekly* chart. First thing you will notice is that there are hardly any gaps. The average weekly chart is perhaps a little less active than its daily counterpart, but you'd be hard-pressed not to find a decent number of setups to make it worth your while. Scan as many stocks as you like, you have all weekend.

Would the *Forex Daily* method work on the Crypto markets?

Price action does not discriminate, so in principle everything works the same on crypto as on any other market. But there are a few snags to be aware of first. Starting with the good part, one undeniable advantage of trading crypto over all other markets, even Forex, is the total absence of overnight gaps (assuming the 24/7 cryptos and not some ETF or futures spin-off). Yet it remains to be seen if this weighs up to the disadvantages often paramount to new or only partially regulated markets: unstable platforms, bad fills, bounced orders, huge spreads, high commissions, lagging executions, and the like.

While perhaps not so relevant for the so-called *hodlers* who believe their coins will eventually rise to great height, such issues can be quite unsavory for swing traders. This was actually the case with Forex too when first introduced to the general public. So in that respect it is only fair to assume that if the crypto markets are here to stay, most of the above will eventually sort itself out.

As for the price action, all the usual themes are there, but it needs no explanation that the crypto markets are highly prone to speculation, leading to countless pump-and-dump schemes. Even the dot.com bubble and the current AI craze pale in comparison. We don't need a history lesson to predict how this will end, but fair is fair, it also offers amazing opportunity, even for total amateurs. One tactic in particular so far has proved to be the gift that keeps on giving: position yourself on the long side after an extensive decline and then hodle for the next wave of speculative buying. Not a bad idea, until you wind up hodling the proverbial bag instead.

As for actual swing trading, my research is too limited to offer meaningful advice. I am sure there are coins that behave almost like regular currencies, so that would be a good place to start. The more liquid coins will likely fall into this category.

Any tips on how to speed up the daily scans?

Start with a template. If you solely trade Forex, make a watchlist of the 28 pairs in alphabetical order and set your platform to open up with the AUDCAD. If the chart opens a little too wide for a pleasant read (vertically), quickly adjust it to your liking. Then take a few seconds to check for barriers, or to see if those already in place are still valid.

Once you become more experienced, a mere glance will often suffice to see if anything is brewing. If nothing stands out, move on to the next chart. Before long it should only take a handful of minutes to scan your entire list.

It might also help to attach a toolbar to your charts that contains a line tool for horizontal and angular barriers and a box tool for estimating targets, plus a green and red arrow with which to mark your long and short positions. You can also add a text icon for potential annotations to keep you on guard.

Whenever a pair calls for action, finish your scan first. Then calmly revisit the chart, check the setup again, and if all looks fine, place your trade.

While in principle you could use a phone or a tablet, it is strongly advised to do your scanning and all the initial training on a desktop PC or at least a device with a mouse attached as that will make it so much easier to scroll through charts, draw barriers, calculate distances, or mark entries. Not to mention placing orders.

Any advice for struggling swing traders?

Don't be too hard on yourself if things do not go as planned right out of the gate. If it is your own doing, just accept. As with all new endeavors, and most certainly in trading, some lessons simply need to be learned the hard way, and possibly a few times over, before they finally sink in. So rather than feel frustrated, look upon it as a challenge to fix whatever needs fixing. There is no reason for shame, we've all been through it; do be honest with yourself as you examine what exactly it is that is holding you back.

And for what it is worth, not every year will offer equal opportunities, that is just how it is. So don't freak out if halfway through you find your results a bit lacking; and besides, you never know what the next quarter will bring. Focus on executing your method. As that is the one thing in trading you truly control.

* * *

chapter **16**

Final Thoughts

If this guide has proven anything, it is that swing trading Forex is by all means a viable pursuit. Frankly, that is quite an understatement. The ranging nature of currency pairs is practically built for the swing trader, with highly repetitive themes and setups that are easy to spot. And let's not forget, the daily scans take just minutes to complete!

Should you take a liking to this style of trading, feel free to copy the *Forex Daily* method as is, but don't hesitate to experiment with alternative ideas. For example, there is no need to stick to a 1:2 risk-to-reward. Aim for bigger targets if you wish, if only on occasion; or perhaps become a one-point specialist. It's all good. Take all the time you need to figure out which style suits you best.

When that pleasant moment comes to test your chops in the markets, don't make the classic mistake of diving in headfirst. Get your toes wet first. Unless you are among that rare breed of natural-born traders, trading live will take some getting used to; some even view it as a rite of passage. If by any chance it turns out that you're *not* yet ready, for whatever reason, it is better to find out on the cheap.

My final advice is to always remain humble as a trader—and never stop studying. Accept the occasional setbacks as a cost of business, and feel proud of every step forward.

All the best on your journey,
Bob Volman

appendix

All pairs 2018–2024

As promised, included here are the seven follow-up years. (Subsequent years will be posted on ***www.bobvolman.me***.) As you browse through these charts, rather than just focus on the setups, see if you can identify the dominant theme first. It's excellent practice.

All bars are again based on the EU close, which is two hours behind the US close and one hour ahead of the UK close. Small arrows point to the entries—always a few pips above or below the signal bar. The stops are marked by a little dash at the other end of the signal bar, or, in case of insurance, a bar nearby. Unless indicated otherwise, the target is our trusted two-pointer. (FYI, the annotations point at the trade idea more than any particular setup category.)

As you will soon see, these seven years also produced countless setups of the highest quality, fairly close to our earlier average of about one trade per market per year. Two years lagged behind, most notably 2020, which is perhaps not so strange if we consider the global pandemic and the mayhem it caused on the markets worldwide. It is reassuring to find, though, that even after a slow start that year still ended very profitably. It teaches us a valuable lesson: for us swing traders, patience is a must. So always keep in mind that long-term objective.

Don't be alarmed if you frequently miss a few setups in your own analysis. While you may have the principles down pat, it still takes time and experience to master any craft. Yet the good part, and this cannot be stressed enough, is that catching even half of the yearly setups would already make for a fantastic bottom line. That's the power of quality over quantity. Enjoy!

2018

Fig A1 AUDCAD 2018 Daily Chart

Fig A2 AUDCHF 2018 Daily Chart

Fig A3 AUDJPY 2018 Daily Chart

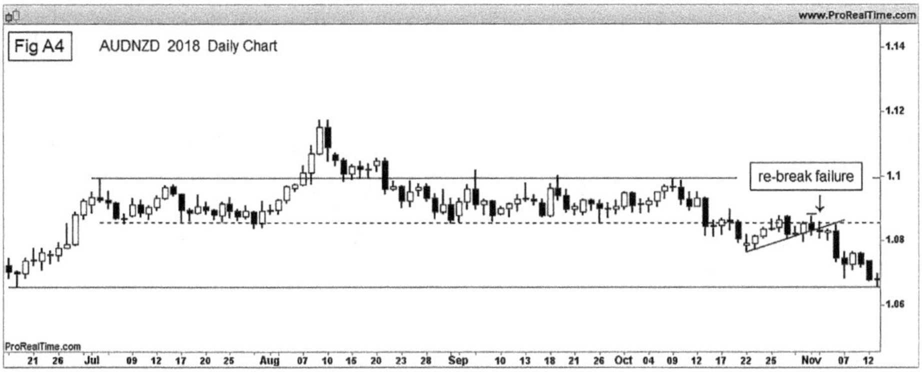

Fig A4 AUDNZD 2018 Daily Chart

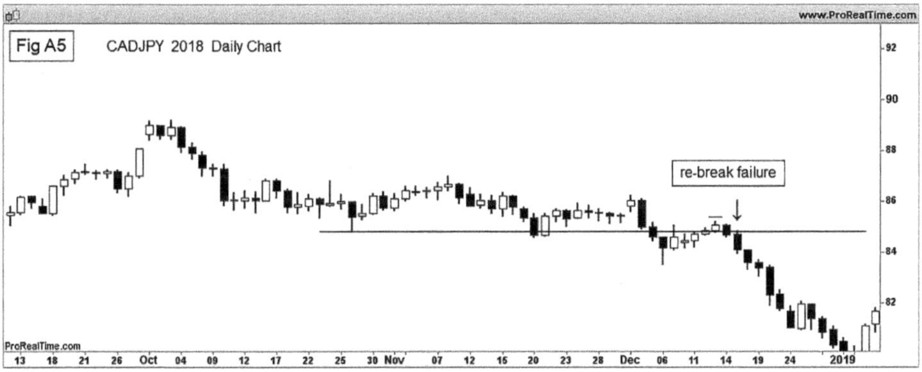

Fig A5 CADJPY 2018 Daily Chart

Fig A6 CHFJPY 2018 Daily Chart

Fig A7
EURAUD 2018 Daily Chart
re-break failure
www.ProRealTime.com

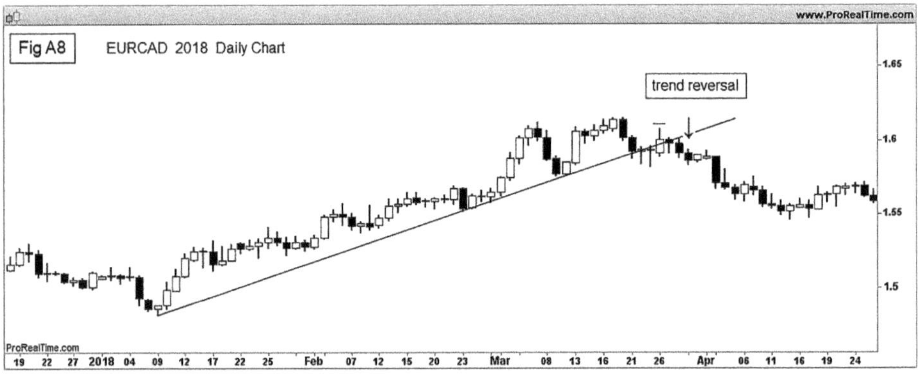
Fig A8
EURCAD 2018 Daily Chart
trend reversal
www.ProRealTime.com

Fig A9
EURCAD 2018 Daily Chart
re-break failure
take profit
www.ProRealTime.com

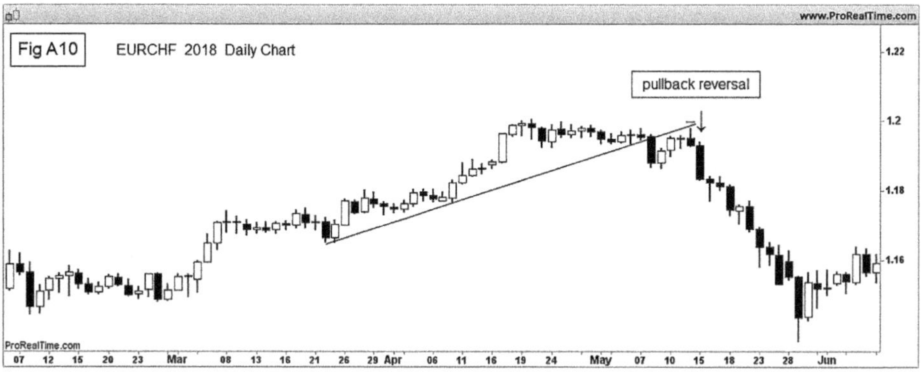
Fig A10
EURCHF 2018 Daily Chart
pullback reversal
www.ProRealTime.com
ProRealTime.com

Fig A11
EURCHF 2018 Daily Chart
range reversal
www.ProRealTime.com
ProRealTime.com

Fig A12
EURGBP 2018 Daily Chart
range reversal
www.ProRealTime.com
ProRealTime.com

Fig A13
EURJPY 2018 Daily Chart
re-break failure
www.ProRealTime.com
ProRealTime.com

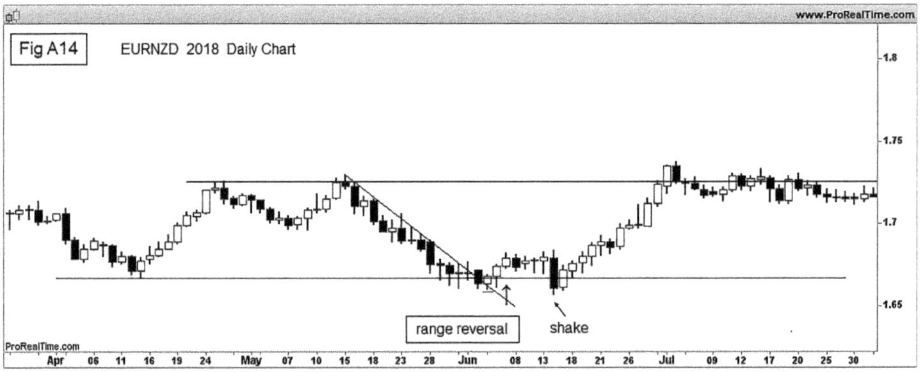

Fig A14
EURNZD 2018 Daily Chart
range reversal
shake
www.ProRealTime.com
ProRealTime.com

Fig A15
EURUSD 2018 Daily Chart
M-top reversal
www.ProRealTime.com
ProRealTime.com

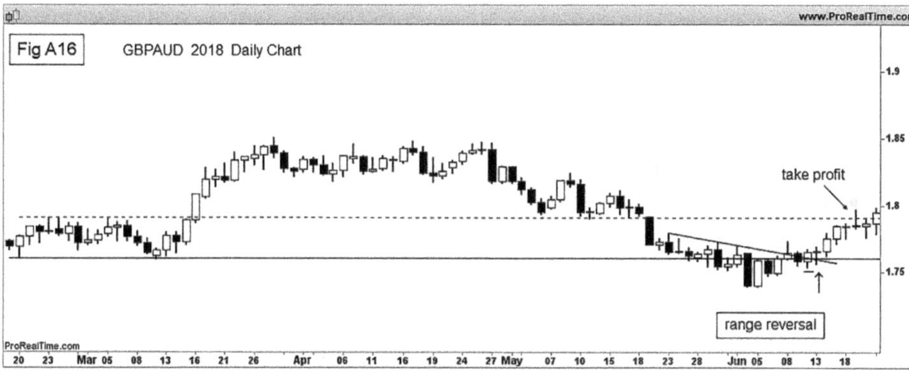
www.ProRealTime.com
Fig A16
GBPAUD 2018 Daily Chart
take profit
range reversal
ProRealTime.com

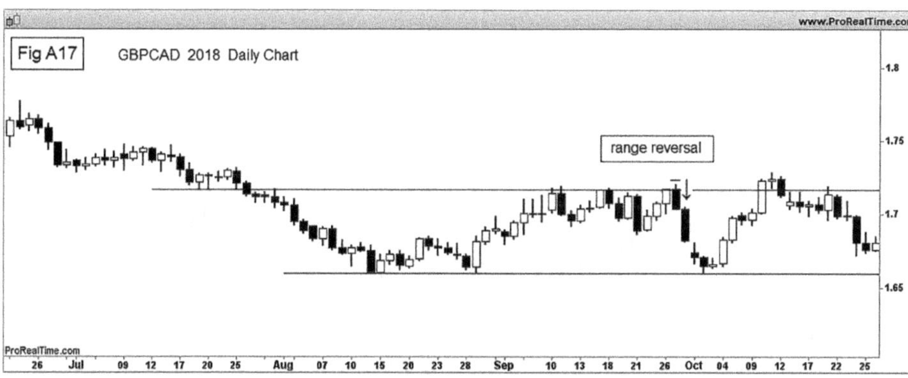
www.ProRealTime.com
Fig A17
GBPCAD 2018 Daily Chart
range reversal
ProRealTime.com

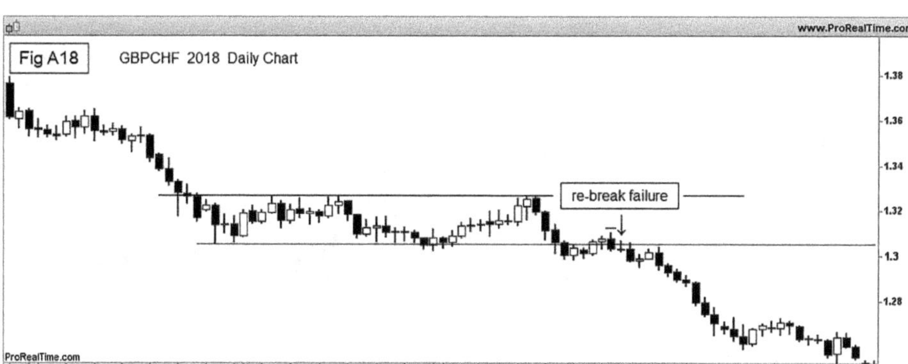
www.ProRealTime.com
Fig A18
GBPCHF 2018 Daily Chart
re-break failure
ProRealTime.com

Fig A19
GBPJPY 2018 Daily Chart
pullback reversal
might have
just missed target

Fig A20
GBPNZD 2018 Daily Chart
range reversal

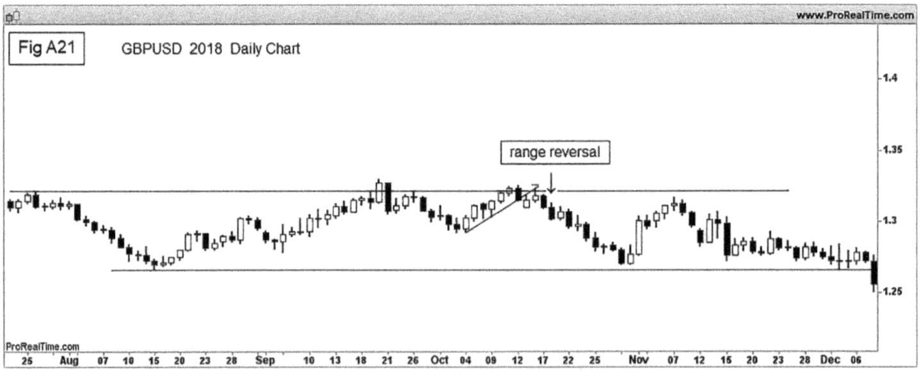
Fig A21
GBPUSD 2018 Daily Chart
range reversal

www.ProRealTime.com
Fig A22
NZDCHF 2018 Daily Chart
range reversal
0.74
0.72
0.7
0.68
0.66
ProRealTime.com
09 12 17 22 25 Feb 07 12 15 20 23 Mar 08 13 16 21 26 Apr 06 11 16 19 24 May 07 10

www.ProRealTime.com
Fig A23
NZDJPY 2018 Daily Chart
pullback reversal
take profit
84
82
80
78
76
74
ProRealTime.com
20 23 28 Dec 06 11 14 19 22 27 2018 04 09 12 17 22 25 Feb 07 12 15 20 23 Mar 08 13 16 21 26

www.ProRealTime.com
Fig A24
USDCHF 2018 Daily Chart
take profit
pullback reversal
1.02
1
0.98
0.96
ProRealTime.com
21 26 Apr 06 11 16 19 24 May 07 10 15 18 23 28 Jun 05 08 13 18 21 26 Jul 09 12 17

www.ProRealTime.com
Fig A25
USDJPY 2018 Daily Chart
114
112
110
108
106
104
trend reversal
ProRealTime.com
09 12 17 22 25 30 Feb 07 12 15 20 23 Mar 05 08 13 16 21 26 29 Apr 06 11 16 19 24 27 May

2019

Fig A26 AUDCAD 2019 Daily Chart

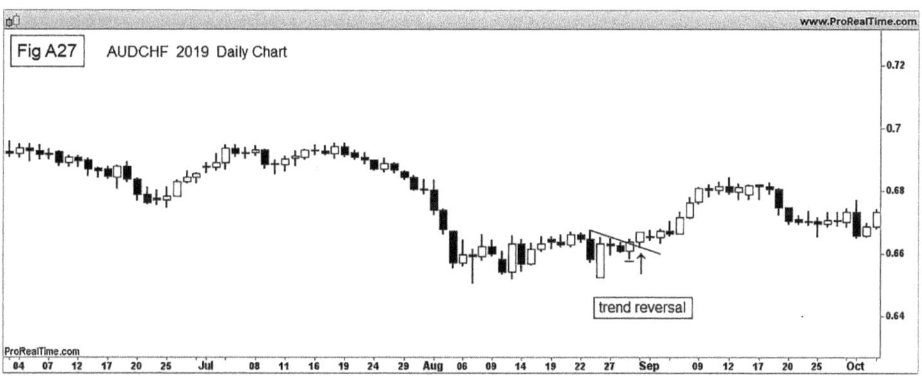

Fig A27 AUDCHF 2019 Daily Chart

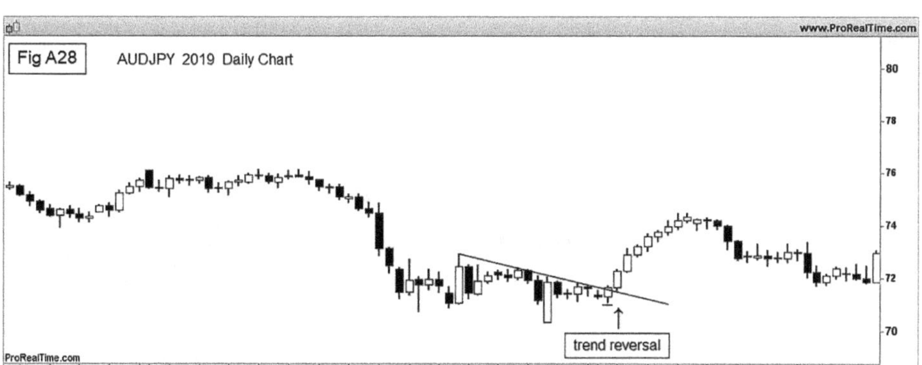

Fig A28 AUDJPY 2019 Daily Chart

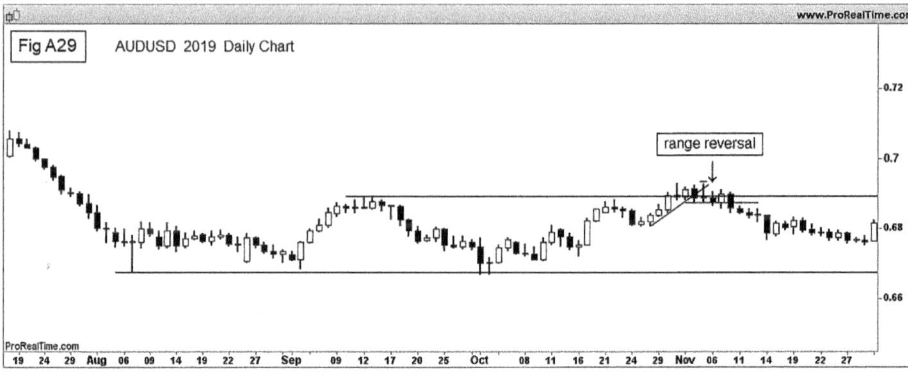
www.ProRealTime.com
Fig A29
AUDUSD 2019 Daily Chart
range reversal
0.72
0.7
0.68
0.66
ProRealTime.com
19 24 29 Aug 06 09 14 19 22 27 Sep 09 12 17 20 25 Oct 08 11 16 21 24 29 Nov 06 11 14 19 22 27

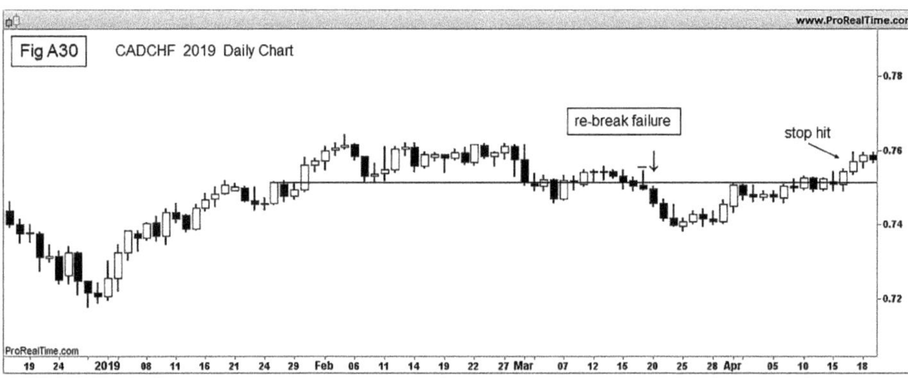
www.ProRealTime.com
Fig A30
CADCHF 2019 Daily Chart
re-break failure
stop hit
0.78
0.76
0.74
0.72
ProRealTime.com
19 24 2019 08 11 16 21 24 29 Feb 06 11 14 19 22 27 Mar 07 12 15 20 25 28 Apr 05 10 15 18

www.ProRealTime.com
Fig A31
CADCHF 2019 Daily Chart
re-break failure
0.79
0.78
0.77
0.76
0.75
0.74
0.73
ProRealTime.com
14 19 22 Mar 07 12 15 20 25 Apr 05 10 15 18 23 26 May 06 09 14 17 22 27 Jun 07 12

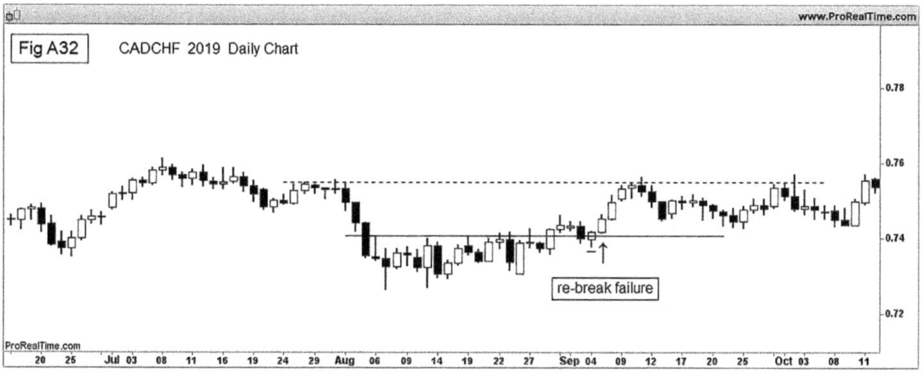
www.ProRealTime.com
Fig A32
CADCHF 2019 Daily Chart
re-break failure
ProRealTime.com
0.78
0.76
0.74
0.72
20 25 Jul 03 08 11 16 19 24 29 Aug 06 09 14 19 22 27 Sep 04 09 12 17 20 25 Oct 03 08 11

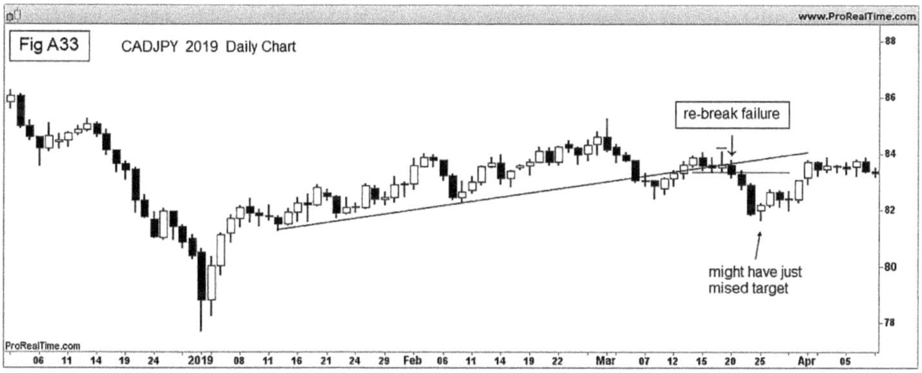
www.ProRealTime.com
Fig A33
CADJPY 2019 Daily Chart
re-break failure
might have just
mised target
ProRealTime.com
88
86
84
82
80
78
06 11 14 19 24 2019 08 11 16 21 24 29 Feb 06 11 14 19 22 Mar 07 12 15 20 25 Apr 05

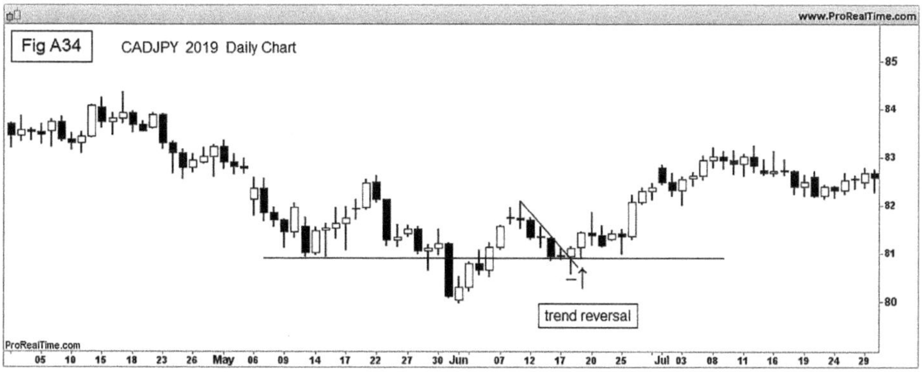
www.ProRealTime.com
Fig A34
CADJPY 2019 Daily Chart
trend reversal
ProRealTime.com
85
84
83
82
81
80
05 10 15 18 23 26 May 06 09 14 17 22 27 30 Jun 07 12 17 20 25 Jul 03 08 11 16 19 24 29

www.ProRealTime.com
Fig A35
CHFJPY 2019 Daily Chart
trend reversal
ProRealTime.com

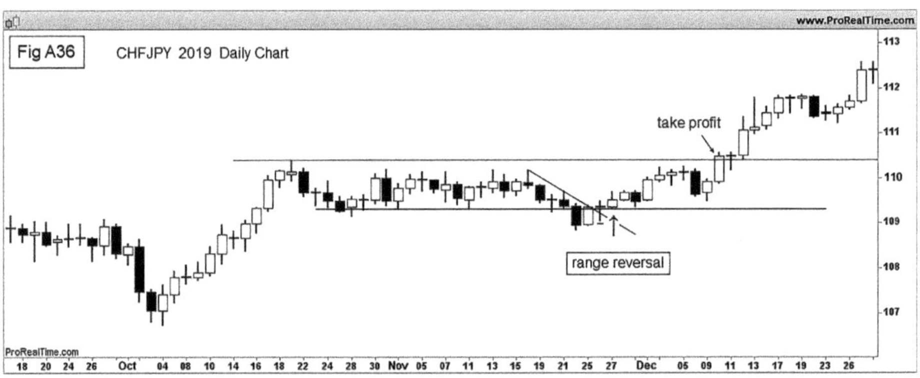
www.ProRealTime.com
Fig A36
CHFJPY 2019 Daily Chart
take profit
range reversal
ProRealTime.com

www.ProRealTime.com
Fig A37
EURAUD 2019 Daily Chart
pullback reversal
ProRealTime.com

www.ProRealTime.com
Fig A38
EURGBP 2019 Daily Chart
pullback reversal
0.94
0.92
0.9
0.88
0.86
0.84
ProRealTime.com
23 28 Dec 06 11 14 19 24 2019 08 11 16 21 24 29 Feb 06 11 14 19 22 Mar 07 12 15 20 25 28

www.ProRealTime.com
Fig A39
EURJPY 2019 Daily Chart
range breakout
128
126
124
122
120
118
ProRealTime.com
15 18 23 26 May 06 09 14 17 22 27 Jun 07 12 17 20 25 Jul 08 11 16 19 24 29 Aug 06 09 14

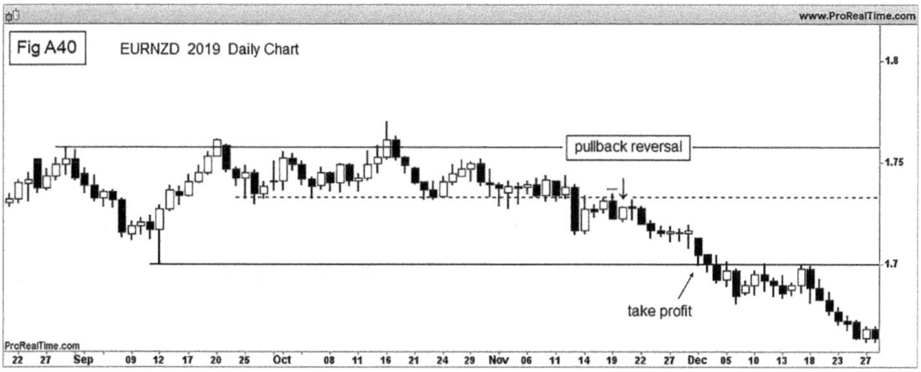
www.ProRealTime.com
Fig A40
EURNZD 2019 Daily Chart
pullback reversal
take profit
1.8
1.75
1.7
ProRealTime.com
22 27 Sep 09 12 17 20 25 Oct 08 11 16 21 24 29 Nov 06 11 14 19 22 27 Dec 05 10 13 18 23 27

www.ProRealTime.com
Fig A41
EURUSD 2019 Daily Chart
range reversal
cluster breakout
1.15
1.14
1.13
1.12
1.11
1.1
1.09
ProRealTime.com
27 Sep 04 09 12 17 20 25 Oct 03 08 11 16 21 24 29 Nov 06 11 14 19 22 27 Dec 05 10 13 18

www.ProRealTime.com
Fig A42
GBPCAD 2019 Daily Chart
range breakout
1.85
1.8
1.75
1.7
1.65
ProRealTime.com
06 11 14 19 22 Mar 07 12 15 20 25 Apr 05 10 15 18 23 26 May 06 09 14 17 22 27 Jun 07 12 17 20 25

www.ProRealTime.com
Fig A43
GBPCHF 2019 Daily Chart
range reversal
1.35
1.3
1.25
ProRealTime.com
21 26 Oct 04 09 12 17 22 25 Nov 07 12 15 20 23 28 Dec 06 11 14 19 24 2019 08 11 16 21 24

Fig A44
GBPUSD 2019 Daily Chart
take profit
pullback reversal
www.ProRealTime.com
ProRealTime.com

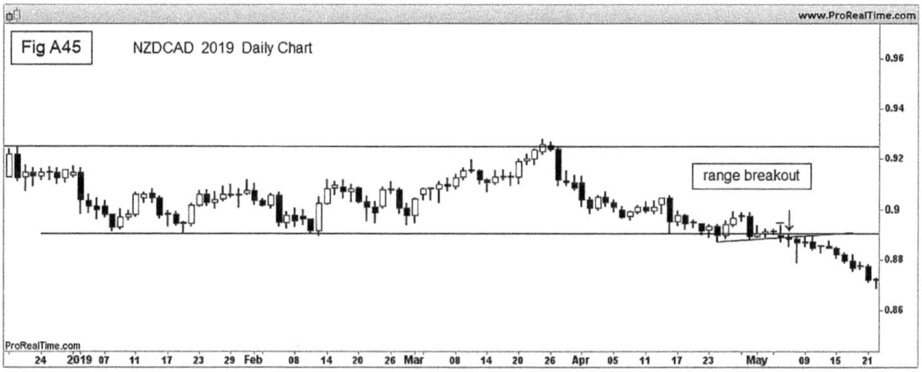
Fig A45
NZDCAD 2019 Daily Chart
range breakout
www.ProRealTime.com
ProRealTime.com

Fig A46
NZDCHF 2019 Daily Chart
range reversal
www.ProRealTime.com
ProRealTime.com

Fig A47
NZDJPY 2019 Daily Chart
range breakout
www.ProRealTime.com
ProRealTime.com

Fig A48
NZDJPY 2019 Daily Chart
pullback reversal
www.ProRealTime.com
ProRealTime.com

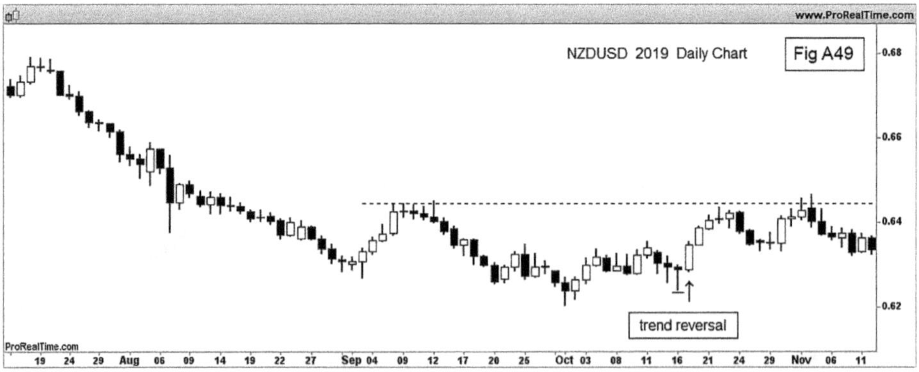
NZDUSD 2019 Daily Chart
Fig A49
trend reversal
www.ProRealTime.com
ProRealTime.com

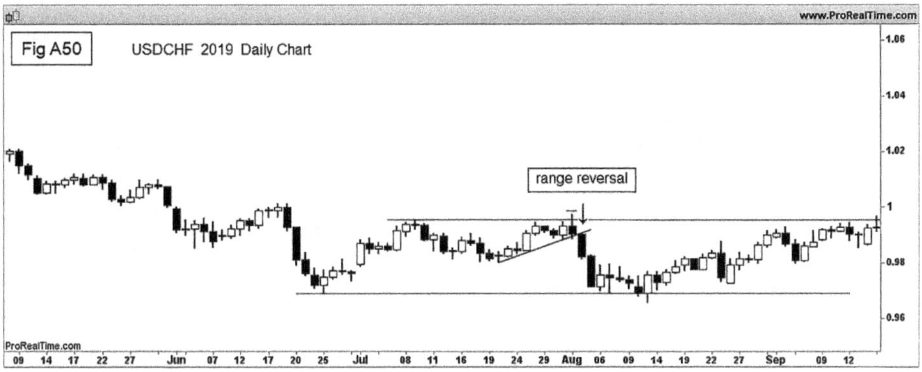
Fig A50
USDCHF 2019 Daily Chart
range reversal
www.ProRealTime.com
ProRealTime.com
1.06
1.04
1.02
1
0.98
0.96
09 14 17 22 27 Jun 07 12 17 20 25 Jul 08 11 16 19 24 29 Aug 06 09 14 19 22 27 Sep 09 12

2020

Fig A51
AUDCHF 2020 Daily Chart
pullback reversal

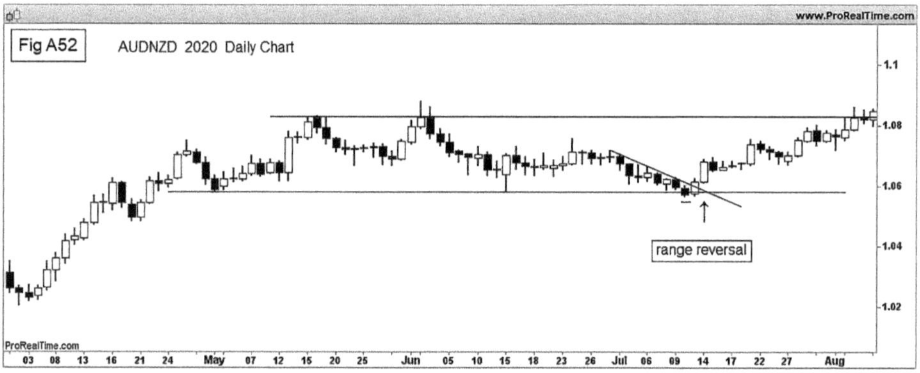
Fig A52
AUDNZD 2020 Daily Chart
range reversal

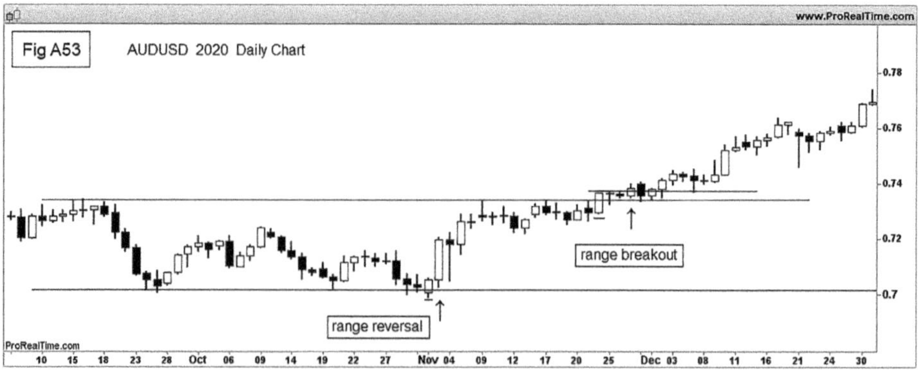
Fig A53
AUDUSD 2020 Daily Chart
range breakout
range reversal

Fig A54
CHFJPY 2020 Daily Chart
re-break failure
www.ProRealTime.com
ProRealTime.com

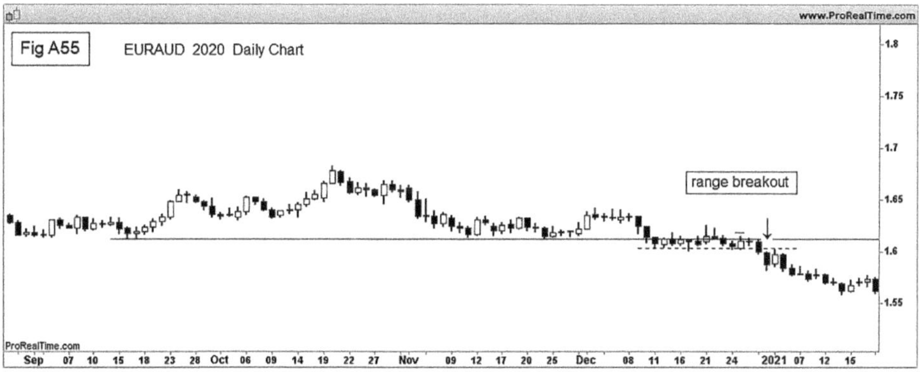

Fig A55
EURAUD 2020 Daily Chart
range breakout
www.ProRealTime.com
ProRealTime.com

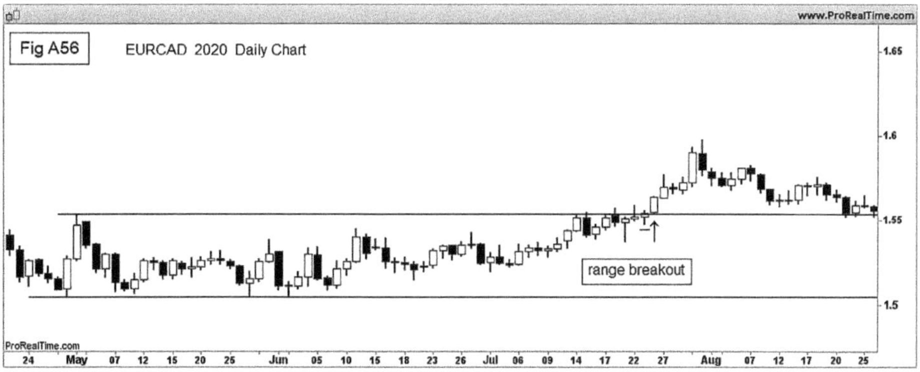

Fig A56
EURCAD 2020 Daily Chart
range breakout
www.ProRealTime.com
ProRealTime.com

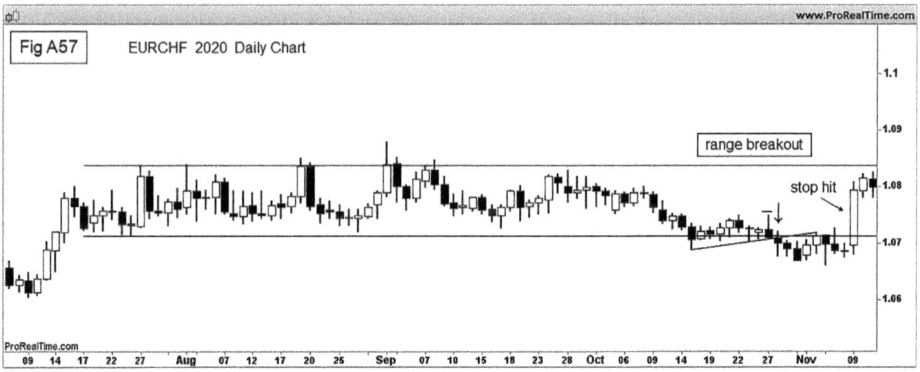
Fig A57
EURCHF 2020 Daily Chart
range breakout
stop hit

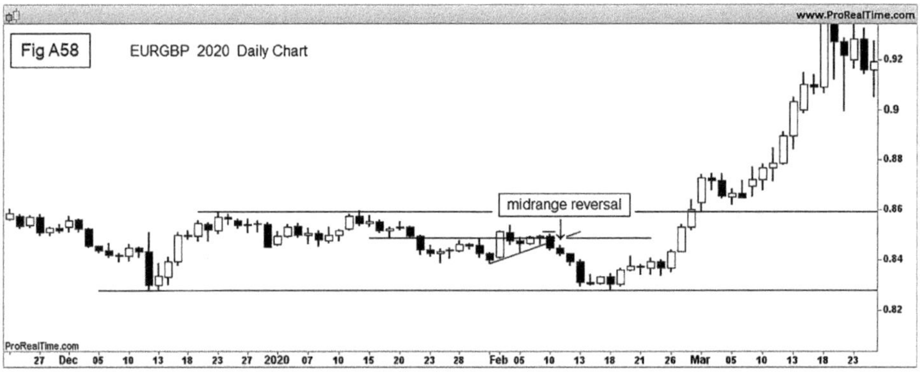
Fig A58
EURGBP 2020 Daily Chart
midrange reversal

Fig A59
EURJPY 2020 Daily Chart
take profit
range reversal

Fig A60 GBPAUD 2020 Daily Chart

Fig A61 GBPNZD 2020 Daily Chart

Fig A62 GBPUSD 2020 Daily Chart

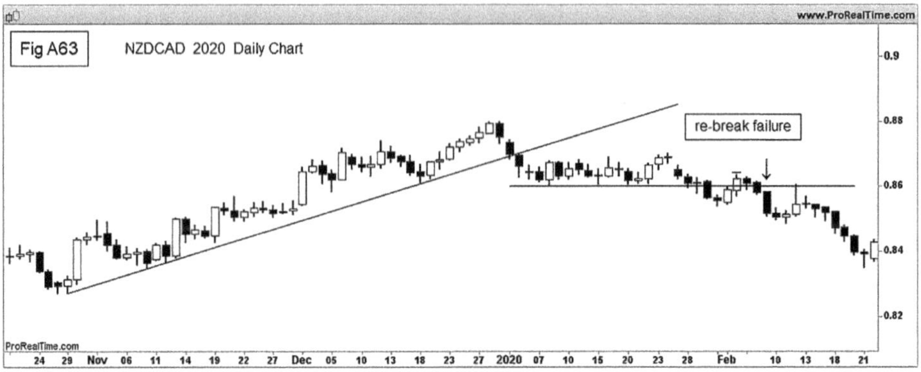
Fig A63
NZDCAD 2020 Daily Chart
re-break failure
www.ProRealTime.com

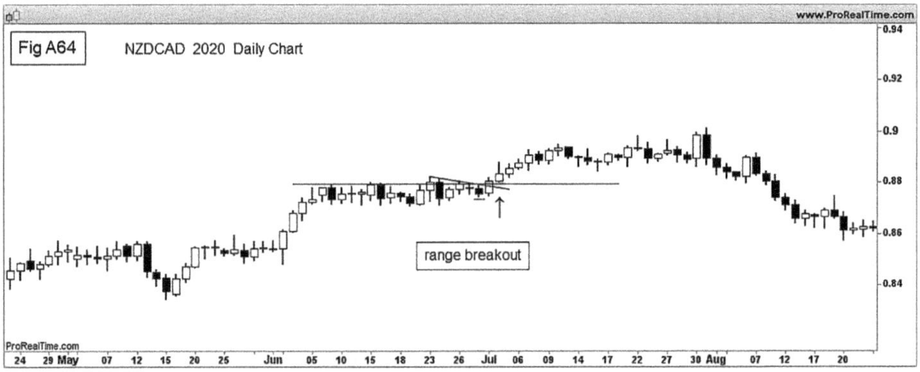
Fig A64
NZDCAD 2020 Daily Chart
range breakout
www.ProRealTime.com

Fig A65
USDCHF 2020 Daily Chart
range breakout
www.ProRealTime.com

2021

Fig A66 AUDCHF 2021 Daily Chart

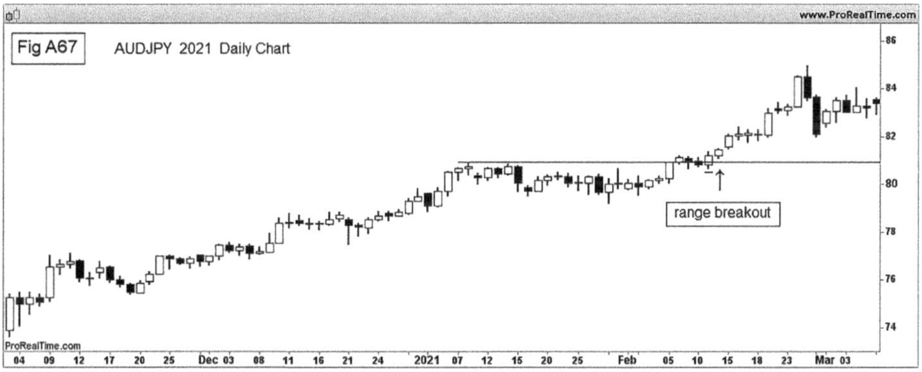

Fig A67 AUDJPY 2021 Daily Chart

Fig A68 CADCHF 2021 Daily Chart

Fig A69
CADJPY 2021 Daily Chart
range breakout
www.ProRealTime.com

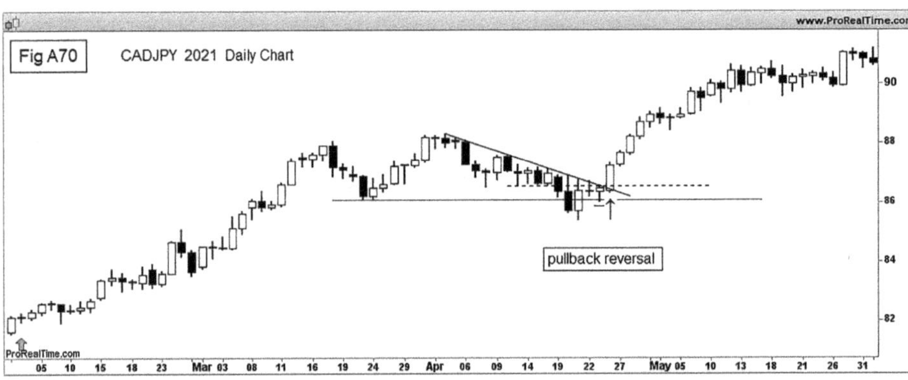
Fig A70
CADJPY 2021 Daily Chart
pullback reversal
www.ProRealTime.com

Fig A71
CADJPY 2021 Daily Chart
re-break failure
www.ProRealTime.com

Fig A72
CHFJPY 2021 Daily Chart
range reversal
take profit
www.ProRealTime.com

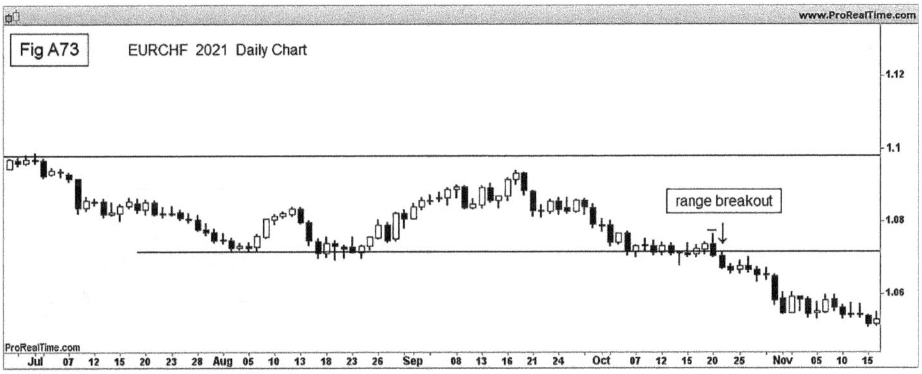
Fig A73
EURCHF 2021 Daily Chart
range breakout
www.ProRealTime.com

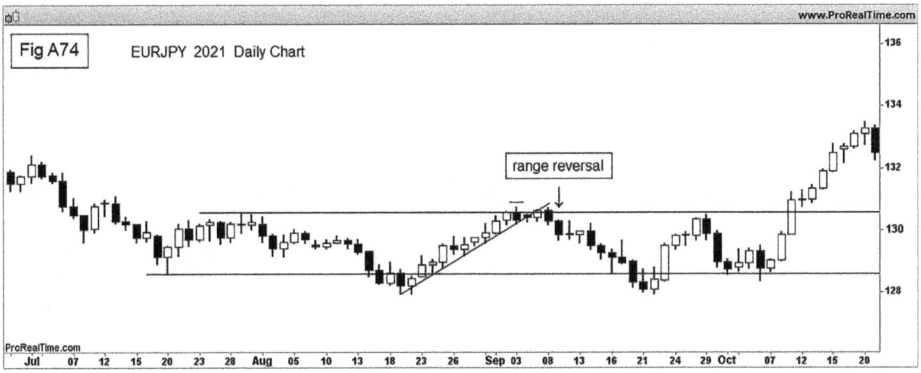
Fig A74
EURJPY 2021 Daily Chart
range reversal
www.ProRealTime.com

Fig A75
EURUSD 2021 Daily Chart
re-break failure

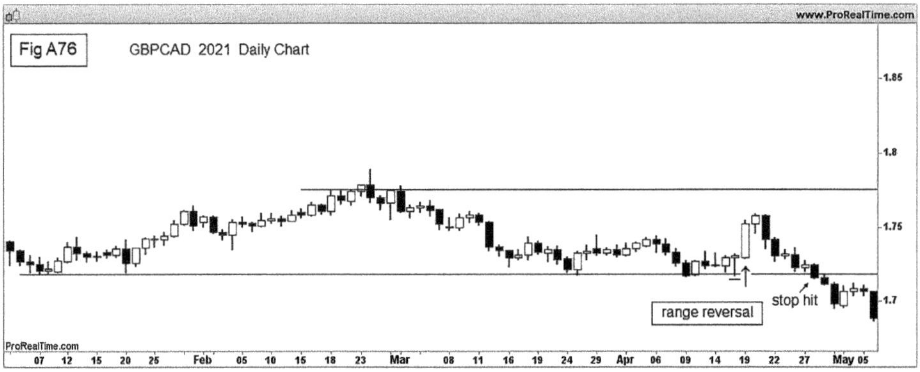
Fig A76
GBPCAD 2021 Daily Chart
range reversal
stop hit

Fig A77
GBPCHF 2021 Daily Chart
pullback reversal

Fig A78
GBPJPY 2021 Daily Chart
range breakout
www.ProRealTime.com

Fig A79
GBPJPY 2021 Daily Chart
pullback reversal
www.ProRealTime.com

Fig A80
GBPNZD 2021 Daily Chart
just missed target
range breakout
stop hit
www.ProRealTime.com

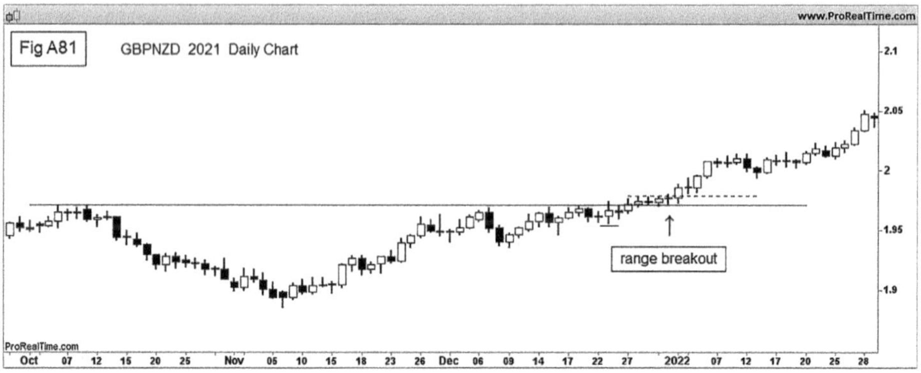
Fig A81
GBPNZD 2021 Daily Chart
range breakout

Fig A82
GBPUSD 2021 Daily Chart
pullback reversal

Fig A83
NZDCAD 2021 Daily Chart
pullback reversal

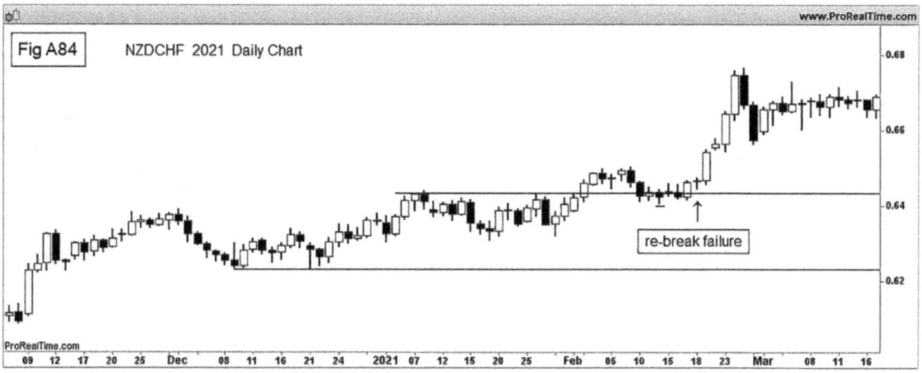
www.ProRealTime.com
Fig A84
NZDCHF 2021 Daily Chart
re-break failure
0.68
0.66
0.64
0.62
ProRealTime.com
09 12 17 20 25 Dec 08 11 16 21 24 2021 07 12 15 20 25 Feb 05 10 15 18 23 Mar 08 11 16

www.ProRealTime.com
Fig A85
NZDUSD 2021 Daily Chart
pullback reversal
take profit
range reversal
0.76
0.74
0.72
0.7
0.68
0.66
ProRealTime.com
05 11 17 23 Dec 09 15 21 28 2021 07 13 19 25 Feb 04 10 16 22 Mar 04 10 16 22 26 Apr 07 13 19

www.ProRealTime.com
Fig A86
NZDUSD 2021 Daily Chart
range reversal
0.76
0.74
0.72
0.7
0.68
ProRealTime.com
26 Jun 08 11 16 21 24 Jul 07 12 15 20 23 28 Aug 05 10 13 18 23 26 Sep 08 13 16 21 24 Oct 07 12 15

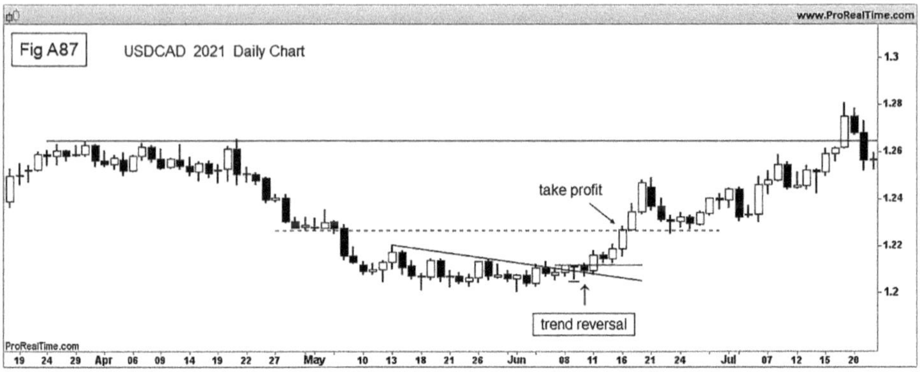
Fig A87
USDCAD 2021 Daily Chart
take profit
trend reversal
www.ProRealTime.com

Fig A88
USDCHF 2021 Daily Chart
pullback reversal
www.ProRealTime.com

Fig A89
USDCHF 2021 Daily Chart
pullback reversal
take profit
www.ProRealTime.com

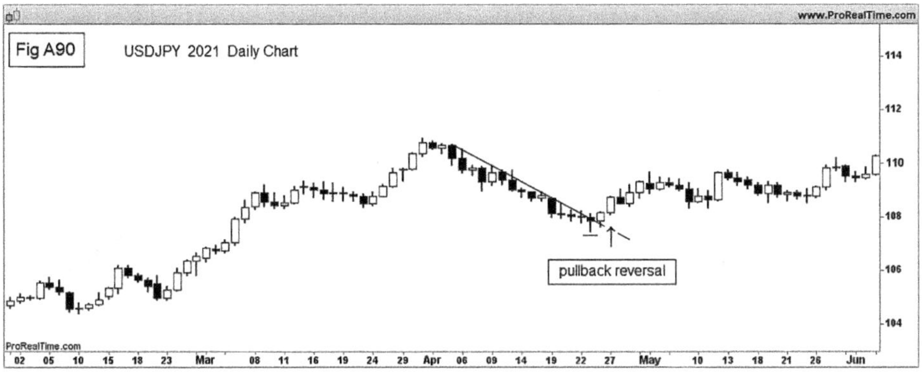

www.ProRealTime.com
Fig A90
USDJPY 2021 Daily Chart
pullback reversal
114
112
110
108
106
104
ProRealTime.com
02 05 10 15 18 23 Mar 08 11 16 19 24 29 Apr 06 09 14 19 22 27 May 10 13 18 21 26 Jun

2022

Fig A91
AUDCAD 2022 Daily Chart
re-break failure
www.ProRealTime.com
ProRealTime.com

Fig A92
AUDCHF 2022 Daily Chart
range reversal
www.ProRealTime.com
ProRealTime.com

Fig A93
AUDJPY 2022 Daily Chart
range breakout
www.ProRealTime.com
ProRealTime.com

Fig A94 AUDJPY 2022 Daily Chart

Fig A95 AUDNZD 2022 Daily Chart

Fig A96 AUDUSD 2022 Daily Chart

Fig A97
CHFJPY 2022 Daily Chart
range breakout
www.ProRealTime.com

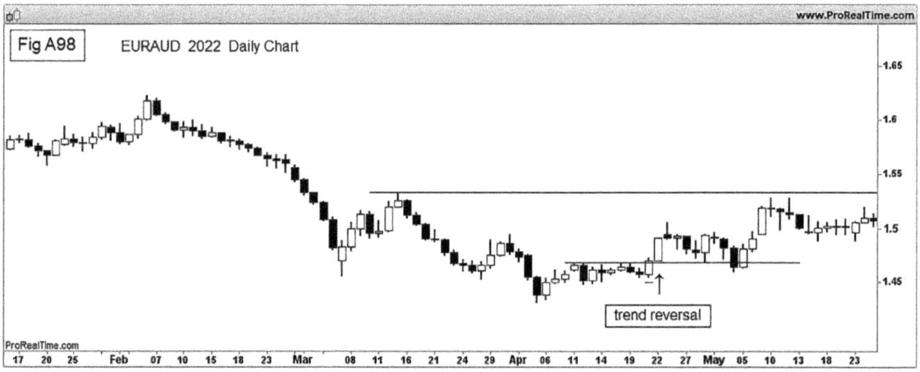
Fig A98
EURAUD 2022 Daily Chart
trend reversal
www.ProRealTime.com

Fig A99
EURAUD 2022 Daily Chart
range reversal
www.ProRealTime.com

www.ProRealTime.com
Fig A100
EURGBP 2022 Daily Chart
range breakout
ProRealTime.com

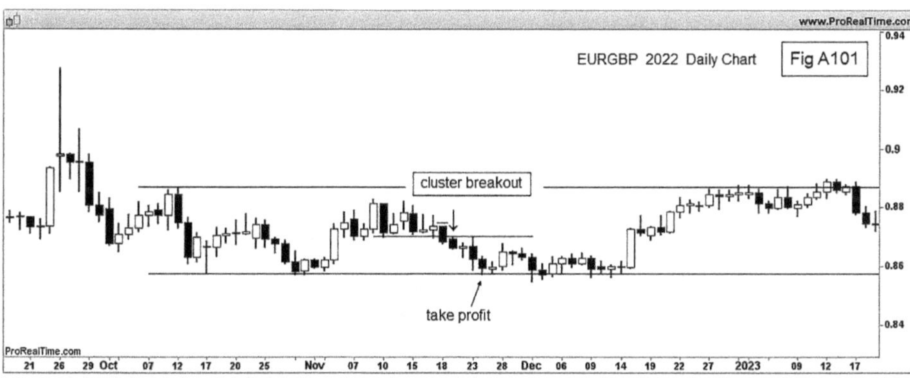
www.ProRealTime.com
EURGBP 2022 Daily Chart
Fig A101
cluster breakout
take profit
ProRealTime.com

www.ProRealTime.com
Fig A102
EURJPY 2022 Daily Chart
pullback reversal
ProRealTime.com

Fig A103
EURJPY 2022 Daily Chart
pullback reversal
www.ProRealTime.com
ProRealTime.com

Fig A104
EURUSD 2022 Daily Chart
Mm-top reversal
take profit
www.ProRealTime.com
ProRealTime.com

Fig A105
GBPAUD 2022 Daily Chart
re-break failure
www.ProRealTime.com
ProRealTime.com

Fig A106
GBPAUD 2022 Daily Chart
re-break failure
www.ProRealTime.com
ProRealTime.com

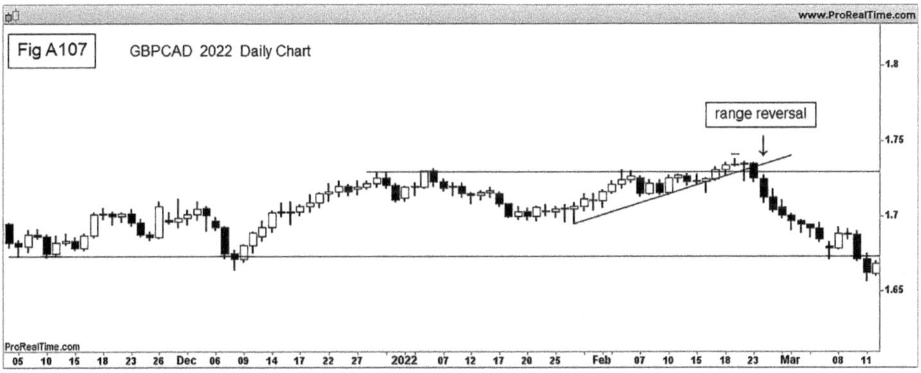
Fig A107
GBPCAD 2022 Daily Chart
range reversal
www.ProRealTime.com
ProRealTime.com

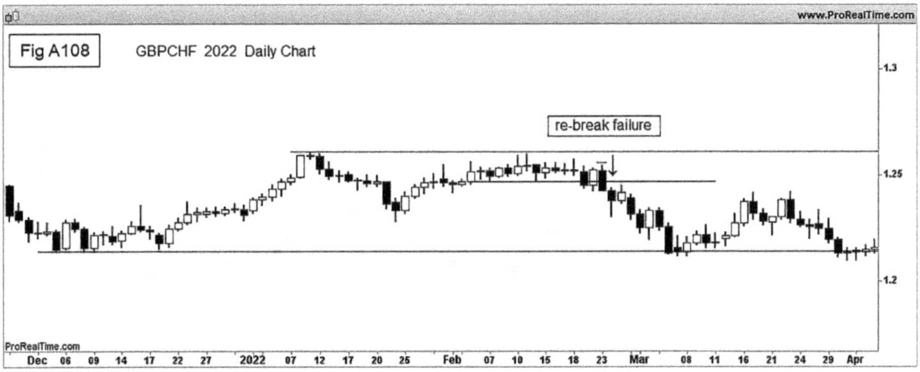
Fig A108
GBPCHF 2022 Daily Chart
re-break failure
www.ProRealTime.com
ProRealTime.com

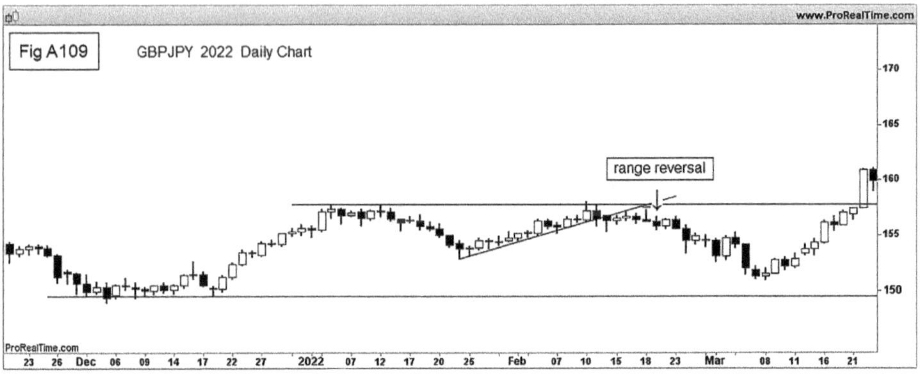
www.ProRealTime.com
Fig A109
GBPJPY 2022 Daily Chart
range reversal
ProRealTime.com

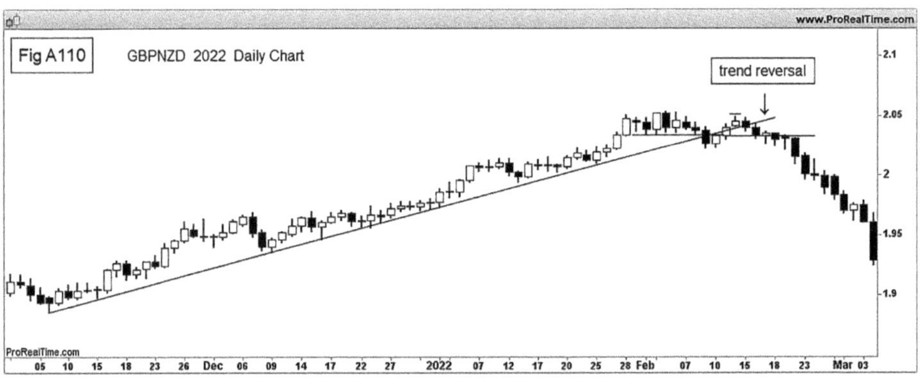
www.ProRealTime.com
Fig A110
GBPNZD 2022 Daily Chart
trend reversal
ProRealTime.com

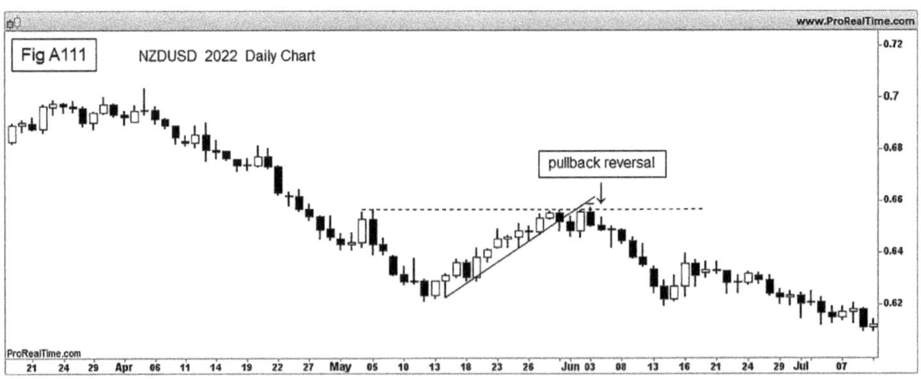
www.ProRealTime.com
Fig A111
NZDUSD 2022 Daily Chart
pullback reversal
ProRealTime.com

www.ProRealTime.com
Fig A112
USDCAD 2022 Daily Chart
pullback reversal
ProRealTime.com

www.ProRealTime.com
Fig A113
USDCAD 2022 Daily Chart
range reversal
ProRealTime.com

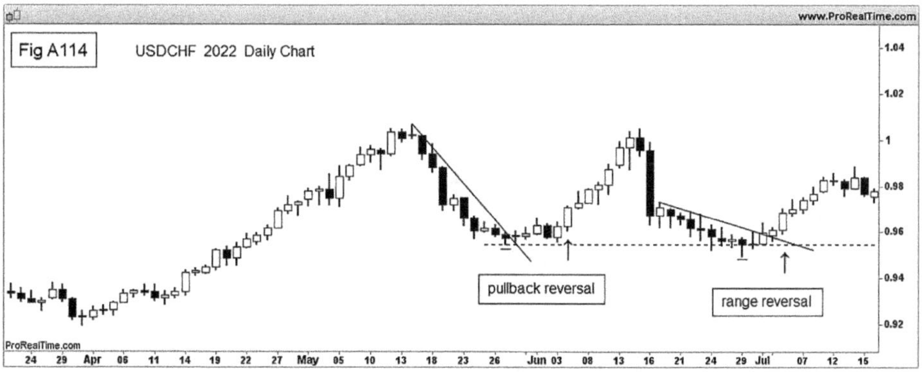
www.ProRealTime.com
Fig A114
USDCHF 2022 Daily Chart
pullback reversal
range reversal
ProRealTime.com

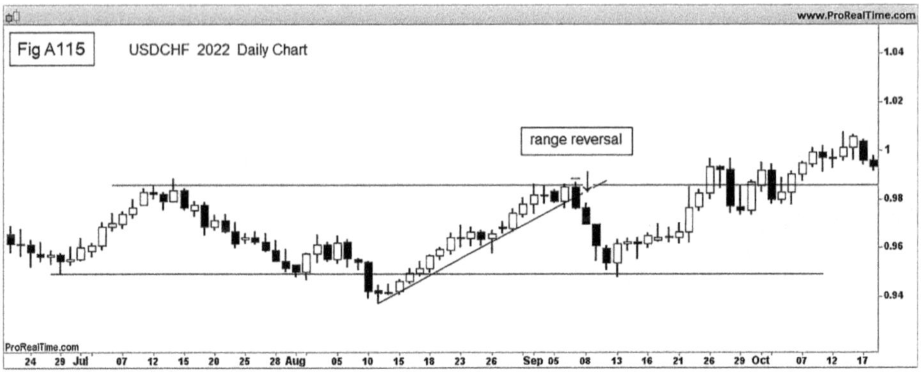
Fig A115
USDCHF 2022 Daily Chart
range reversal
www.ProRealTime.com

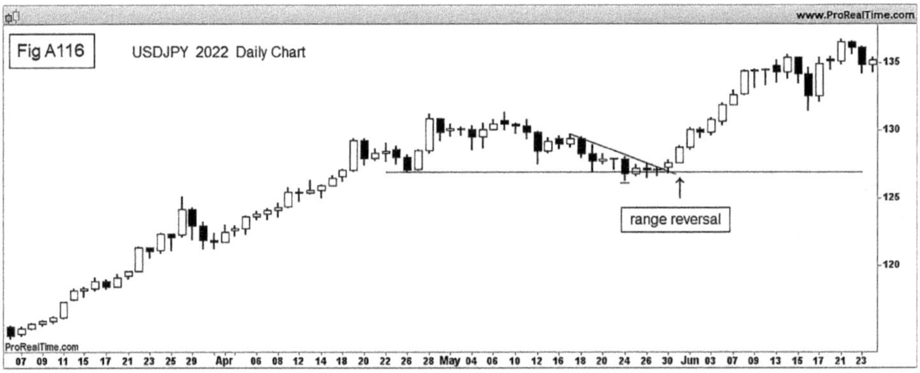
Fig A116
USDJPY 2022 Daily Chart
range reversal
www.ProRealTime.com

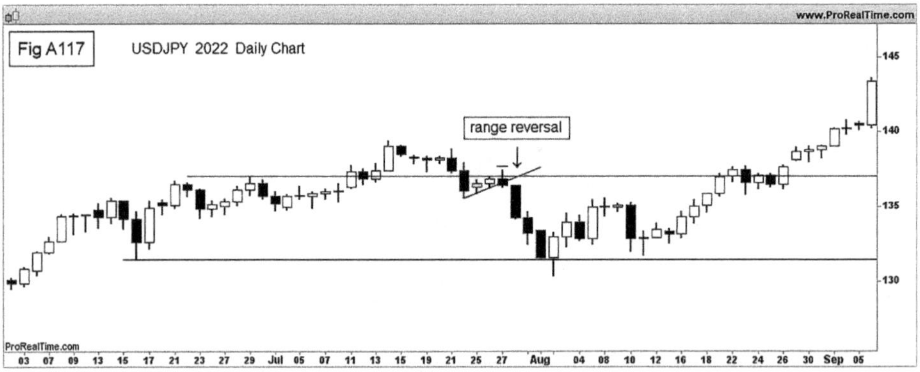
Fig A117
USDJPY 2022 Daily Chart
range reversal
www.ProRealTime.com

2023

www.ProRealTime.com
Fig A118
AUDCAD 2023 Daily Chart
range breakout
stop hit
ProRealTime.com

www.ProRealTime.com
Fig A119
AUDCAD 2023 Daily Chart
cluster breakout
ProRealTime.com

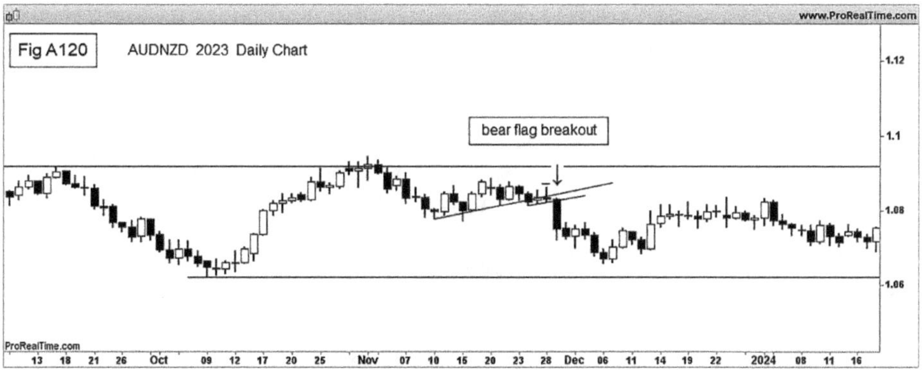
www.ProRealTime.com
Fig A120
AUDNZD 2023 Daily Chart
bear flag breakout
ProRealTime.com

www.ProRealTime.com
Fig A121
CADCHF 2023 Daily Chart
range reversal
0.72
0.7
0.68
0.66
0.64
ProRealTime.com

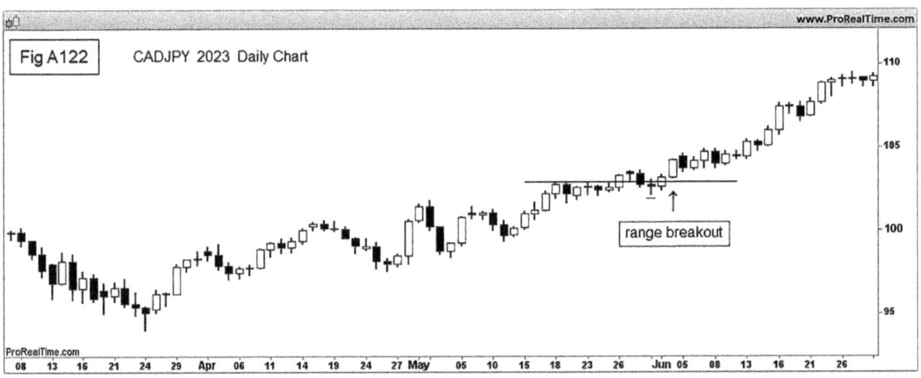
www.ProRealTime.com
Fig A122
CADJPY 2023 Daily Chart
range breakout
110
105
100
95
ProRealTime.com

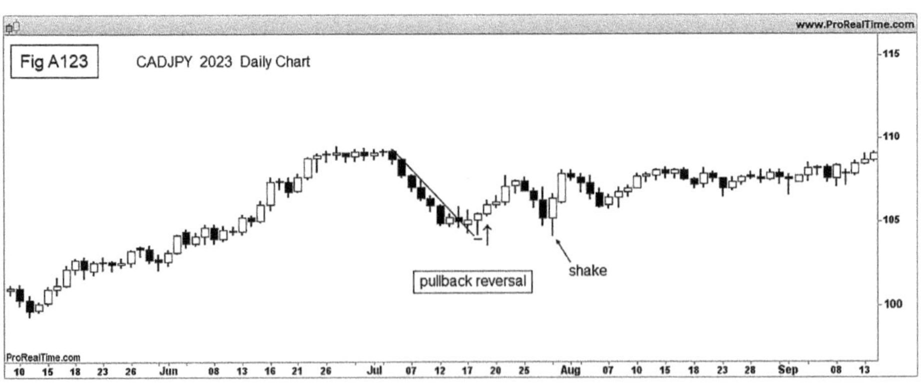
www.ProRealTime.com
Fig A123
CADJPY 2023 Daily Chart
pullback reversal
shake
115
110
105
100
ProRealTime.com

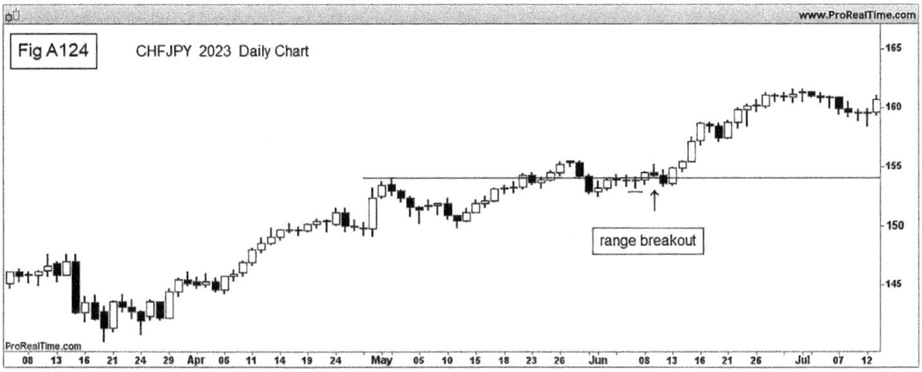
Fig A124
CHFJPY 2023 Daily Chart
range breakout
www.ProRealTime.com
ProRealTime.com

Fig A125
EURGBP 2023 Daily Chart
midrange reversal
take profit
www.ProRealTime.com
ProRealTime.com

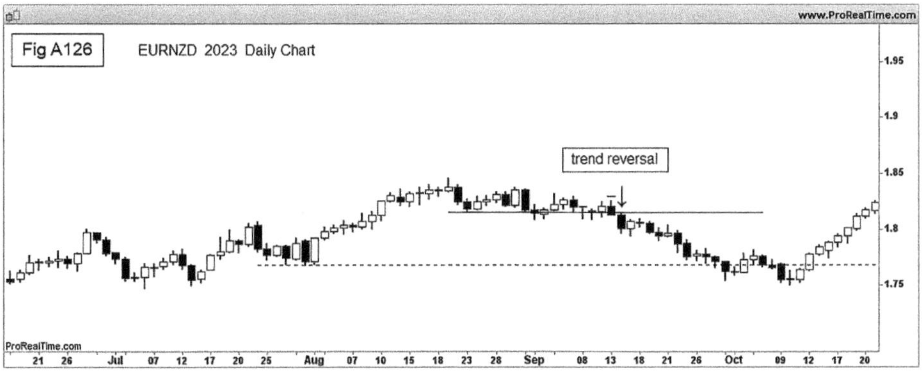
Fig A126
EURNZD 2023 Daily Chart
trend reversal
www.ProRealTime.com
ProRealTime.com

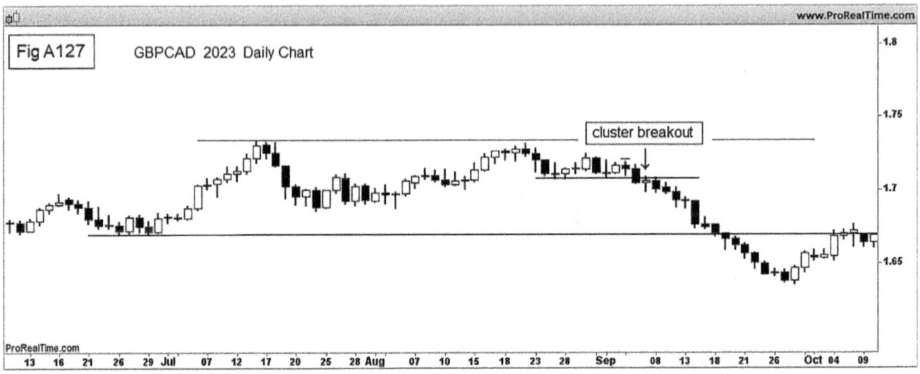
Fig A127
GBPCAD 2023 Daily Chart
cluster breakout
www.ProRealTime.com
ProRealTime.com

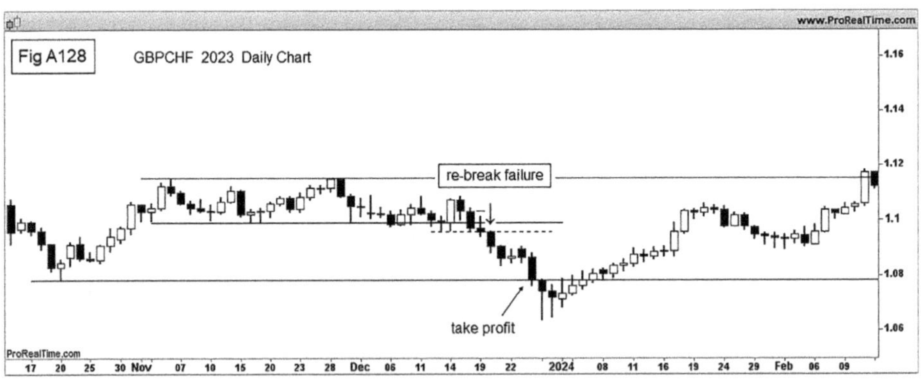
Fig A128
GBPCHF 2023 Daily Chart
re-break failure
take profit
www.ProRealTime.com
ProRealTime.com

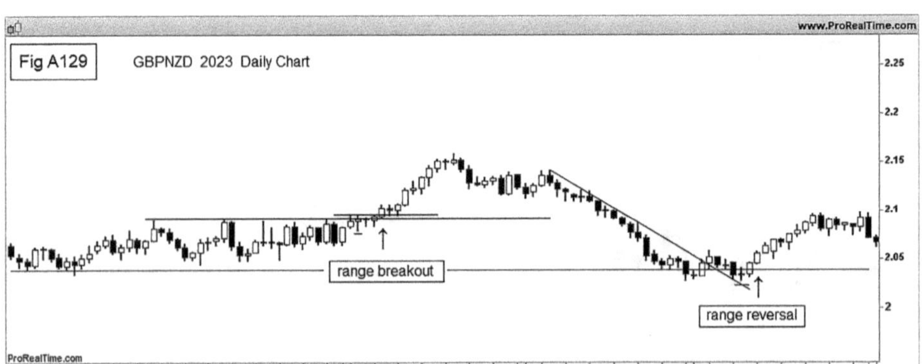
Fig A129
GBPNZD 2023 Daily Chart
range breakout
range reversal
www.ProRealTime.com
ProRealTime.com

www.ProRealTime.com
Fig A130
GBPUSD 2023 Daily Chart
range breakout
ProRealTime.com
1.34
1.32
1.3
1.28
1.26
1.24
1.22
29 Apr 06 11 14 19 24 May 05 10 15 18 23 26 Jun 08 13 16 21 26 Jul 07 12 17 20 25 28

www.ProRealTime.com
Fig A131
NZDUSD 2023 Daily Chart
range reversal
ProRealTime.com
0.68
0.66
0.64
0.62
0.6
03 08 13 16 21 24 29 Apr 06 11 14 19 24 May 05 10 15 18 23 26 Jun 08 13 16 21 26 Jul 07 12 17

www.ProRealTime.com
Fig A132
NZDUSD 2023 Daily Chart
take profit
range reversal
ProRealTime.com
0.66
0.64
0.62
0.6
0.58
17 20 25 Aug 07 10 15 18 23 28 Sep 08 13 18 21 26 Oct 09 12 17 20 25 Nov 07 10 15 20 23

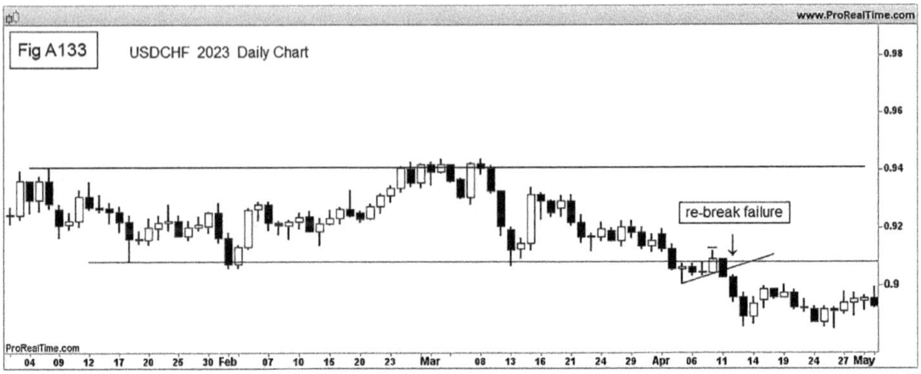
Fig A133
USDCHF 2023 Daily Chart
re-break failure
www.ProRealTime.com

Fig A134
USDCHF 2023 Daily Chart
bear flag breakout
www.ProRealTime.com

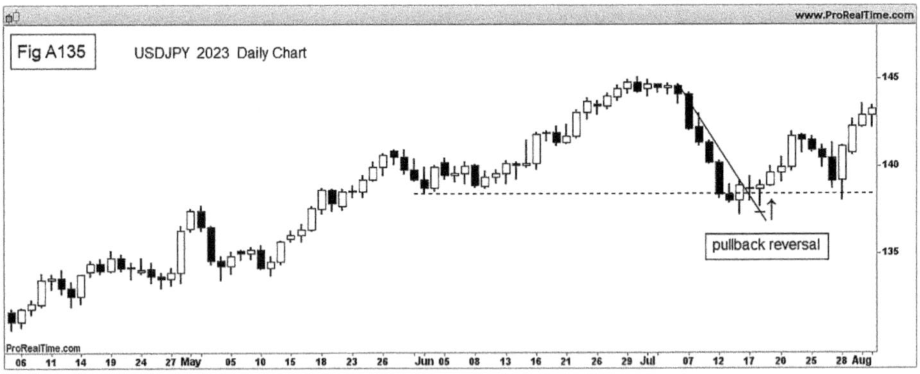
Fig A135
USDJPY 2023 Daily Chart
pullback reversal
www.ProRealTime.com

2024

www.ProRealTime.com
Fig A136
AUDCAD 2024 Daily Chart
range reversal
ProRealTime.com

www.ProRealTime.com
Fig A137
CADCHF 2024 Daily Chart
M-top reversal
take profit
ProRealTime.com

www.ProRealTime.com
Fig A138
CHFJPY 2024 Daily Chart
cluster breakout
ProRealTime.com

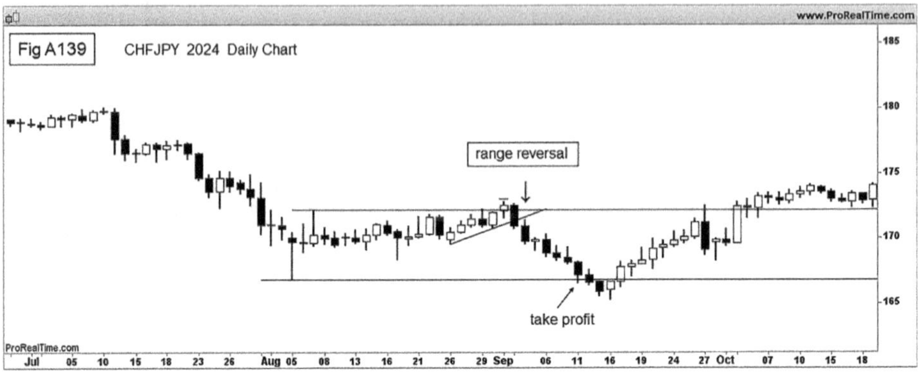
www.ProRealTime.com
Fig A139
CHFJPY 2024 Daily Chart
range reversal
take profit
ProRealTime.com

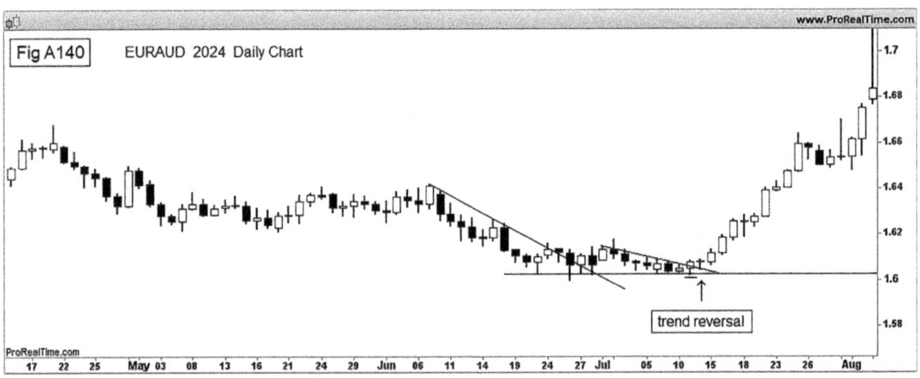
www.ProRealTime.com
Fig A140
EURAUD 2024 Daily Chart
trend reversal
ProRealTime.com

www.ProRealTime.com
Fig A141
EURAUD 2024 Daily Chart
bear flag breakout
ProRealTime.com

Fig A142
EURCAD 2024 Daily Chart
re-break failure
take profit
www.ProRealTime.com

Fig A143
EURCHF 2024 Daily Chart
pullback reversal
www.ProRealTime.com

Fig A144
EURGBP 2024 Daily Chart
range reversal
www.ProRealTime.com

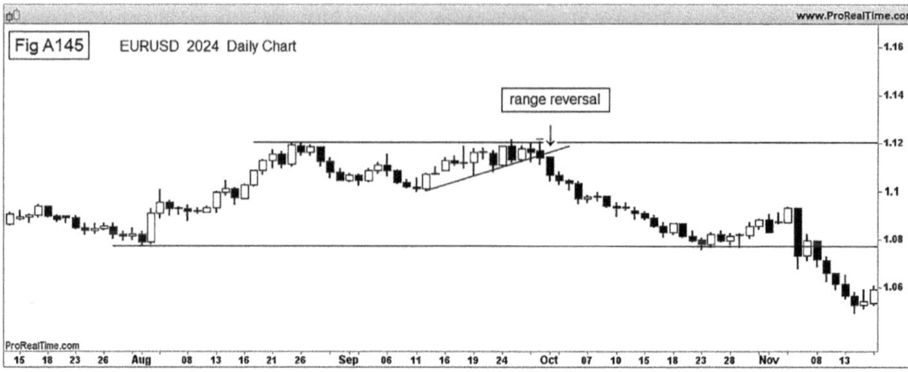
www.ProRealTime.com
Fig A145
EURUSD 2024 Daily Chart
range reversal
ProRealTime.com

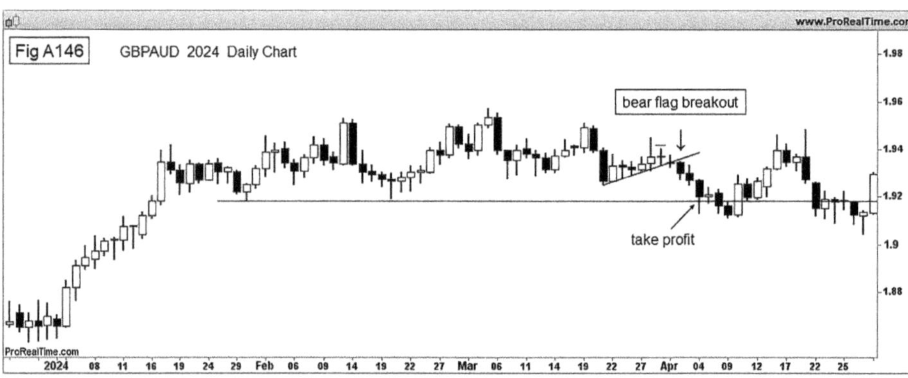
www.ProRealTime.com
Fig A146
GBPAUD 2024 Daily Chart
bear flag breakout
take profit
ProRealTime.com

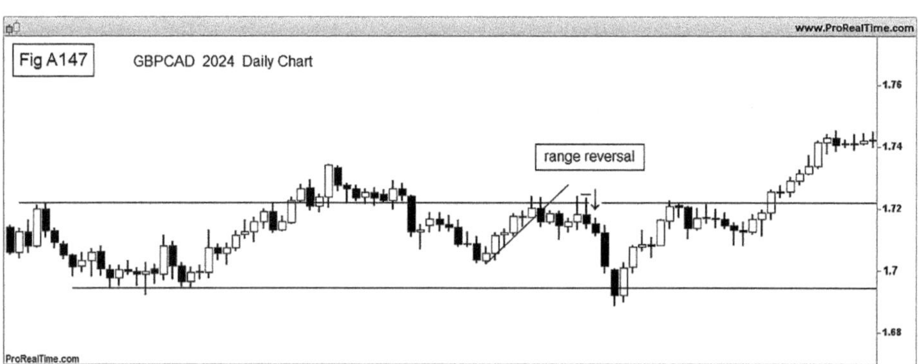
www.ProRealTime.com
Fig A147
GBPCAD 2024 Daily Chart
range reversal
ProRealTime.com

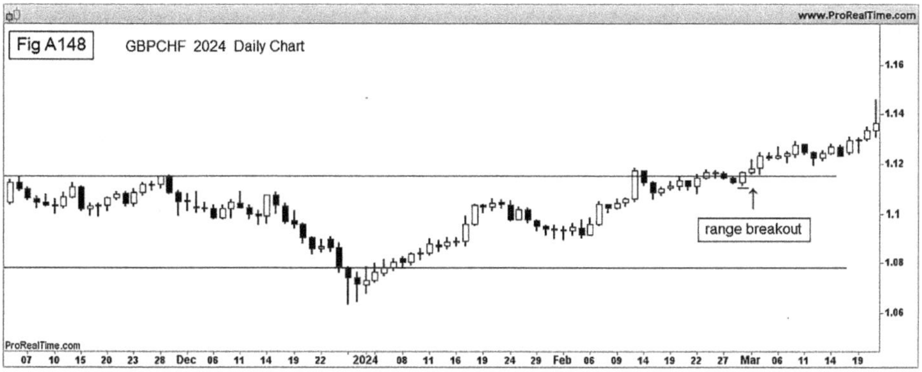
Fig A148
GBPCHF 2024 Daily Chart
range breakout
www.ProRealTime.com
ProRealTime.com

Fig A149
GBPJPY 2024 Daily Chart
pullback reversal
might have just missed target
www.ProRealTime.com
ProRealTime.com

Fig A150
GBPNZD 2024 Daily Chart
range breakout
www.ProRealTime.com
ProRealTime.com

Fig A151

Fig A152

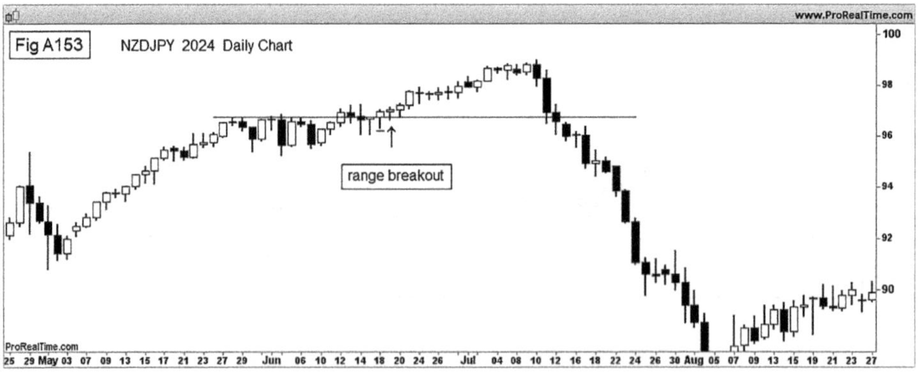

Fig A153

Fig A154
NZDUSD 2024 Daily Chart
midrange reversal
www.ProRealTime.com

Fig A155
USDCHF 2024 Daily Chart
range breakout
www.ProRealTime.com

Index

Note: Since many of the following references appear on a continual basis throughout the entire book, the page numbers refer to where they are first introduced and/or explained with the most attention for detail.

www.ingramcontent.com/pod-product-compliance
Lightning Source LLC
Chambersburg PA
CBHW061205240926
51846CB00006B/1116
* 9 7 8 9 0 8 2 2 7 8 6 3 7 *